'A scholarly, compassionate and courageous examination of a subject that's sparked an unhelpful civil war within the LGBTQ community. Unlike those of her online counterparts, Joyce's arguments are well researched, soundly made and avoid the toxicity that mars so much conversation on this topic.'

Observer, Books of the Year 2021

'Anyone wanting to understand how transgender rights became such a flashpoint in identity politics – and why a generation of feminists is so determined to stand its ground – should start here with this polemical book by Helen Joyce.'

Patrick Maguire, *The Times*, Books of the Year 2021

'I was knocked out by *Trans*... Joyce is always cool, calm and in complete possession of her extensive collection of facts.'

Spectator, Books of the Year

'A frighteningly necessary book: well-written, thoroughly-researched, passionate and very brave.'

Richard Dawkins

'A courageous, intelligent and important work, rooted in good science and common sense.'

Jenni Murray

'Reasonable, methodical, sane, and utterly unintimidated by extremist orthodoxy, *Trans* is also a riveting read.'

Lionel Shriver

TRANS

Gender Identity and the New Battle for Women's Rights

Helen Joyce

ONEWORLD

A Oneworld Book

First published by Oneworld Publications in 2021
This updated paperback edition published 2022
Reprinted, 2022, 2023

ISBN 978-0-86154-372-4
eISBN 978-0-86154-050-1

Typeset by Hewer Text UK Ltd, Edinburgh
Printed and bound in Great Britain by Clays Ltd, Elcograf S.p.A.

Oneworld Publications
10 Bloomsbury Street
London WC1B 3SR
England

Stay up to date with the latest books,
special offers, and exclusive content from
Oneworld with our newsletter

Sign up on our website
oneworld-publications.com

'When I dare to be powerful, to use my strength in the service of my vision, then it becomes less and less important whether or not I am afraid.'

Audre Lorde

'Freedom is the freedom to say that two plus two make four. If that is granted, all else follows.'

George Orwell

Dedicated to Stephanie Davies-Arai,
with admiration and gratitude

CONTENTS

FOREWORD

February 2022

The arguments in this book are based on facts that until recently were universally accepted: that humans cannot change sex; that males are on average much stronger than females and commit nearly all violent and sexual crime. Yet when the hardback edition was published in July 2021, I came under vicious attack. I was accused of thinking women were inferior to men, of branding all men rapists and of calling for the death of trans people. My arguments were compared with racism and homophobia. I was branded a bigot and a liar.

One reason for this backlash, I realised, was selective compassion. Activists who expressed genuine and reasonable concern for the struggles of trans-identified people would simultaneously dismiss women's desire for safety, privacy, dignity and fair competition. Unlike those activists, I feel compassion both for people who feel at odds with their sexed bodies, and for the people, mainly women and children, who are harmed when sexual dimorphism is denied.

At first I was puzzled that well-educated young women were the most ardent supporters of this new policy of gender self-identification, even though it is very much against their interests. A man may be embarrassed if a female person uses a male changing room; a male in a communal female facility can inspire fear. I came to see it as the rising generation's 'luxury belief' – a creed espoused by members of an elite to enhance their status in each other's eyes, with the harms experienced by the less fortunate. If you have social and financial capital, you can buy your way out of problems – if a facility you use jeopardises your safety or privacy, you will simply switch. It is poorer and older women who are stuck with the consequences of self-ID in women's prisons, shelters and refuges, hospital wards and care homes.

And some women's apparent support for self-ID is deceptive, expressed for fear of what open opposition would bring. The few male academics and journalists who write critically on this topic tell me that they get only a fraction of the hate directed at their female peers (and are spared the sexualised insults and rape threats). This dynamic is reinforced by ageism, which is inextricably intertwined with misogyny – including internalised misogyny. I was astonished by the young female reviewer who described my book's tone as 'harsh' and 'unfortunate'. I wondered if she knew that sexists often say they would have listened to women if only they had stated their demands more nicely and politely, and whether she realised that once she is no longer young and beautiful, the same sorts of things will be said about her, too.

Writing this book has meant abandoning much of what I thought I knew. I had no idea that so few people who engage in online debates genuinely cared about facts and logic, nor that so many people would put partisan politics ahead of any concept of societal good. I did not know that self-censorship was so common. I've received many emails, always in confidence, detailing legal troubles, blacklisting and loss of employment. I got used to being told 'you're right,' followed by 'but I can't say so in public.'

Since *Trans* was first published, I have become far more critical of journalism, the field I work in, and academia, which I left for it. Both are supposed to be meaning-making institutions that reveal and explain us to ourselves and our fellow citizens. But large swathes of both have abandoned this mission, and instead promote ideological narratives divorced from reality.

I have lost friends, though hearteningly few. Most of the people whose opinions I valued turned out either to agree with me, or to accept that people can think differently. And I gained new friends. I have been touched by the many people who told me how much the book meant to them. They included gay men and women who sense they might have felt the pressure to medically transition had they been born only a decade or two later, parents and teachers hungry for information, and young women working up the courage to argue with their peers.

A novel belief system is upending the legal and societal order, from education and sports to criminal justice and employment law. It has both fed off and worsened political polarisation. When a story is this big, you expect to see dozens of journalists and academics scrabbling to find a novel angle. Instead, the viciousness of the attacks on anyone who dares to criticise the latest social-justice dogma cleared the field for me and a handful of other authors.

I am often asked why I took the risk of writing this book, and occasionally why I felt I had the right. The issue does not touch me closely. I'm not trans. I don't have a trans-identified child. I'm not a detransitioner, or an athlete forced to compete against transwomen, or a lesbian seeking a partner on dating sites that are now filled with males.

The answer to both questions is simple: I wrote this book because, unlike many other people, I could. Parents of children caught up in the gender-identity social contagion stay silent to protect their relationships. The detransitioners I know are traumatised. Many critics of this ideology can say nothing without risking their jobs. All these people need someone else to articulate what is happening. And though it's been demoralising to hear the same terrible arguments for the hundredth time, and sometimes devastating to see the harm done, I've been invigorated by witnessing the resurgence of grassroots feminist activism in the UK, and by being part of something that matters. 'Never doubt that a small group of thoughtful, committed citizens can change the world,' said the anthropologist Margaret Mead. 'Indeed, it's the only thing that ever has.'

INTRODUCTION

This is a book about an idea, one that seems simple but has far-reaching consequences. The idea is that people should count as men or women according to how they feel and what they declare, instead of their biology. It's called gender self-identification, and it is the central tenet of a fast-developing belief system which sees everyone as possessing a gender identity that may or may not match the body in which it is housed. When there is a mismatch, the person is 'transgender' – trans for short – and it is the identity, not the body, that should determine how everyone else sees and treats them.

The origins of this belief system date back almost a century, to when doctors first sought to give physical form to the yearnings of a handful of people who longed to change sex. For decades such 'transsexuals' were few and far between, the concern of a handful of maverick clinicians, who would provide hormones and surgeries to reshape their patients' bodies to match their desires as closely as possible. Bureaucrats and governments treated them as exceptions, to be accommodated in society with varying degrees of competence and compassion.

But since the turn of the century, the exception has become the rule. National laws, company policies, school curricula, medical protocols, academic research and media style guides are being rewritten to privilege self-declared gender identity over biological sex. Facilities that used to be sex-separated, from toilets and changing rooms to homeless shelters and prisons, are switching to gender self-identification. Meanwhile more and more people are coming out as trans, usually without undergoing any sort of medical treatment. This book explains why this has happened, and how it happened so fast.

Developments in academia played a central role. Feminists used to use the word 'gender', and some still do, to denote the societal framing of female people as inferior and subordinate to male ones. Roughly, sex is a biological category, and gender a historical category; sex is *why* women are oppressed, and gender is *how* women are oppressed.

But in the 1990s the word was borrowed to signify a *discourse* – or, in the words of Judith Butler, the doyenne of gender studies and queer theory, 'an imitation for which there is no original'. And so in these academic fields, which developed on American campuses out of 1960s French postmodernism, a man or woman came to mean someone who performed manhood or womanhood, which were sets of stereotypes – matters of self-presentation, such as clothing and hairstyle, and behaviours, such as choice of hobbies and career – that were meaningful simply because they were performed over and over again. In the past decade, even the tenuous link with objective reality provided by those stereotypes has been severed. In the simplistic version of the new creed that has hardened into social-justice orthodoxy, gender is no longer even something that is performed. It is innate and ineffable: something like a sexed soul.

When the only people who identified out of their sex were

the tiny number of post-operative transsexuals, they had little impact on others. But the gender identity that is posited by today's ideology is entirely subjective, and the group of trans people is far larger. It includes part-time cross-dressers and even people who present as a typical member of their sex, but identify to the contrary – or declare a novel identity, such as non-binary or gender-fluid. What is being demanded is no longer flexibility, but a redefinition of what it means for anyone to be a man or woman – a total rewrite of societal rules.

Gender self-identification is often described as this generation's civil-rights battle. And it is promoted by some of the same organisations that fought for women's suffrage, desegregation in the American South and gay marriage. But demanding that self-declared gender identity be allowed to override sex is not, as with genuine civil-rights movements, about extending privileges unjustly hoarded by a favoured group to a marginalised one.

In no society – anywhere, ever – have people been oblivious to the sex of those around them, and certainly not in situations involving nakedness or physical contact. And in all societies – everywhere, always – the overwhelming majority of violence, sexual assault and harassment suffered by female people has been perpetrated by male ones. Single-sex spaces exist for these reasons, not to prop up privilege or pander to prejudice. And it is logically impossible to admit people of one sex to spaces intended for the other while keeping them single-sex. All this is so obvious that it is remarkable to have to say it – and until a few years ago, when gender self-identification started to catch on, there would have been no need.

Most people are in the dark about what is being demanded by transactivists. They understand the call for 'trans rights' to mean compassionate concessions that enable a suffering minority to live full lives, in safety and dignity. I, alongside every critic of

3

gender-identity ideology I have spoken to for this book, am right behind this. Most, including me, also favour bodily autonomy for adults. A liberal, secular society can accommodate many subjective belief systems, even mutually contradictory ones. What it must never do is impose one group's beliefs on everyone else.

The other belief systems accommodated in modern democracies are, by and large, held privately. You can subscribe to the doctrine of reincarnation or resurrection alongside fellow believers, or on your own. Gender self-identification, however, is a demand for validation *by others*. The label is a misnomer. It is actually about requiring others to identify you as a member of the sex you proclaim. Since evolution has equipped humans with the ability to recognise other people's sex, almost instantaneously and with exquisite accuracy, very few trans people 'pass' as their desired sex. And so to see them as that sex, everyone else must discount what their senses are telling them.

Underlying my objections to gender self-identification is a scientific fact: that biological sex has an objective basis lacked by other socially salient categories, such as race and nationality. Sexual dimorphism – the two sexes, male and female – first appeared on Earth 1.2 billion years ago. Mammals – animals like humans that grow their young inside them, rather than laying eggs – date back 210 million years. In all that time, no mammal has ever changed sex (some non-mammals can, for example crocodiles and clownfish). Men and women have therefore evolved under differing selection pressures for an extremely long time, and these have shaped male and female bodies and psyches in ways that matter profoundly for health and happiness. The distinction between the sexes is not likely to be at all amenable to social engineering, no matter how much some people want it to be.

*

This is not a book about trans people. I will present the scientific research into what causes gender dysphoria and cross-sex identification. But I will not seek to balance stories of those for whom transition has been a success, and those for whom it has been a failure. Whether or not transition makes people happier is an important question for individuals and clinicians, especially when it involves irreversible hormonal or surgical interventions. But it is irrelevant to evaluating the truth of gender-identity ideology, and to whether self-declared gender should replace sex across society. To draw another analogy, whether a religion makes its believers happy is irrelevant to the question of whether its god exists, or whether everyone else should be compelled to pay it lip service.

This is, rather, a book about transactivism. It is a story of policy and institutional capture; of charitable foundations controlled by billionaires joining forces with activist groups to pump money into lobbying behind the scenes for legal change. They have won over big political parties, notably America's Democrats, and big businesses, including tech giants. They are backed, too, by academics in gender studies, queer theory and allied fields, and by the pharmaceutical and health-care industries, which have woken up to the fortunes to be made from 'gender-affirmative' medicine.

This powerful new lobby far outnumbers the trans people it claims to speak for. And it serves their interests very poorly. Its ideological focus means it seeks to silence anyone who does not support gender self-identification – which includes many post-operative transsexuals, who are under no illusion as to how much bodies matter. It also ignores other possible solutions to problems faced by trans people – research into the causes and treatment of gender dysphoria, for instance, or adding unisex facilities alongside single-sex ones. Its overreach is likely to provoke a backlash that will harm ordinary trans people, who simply want safety and social acceptance. When the general public finally realises what is being demanded, the blame may not land with the activists, where it belongs.

One place I expect to see a backlash soon is in women's sports. Their entire purpose is to enable fair competition, since the physical differences between the sexes give males an overwhelming athletic advantage, and competing separately is the only way that exceptional females can get their due. Allowing males to identify as women for the purposes of entry to women's competitions makes no more sense than allowing heavyweights to box as flyweights, or able-bodied athletes to enter the Paralympics, or adults to compete as under-eighteens. And yet, under pressure from transactivists, almost every sporting authority right up to the International Olympic Committee has moved to gender self-identification.

The sight of stronger, heavier, faster males easily beating the world's best female athletes is sure to outrage deep-seated intuitions about fair play – once it comes to wider notice. As this book went to press, it was unclear where that would happen first, but clear that it would happen soon.

A handful of males were expected to compete in women's events at the Tokyo Olympics, postponed in 2020 – and, judging from recent regional competitions, to place far better than they used to when competing as men. Meanwhile, duelling lawsuits are heading towards America's Supreme Court, seeking on the one hand to block states from allowing male athletes to compete as women, and on the other to force states to do so.

Another backlash is imminent in paediatric gender medicine. Until recently, hardly any children presented at gender clinics, but in the past decade the number has soared. Every one of the dozen or so studies of children with gender dysphoria

– discomfort and misery caused by one's biological sex – has found that most grow out of it, as long as they are supported in their gender non-conformity and not encouraged in a cross-sex identification. Many of these 'desisters' are destined to grow up gay: there is copious evidence of a strong link between early gender non-conformity and adult homosexuality.

But as gender clinics have come under activists' sway, the treatment they offer has taken an ideological turn. Instead of advising parents to watch and wait with sympathy and kindness, they now work on the assumption that childhood gender dysphoria destines someone to trans adulthood. They recommend immediate 'social transition' – a change of name, pronouns and presentation – followed successively by drugs to block puberty, cross-sex hormones and surgery, often while the patient is still in their teens. This treatment pathway is a fast track to sexual dysfunction and sterility in adulthood.

In the past few years a new group of trans-identifying minors has emerged: teenage girls. Until very recently, this demographic was almost never seen at gender clinics: now it predominates worldwide. And again these girls are fast-tracked to hormones and surgery, even though there is no evidence that these will help – and good reason to think they will not. This is the demographic most prone to social contagions, from the outbreaks of hysterical laughter and fainting that have been documented in girls' schools and convents throughout history, to the eating disorders and self-harm that sometimes sweep through friendship groups in the present day. Now another is under way, this time spread by social-justice warriors on social media alongside the medical profession and schools, which have added gender-identity ideology to the curriculum.

Early signs suggest that the number of children appearing at gender clinics is levelling off in Sweden, where clinicians have started to become concerned about the uncritical promotion of trans identification across society. And in late 2020, an English court ordered the country's sole paediatric gender clinic to seek judicial approval before offering children puberty-blocking drugs. These, it ruled, were part of a treatment pathway leading to irreversible harms that very few under-sixteens could possibly have the maturity to understand and consent to. But in the United States, where regulation is light and the health-care lobby is powerful, clinicians are abandoning even the last vestiges of caution. This story will end in shattered lives – and lawsuits.

I know that I will be called unkind, and worse, for writing this book. Some of what I say is bound to be perceived as deeply hurtful by some: that it is rare to be able to pass as a member of the opposite sex, especially if you are male; that the feeling of being a member of the opposite sex, no matter how deep and sincere, cannot change other people's instinctive perceptions; that such a feeling does not constitute licence to use facilities or services intended for the sex that you are not; that children who suffer distress at their sex are ill-served by being told that they can change it.

My intention is not to be unkind to trans people, but to prevent greater unkindness. As gender self-identification is written into laws around the world, the collateral damage is mounting. Males who raped and murdered women are gaining transfers to women's prisons. Women have lost their jobs for saying that male and female are objective, socially significant categories. I think it is deeply unkind to force female athletes to compete against males, and a scandal to sterilise children. These things are happening partly because of an admirable, but poorly thought-out, sense of compassion for trans people. This compassion is, not coincidentally, mostly demanded of women, who are socialised to put their own needs last and punished more severely than men when they refuse to comply.

What first intrigued me about gender-identity ideology was the circularity of its core mantra, 'transwomen are women', which raises and leaves unanswered the question of what, then, the word 'woman' means. What led me to think further was the vilification of anyone who questioned it. Philosophers, who freely debate such thorny topics as whether it is moral to kill disabled babies or remove kidneys from unwilling people for donation, have, with few exceptions, been cowed into silence regarding the consequences of redefining 'man' and 'woman'. Journalists, who pride themselves on ferreting out the stories that someone, somewhere doesn't want them to print, have taken one look at paediatric transitioning, males winning women's sporting competitions and women being sacked for talking about the reality of biological sex – and, again with just a few exceptions, turned tail.

What finally pushed me to write this book, however, was meeting some of gender-identity ideology's most poignant victims. They are detransitioners: people who took hormonal and sometimes surgical steps towards transition, only to realise that they had made a catastrophic mistake. At the inaugural meeting of the Detransition Advocacy Network, a British self-help group, in Manchester in late 2019, I met some in person. When I heard their stories, I knew I had to amplify them.

Some of those I have spoken with, at that meeting and since, are young lesbians who had previously decided that their gender non-conformity meant they were really men. Others are young gay men whose parents preferred to see their effeminate small boys as 'girls trapped in boys' bodies', rather than as probable future homosexuals. The share with traits suggestive of an autistic-spectrum disorder is much higher than in the general population. These traits include dissociative feelings, which can be misinterpreted as gender dysphoria, and rigid thinking, which can lead someone to conclude that deviating from sex stereotypes makes a person trans. Young women with eating disorders are over-represented. And not a few were simply miserable teenagers seeking in transition a community and validation.

Detransitioners speak of trauma from experimental drugs and surgeries, of having been manipulated and deceived by adults, and of being abandoned by friends when they detransitioned. I have seen them abused and defamed on social media, accused of being transphobes and liars, and of trying to stop genuine trans people getting the treatments they need. In fact, most are simply urging caution, and have no desire to stop others living as they wish. Their most obvious wounds are physical: mastectomies; castration; bodies shaped by cross-sex hormones. But the mental wounds go deeper. They bought into an ideology that is incoherent and constantly shifting, and where the slightest deviation is ferociously punished. They were led to believe that parents who expressed concern about the impact of powerful drugs on developing minds and bodies were hateful bigots, and that the only conceivable alternative to transition was suicide.

Ideas have consequences, and one of the consequences of the idea of gender self-identification is that children are being manipulated and damaged. Once you have seen that, it is hard to look away. The detransitioners I know have suffered greatly. They and their counterparts around the world seem to have settled on the lizard emoji as an informal mascot online: a talisman of rejuvenation, recovery and renewal. Their motive for speaking out is to save other young people from suffering as they did. That is also my motive for writing this book.

1

THE DANISH GIRLS

A brief history of transsexuality

It began with stockings. Gerda's sitter, the actress Anna Larssen, had telephoned to say she was running late for her portrait. Why not use Gerda's husband Einar, Anna suggested teasingly, as a substitute? After all, his legs were as good as Anna's. 'The most perfect ladies' model!' cried Gerda, when she saw Einar transformed into . . . whom? 'What do you say to Lili?' asked Anna, when she finally joined: 'A particularly lovely, musical name.'

Whether this is truth or later mythmaking is impossible to tell. But certainly Einar Wegener – an artist born in 1882 and trained in Copenhagen, and the Danish girl of the eponymous 2015 film starring Eddie Redmayne – dated the birth of Lili Elbe (the surname was inspired by the river) to that 'extravagant joke'. For years afterwards, Einar brought her out for portraits and parties. Hardly anyone knew that Gerda's sultry, sloe-eyed model was her cross-dressing husband.

The couple left Copenhagen to avoid exposure, and settled in Paris in 1912. Lili took to introducing herself as Gerda's sister. Over time, what had started as a game became deadly serious: the persona Einar now thought of as 'the woman in this body' was gaining the upper hand. He went to doctors: they said he was mad – or homosexual, which bothered him more. By his late forties, he was despairing. Within the following year, he decided, he would either find a way to give permanence to Lili's existence or end Einar's.

The year was nearly up when Lili was thrown a lifeline. In February 1930, Einar visited the Institute of Sexual Science in Berlin, where he consulted its founder Magnus Hirschfeld. The Institute combined research with practical services, such as treatment for venereal disease, impotence and infertility. It had an archive like no other. In his memoir of Weimar-era Berlin, Christopher Isherwood recalled its 'whips and chains and torture instruments designed for the practitioners of pleasure-pain; high-heeled, intricately decorated boots for the fetishists; lacy female undies which had been worn by ferociously masculine Prussian officers beneath their uniforms'.

For Wegener, who felt like twin people of opposite sexes inhabiting a single body, Hirschfeld's way of thinking about what distinguished men and women could not have been more congenial. According to the ancient 'one-sex model', men and women were essentially similar, except that women's reproductive anatomy was inverted and inferior. Women have 'exactly the same organs but in exactly the wrong places', wrote Galen, a Greek physician of the second century. By the nineteenth century, as the study of anatomy advanced, this had been supplanted by a 'two-sex' model, in which male and female were understood as separate categories. In the early twentieth century, however, Hirschfeld and a handful of other European sexologists were developing a new model. Surprisingly, their theories were uninformed by, and impossible to reconcile with, evolutionary theory and Charles Darwin's insights into the origin and significance of the two sexes. That foundational error is still visible in much thinking about what it means to be transgender today.

In *The Origin of Species*, published in 1859, Darwin explained the two types of selection that drove evolution: natural and sexual. In the former, it is differential survival rates that cause reproduction rates to vary; in the latter, it is differential success in attracting mates. The theory of evolution underpins all modern biological and medical science, and understands the sexes as ancient categories: reproductive roles shaped by and directed towards survival and reproduction. Male body parts are those directed towards the production of small, motile gametes (in animals, called sperm), and female ones are those directed towards the production of large, immotile gametes (in animals, called ova, or eggs).

Whether an individual has parts of just one sex or both depends on the species. Many plants are self-pollinating, and a single specimen contains both male and female parts. Some animals – earthworms, for example – are hermaphrodites, possessing both male and female sex organs. Others, such as crocodiles and clownfish, have the potential to develop into individuals of either sex in response to environmental cues. But for humans, as for all mammals, individuals are of one sex or the other, and that sex is immutable and determined at conception. The existence of 'intersex' conditions or disorders of sex development (DSDs) – an umbrella term for around forty different developmental conditions of the genitalia and gonads – does not alter this. I will have more to say about these conditions in later chapters.

After Darwin, any definition of 'male' and 'female' other than as developmental pathways directed towards and shaped by reproductive roles should have been dead in the water. But for Hirschfeld and his colleagues at the Institute, it was as if Darwin had never existed. Not only did they ignore the origin of the sexes, they did not even regard them as distinct categories. In Hirschfeld's

13

phrase, all people were 'bisexual', not in the sense of being attracted to both sexes, but in the sense of *being* both sexes. Male and female, Hirschfeld wrote, were 'abstractions, invented extremes'. Homosexuals and 'transvestites' – Hirschfeld's word for anyone from part-time cross-dressers to people with a strong, unremitting identification with the opposite sex – were simply intermediate types, unusually far from those notional end-points.

For someone like Wegener, who wanted to change sex, these ideas were appealing. If the sexes were distinct and non-overlapping, how could you move from one to the other? But if sex was a spectrum, then perhaps you could move far enough along it to be reclassified.

By the time he met Hirschfeld, the Institute had already been experimenting along these lines with genital surgery. Its earliest known patient was Dora (Rudolph) Richter. Born in 1891 to a poor farming family, Rudolph had cross-dressed from very young, and at age six attempted to remove his penis and scrotum with a tourniquet. Under the care of the Institute, in 1922 Rudolph was castrated and in 1931 underwent penectomy and the construction of an artificial vagina. Dora stayed on at the Institute as a demonstration patient and maid.

For Wegener, Hirschfeld wanted to try something more ambitious: a transformation of body chemistry as well as genitals. He was inspired by the work of Eugen Steinach, an Austrian endocrinologist who transplanted testicles into baby female guinea pigs, and ovaries into baby male ones, in the hope of inducing behaviours characteristic of the donor sex. He set Wegener on a gruelling series of operations. First came castration and penectomy, as with Richter; then the implantation of ovaries removed from a young woman; and finally the construction of a 'natural outlet' – probably a neovagina crafted from uterine tissue, or possibly an attempt at a womb transplant.

The details are unclear because the Institute's records were destroyed in the infamous Nazi book-burning in front of the Berlin Opera House in 1933. The only surviving account is *Man into Woman*, Wegener's memoir, which was written between and after the operations, and published under a pseudonym. It seems that either he did not understand what the doctors told him, or they were talking nonsense that went well beyond the theory of 'bisexuality'. For instance, the memoir states that they discovered two ovaries in Wegener's abdomen – impossible, since he also had two external testicles, and the male and female gonads develop from the same foetal tissue. Wegener also believed that, once the operations were complete, Lili would be able to conceive and bear a child with her implanted womb and ovaries. Whether this is what the doctors said to Einar, or a fantasy he constructed, is impossible to say.

If Hirschfeld had absorbed Darwin's insights, he might still have offered Wegener the same treatment, but he would surely have conceptualised and explained it differently. He could have empathised with Wegener's misery, and even sought to alleviate it with surgery that better aligned his body with his wishes, and allowed him to move through the world being taken as a woman in most circumstances – without suggesting that this would shift Wegener towards the female end of a non-existent sex spectrum. A great deal of later confusion would have been avoided – and a great deal of sexism.

I do not mean to be unappreciative of Hirschfeld, who was remarkably brave and forward-thinking. He supported the franchise for women, and campaigned for decriminalising homosexual relations between men, although this put him in grave danger during the Nazis' rise to power. (He was a gay man himself, and a 'transvestite', in his sense, frequenting Berlin's drag scene as Aunt Magnesia.) The problem was that his theory of bisexuality, which set the course for generations of later researchers and clinicians, encoded an understanding of women as naturally inferior and subordinate to men, and of the performance of sex stereotypes as part of what made someone a man or woman.

Those who subscribed to the earlier 'two-sex' model were not any more enlightened, of course: they understood men and women as distinct and immutable groups, with the former naturally dominant and superior. Such a way of thinking is no less sexist – but it is more amenable to correction in light of evidence. If the sexes are distinct, then the existence of a successful woman scientist, poet or leader is a blow against the assumed hierarchy. But if the sexes shade into one another, such women can be dismissed as simply less womanly – exceptions, rather than an argument for parity of esteem. And if altering superficial characteristics such as dress, presentation and behaviour is understood as moving someone along a sex spectrum, then a woman who rejects those stereotypes is making herself less of a woman, rather than demonstrating that they are unnecessary to womanhood.

This baked-in sexism is clearly visible in *Man into Woman*. Lili's claim to womanhood is described as relying partly on the promised anatomical changes – she desires a child 'to convince myself in the most unequivocal manner that I have been a woman from the very beginning'. But it relies mostly on Lili's character, so different from Einar's. He is 'ingenious, sagacious, and interested in everything – a reflective and thoughtful man', and she, a 'thoughtless, flighty, very superficially minded woman, fond of dress and fond of enjoyment . . . carefree, illogical, capricious, female'. Art, Einar's passion, does not interest Lili: 'I do not want to be an artist, but a woman.' That must have stung Gerda, who was both an artist and a woman. And how must she

have felt when Lili declared her heart's desire to be 'the last fulfil-
ment of a real woman; to be protected from life by the sterner
being, the husband'?

After the surgeries, the King of Denmark issued Lili a new
passport stating her sex as female, and annulled Einar's marriage
to Gerda. Lili quickly became engaged to Claude Lejeune, an art
dealer. She did not live to marry him. After an 'abyss of suffering',
on 13 September 1931 she died of heart failure, probably caused
by organ rejection or infection. But to her, it had all been worth-
while. 'That I, Lili, am vital and have a right to life I have proved
by living for fourteen months,' she wrote, close to the end. 'It
may be said that fourteen months is not much, but they seem to
me like a whole and happy human life.'

For two decades after Lili's death, the idea of trying to change
sex seemed in abeyance. In some respects, that was strange,
since medical developments would have made it much less risky.
During the 1930s scientists worked out how to synthesise sex
hormones, and during the 1940s antibiotics came into common
use. The German doctors had claimed it was possible to move
males towards the female end of a putative spectrum. Wegener
had done it – and written the travelogue. Why, then, a handful of
other men with similar yearnings continued to wonder, shouldn't
they?

*

'Ex-GI becomes blonde beauty: operations transform Bronx
youth' blared the *New York Daily News* on 1 December 1952. A
twenty-six-year-old New Yorker, George Jorgensen, had travelled to Europe two years earlier, lured by rumours that Swedish
doctors were providing some sort of treatment for men like
him. While he was visiting relatives in Copenhagen, he met Dr
Christian Hamburger, an endocrinologist familiar with
Hirschfeld's work. Hamburger diagnosed 'transvestism' and

offered to treat him – essentially to experiment on him – without charge.

As a boy, George had seemed quite ordinary. But inwardly, he was miserable, hating masculine clothes and games, and developing crushes on other boys. As an adult, he had homosexual experiences, which he regarded as immoral. He longed to 'relate to men as a woman, not another man', he wrote later. He was drafted into military service after the end of the Second World War, and it turned him off manhood further. He got hold of oestrogen before he ever left for Europe, and started taking it without medical supervision.

Hamburger treated Jorgensen in three steps: psychiatric and physical examinations; more female hormones; and finally, in stages during 1951 and 1952, castration and penectomy, plus plastic surgery to give the appearance of external female genitalia. His final assistance was to help his patient get an American passport in a woman's name. As an expression of gratitude, Jorgensen chose Christine.

Hamburger and his colleagues did not regard themselves as having changed Jorgensen's sex. They understood him as a homosexual man whose 'transvestism' was so deep-rooted that living contentedly required presenting as a woman as completely as possible. It was Jorgensen who claimed womanhood – with the assistance of the American press. When she landed in New York in February 1953, hundreds of well-wishers and journalists were waiting. 'I'm glad to be back,' she told them. 'What American woman wouldn't be?'

Though she complained for the rest of her life about the intrusive coverage, biographers have concluded that she had tipped the reporters off herself. They made her world-famous. In the twenty-five days after the story of her operation broke, news wires sent out fifty thousand words about her. A first-person account, serialised in the *American Weekly*, a Sunday-newspaper supplement, earned her $25,000 (a cool $240,000 in today's money) and appeared in seventy countries. 'Sex change' quickly became known as 'the Christine operation'.

Lili Elbe's story had caused a sensation, but was quickly forgotten in the horror that swept across Europe soon after her death. By contrast Jorgensen's, a very American one of self-actualisation and reinvention, suggested a hitherto unimaginable possibility to other men who might previously have dismissed their cross-sex yearnings, or buried any thought of their 'woman inside'. And it opened a new chapter in the multi-decade reconceptualisation of sex as blurred and mutable, rather than binary and fixed.

The shaping of this narrative was now in the hands of journalists as well as doctors. They praised Jorgensen's looks – and skated over what the operations had involved, and their partial results. (The procedure in Denmark had left her with external genitalia only. In 1954 she underwent one more operation, in New Jersey, in which a shallow neo-vagina was constructed using skin from her thighs.) Many of their readers no doubt interpreted the phrase 'sex change' literally. They also credulously repeated Jorgensen's vague claims of a congenital intersex condition, and her insistence that sex was a spectrum. In a letter to her parents that was republished widely, she said that she had been diagnosed with a hormonal imbalance. 'Nature', she wrote, 'made the mistake which I have corrected and now I am your daughter.' In 1957 she told an interviewer that 'people, both men and women, are both sexes. The most any man or woman can be is eighty percent masculine or feminine.'

Christian Hamburger, who had treated Jorgensen in Denmark, found himself besieged with requests from other men all over the world, but turned them all down. It was a doctor practising in New York who hitched himself to Jorgensen's fame, and whose lasting influence on gender medicine has been greater than any other's.

Harry Benjamin, a German endocrinologist who had invited Hirschfeld for a speaking tour of the US shortly before Lili Elbe's death, had started his career as an out-and-out quack. He arrived in New York in 1913 as the assistant of a swindler selling the 'turtle treatment', a fake tuberculosis vaccine. That fraud was exposed, and Benjamin moved on to touting testosterone supplements and vasectomy as anti-ageing treatments. (Neither worked – though he tried both on himself, and was quite an advertisement for his wares, living to 101.)

After meeting Jorgensen at a dinner party in 1953, Benjamin became her endocrinologist. He had already been preaching Hirschfeldian notions for some years; now her fame amplified his voice. At a 1954 symposium sponsored by the *American Journal of Psychotherapy*, he argued that everyone was made up of a 'mixture of male and female components', and that male 'transsexualists' had a 'constitutional femininity, perhaps due to a chromosomal sex disturbance'. Like Hirschfeld, he thought it reasonable to treat them with hormones and surgery, though for quite some time he could not find a surgeon to co-operate. Most other doctors thought such people were mad – and treated them with the usual barbarism of the day, including mega-doses of their own sex's hormones and electric shocks.

In 1963 Benjamin took on another patient who expressed a cross-sex identification, and who was to play as big a part in his career as Jorgensen, although behind the scenes. Reed (Rita) Erickson, a transsexual man who had been born a girl in 1917, was heir to a fortune, and funded a series of research symposia run by Benjamin. A decade later these became a standing body, the Harry Benjamin Foundation, which in 2006 was renamed the World Professional Association for Transgender Health (WPATH). It is still the world's most influential organisation in the field. Erickson also funded a research group led by Benjamin that aimed to set up an American sex-change programme. Among its other members was John Money, a New Zealander who had studied psychology at Harvard before joining Johns Hopkins University.

In the history of gender medicine, this was one of those moments when astrologers say the stars are aligned. Benjamin believed that sex was a spectrum and that people who wished to be members of the opposite sex might be moved along it by pharmacological and surgical means. Money believed that what made someone a man or woman was not their body at all, but which stereotypical sex roles they were reared in. Together, these ideas constituted a new theory regarding the origin and meaning of cross-sex identification, and what to do about it.

In this way of thinking, girls and women were people who had been taught stereotypical femininity in early childhood and grown up to be decorative, domestic and subservient. Boys and men were those who had been taught stereotypical masculinity and grown up to be active, outgoing and domineering. But sometimes the socialisation might fail to take. A person might grow up highly atypical for their sex, perhaps even feeling like a member of the opposite sex and adopting that sex's social role. In such cases, the wisest and kindest course of action would be to alter the body so that the person could be slotted back into the 'natural' order of things as a member of the opposite sex.

Money's contribution was not merely theoretical. To understand it requires a detour into what is now regarded as one of modern medicine's more inglorious episodes: the sterilisation and sex-reassignment of infants born with ambiguous genitalia – a tiny subset of those with so-called intersex conditions.

Nowadays, treatment is usually conservative. Doctors use scans, blood tests and karyotyping (working out what chromosomes someone has) to discover the child's true sex and diagnose their condition. Cosmetic surgery is increasingly delayed until the child is old enough to consent. But Money's theories led to an interventionist approach – one with dire consequences for infants' future fertility, sexual health and well-being.

Money believed that what he called gender roles, meaning 'all those things that a person says or does to disclose himself or herself as having the status of boy or man, girl or woman', were malleable in the first thirty months of life – and after that unchangeable. He therefore concluded that a baby boy with a micropenis, or a baby girl with an enlarged clitoris, would be equally happy brought up as either sex as long as the decision was made early and the parents did not waver. Since it was much easier to make genitals look female rather than male, it was mostly infant boys whose sex he 'reassigned'. He routinely advised the parents of those with normal chromosomes, but abnormal genitalia, to have them castrated and operated on to appear female, and to raise them as girls.

In 1967 Money met the patient who would make, and ultimately break, his reputation. In late 1965 the Reimers, a Canadian couple, had become the parents of identical twin boys. When the infants were seven months old they underwent routine circumcision. A power surge to the cauterising equipment burnt the elder boy's penis beyond repair. As the couple agonised about what to do, they chanced to see Money presenting his theories on television. They wrote to him, and he assured them that if the child was brought up as a girl, then that is what 'she' would believe herself to be. Reluctantly, they agreed.

The castration was carried out, the child's name was changed from Bruce to Brenda, and the Reimers tried to forget they had ever had twin boys. For more than a decade Money wrote about what he called the 'John/Joan' case in glowing terms. The little 'girl' was happy and feminine; fond of dolls and housework. Her twin brother was a normal, rough-and-tumble boy. The case was cited endlessly as proof that sex identities were socially constructed in early childhood.

In reality, however, the sex-reassigned twin was neither happy nor at all feminine. Money exaggerated any indication that the child was settling into girlhood, and concealed the awkward truth that in puberty 'she' had started to insist on being regarded as a boy. Eventually, the Reimers told their child the truth, and he took the name David and reclaimed a male identity. As an adult he underwent operations to construct a neo-penis, married a woman who already had children and tried to settle down.

The story became public after Milton Diamond, an academic sexologist convinced that Money's theories were rubbish, tracked David Reimer down. In 1997 it was written up by journalist John Colapinto in an award-winning article in *Rolling Stone* magazine, and then in a book. There were tragic addenda: in 2002 Brian, David's twin, died of an overdose of antidepressants and two years later, aged thirty-eight, David killed himself with a gunshot to the head. Between his sex reassignment and death, thousands of children worldwide had been sterilised and brought up as members of the other sex, in part because his life as a girl had supposedly been such a wonderful success.

The case of David Reimer is sometimes used today to argue that a sense of sex is innate – after all, even when told he was a girl, he somehow knew he was really a boy – and to argue that people experience cross-sex identification when that inner sense does not match their biology. But the conclusion does not follow. The fact is that Reimer *was* actually a boy, and when Money and his parents said otherwise, they were lying. What made him a boy was not that inner feeling, and a similar inner feeling of 'boyness' in a biological girl would not make her a boy. I will have more to say about the significance of such cross-sex feelings in children in the next chapter.

David Reimer had not yet been born when Benjamin, Money and their research group first met. But similar operations on other infants had already equipped surgeons at Johns Hopkins to 'reassign' the sex of adults. The first such operation was carried out in 1965 without fanfare. It did not long remain secret. In October 1966 Avon Wilson, a 'stunning girl who admits she was a male less than one year ago', featured in the gossip column of the *New York Daily News*.

Benjamin's magnum opus, *The Transsexual Phenomenon*, appeared the same year. David Cauldwell, a sexologist who opposed 'sex-change' surgery, had coined the word 'transsexual', but it was Benjamin who popularised it, and it quickly caught on. Reading the book more than half a century later gives a sense of déjà vu. It mixes and matches explanations for transsexuality, none of them compatible with current understandings of evolutionary theory, developmental biology or child psychology, but all of them still cited, in one form or another, today.

One is a version of Hirschfeld's sex spectrum. 'Every Adam contains elements of Eve and every Eve harbours traces of Adam, physically as well as psychologically,' Benjamin writes. He also describes transsexuals as suffering from a mind–body mismatch: 'Their anatomical sex, that is to say their body, is male. Their psychological sex, that is to say their mind, is female.' Elsewhere, he introduces a new model of sex as an additive property with several constituents: 'chromosomal, genetic, anatomical, legal, gonadal, germinal [meaning the production of ova or sperm], endocrine [hormonal], psychological, and social'. And lastly, he nods to Money's theories. Once 'gender-feeling'

– some sort of amalgam of 'feelings, attitudes, desires and self-identification' – has become settled, if there is a mismatch with biological sex, then it is sex that must 'yield'.

It was anything but easy to get approved for surgery at Benjamin's new clinic. Patients had to be mentally stable, and to have identified as the opposite sex for several years. Unless the doctors thought they would 'pass' and live as heterosexuals in their acquired sex, they were turned away. It never carried out many surgeries – just twenty-four in its first thirty months, out of more than two thousand applications. Nor did it survive long. It had got off the ground despite internal opposition and was closed down in 1979.

But by then the US had at least fifteen sex-change clinics – many run by staff trained at Johns Hopkins – and perhaps a thousand post-operative transsexuals. Much more than Lili Elbe, with her short, pain-filled life, Christine Jorgensen was transsexuality's proof of concept. At the hands of Harry Benjamin, it had indeed become a phenomenon.

*

There has perhaps never been such a quintessentially tabloid story as Corbett v. Corbett, in which Arthur Corbett, later the third Baron Rowallan, convinced a British judge to set aside his marriage to April Ashley. He was an old Etonian, heir to a Scottish title and owner of the Jacaranda Club on the Costa del Sol; she had been born in a Liverpool slum and worked as a dancer in a Paris burlesque club. They married in 1963, but parted almost immediately, and several years later, she demanded maintenance and the villa in Marbella. He wanted the marriage declared void – on the grounds that she was not a woman.

Ashley's early life as George Jamieson shared many features with Wegener's and Jorgensen's: a sad conviction of difference; a preference for girls' company and pastimes. After a short, inglorious career in the Merchant Navy, a failed suicide attempt and committal to a mental hospital, he found his way to the Carrousel nightclub in Paris, where he started performing as a female impersonator in 1955, at the age of twenty, under the name Toni Arthur. Many of the other performers were taking oestrogen to enhance their curves; he did so too. Three years later the star act, Coccinelle ('ladybird' in French), had a sex change in Casablanca with an up-and-coming surgeon, Georges Burou, who asked no questions except whether you could pay – several thousand dollars on arrival, preferably in traveller's cheques. Jamieson started saving, wrote to Burou and, in 1960, got on a plane.

Burou had trained in obstetrics and gynaecology, and drawn on his knowledge of the female pelvic region to invent a revolutionary new technique for surgically altering male anatomy to resemble it. No longer did transsexuals have to undergo a wasteful series of operations, in which the penis and scrotum were discarded and skin was harvested from elsewhere to line a neovaginal cavity. Instead, in a single 'vaginoplasty' operation Burou removed the internal parts of the penis and scrotum, retaining the skin and nerves to construct an unprecedentedly convincing simulacrum of a vagina and labia. He did not insist that males seeking sex-change surgery had previously presented as women or received any counselling; his only condition was that, to him, they looked like women. 'I turn away many people if I am not satisfied they have a feminine aspect and appearance', he told a journalist from the *Sunday Mirror* in 1970.

Perhaps the most famous of Burou's patients was Jan Morris, who as James had been the only journalist to accompany the 1953 expedition that conquered Everest. Morris underwent surgery in Casablanca in 1972, and her autobiography, *Conundrum*, published two years later, did much to spread the word of Burou's prowess. At his peak, Burou received at least two applications for surgery a day and each operation took just an hour. For years he guarded his methods as a trade secret. But after he presented them at a conference in Stanford in 1974, they became copied worldwide.

From Casablanca, Jamieson returned to Paris. There she met Arthur Corbett, who was married with four children, though far from faithful to his wife. He had long cross-dressed for erotic purposes, and sought out Ashley because he was fascinated by her transformation, which he heard about on the transvestite grapevine. He helped her change her name to April Ashley by deed poll and get a new passport stating her sex as female. His obsession with her brought his marriage to an end.

Ashley started to work as a fashion model. Then an acquaintance spotted the similarity with Toni Arthur, the female impersonator, and tipped off the *Sunday People*. The modelling work dried up and her nascent acting career died a sudden death. But the publicity did not deter Corbett. Indeed, Ashley's transsexuality was the draw, and he gave lengthy interviews to the tabloids about their engagement. In 1963 they married, proving her identity with her new passport. But they parted after two months, and when some years later she demanded the deeds to the house she said he had promised her, he sought to get the marriage annulled.

For Ashley, the hearing in 1969 was an utter humiliation. 'Intercourse using the completely artificially constructed cavity could never constitute true intercourse', Lord Justice Ormrod ruled. Her deportment was 'reminiscent of the accomplished female impersonator'. Most devastatingly, he concluded that 'the respondent is not, and was not, a woman at the date of the ceremony of marriage, but was, at all times, a male'. It was irrelevant, he said, that Corbett had known Ashley was transsexual.

Only the union of a man and a woman constituted marriage. And Ashley and Corbett were both men.

The ruling established in British law that, at least for the purposes of marriage, man and woman were purely biological terms. Since no operation could change biological sex, no transsexual would be allowed to marry in their new sex role. Since the National Health Service was already carrying out the occasional sex-change operation, that meant the British state was willing to pay for a man's body to be reshaped to approximate a woman's, but not to enable that person to marry, since a union with a woman would be practically and socially impossible, and one with a man would be unlawful. (At the time the obvious solution – to allow same-sex marriage – was inconceivable.)

Looking back on the first half-century of transsexualism, it is clear that for a long time officials understood what they were doing as resolving a tiny number of anomalous situations, a task they accomplished with varying degrees of compassion and logical coherence. Two long-term societal trends influenced their decisions, though they did not tend to acknowledge this: the growth of bureaucracy and the shift to individual, rather than communal, conceptions of personhood.

To be a man or a woman had always had legal significance, since governments had always treated men and women differently, and not just when it came to marriage – in voting, for example, and in land ownership and inheritance, and laws about which spouse could beat or lock away the other, and who controlled the money. But these laws – almost invariably to women's detriment – did not actually define the sexes. It did not seem necessary: men and women could almost always be distinguished by eye. The few people who managed to cross-dress and 'pass' as members of the opposite sex ran the constant risk of discovery. Unclothed, the body could not lie.

The obvious thing that changed with Lili Elbe was that, after the operations, she was no longer merely a cross-dresser whose artifice would be revealed in nakedness. Less obviously, the relationship between individuals and governments was becoming more formalised. Starting in the nineteenth century, governments recorded and licensed ever more aspects of people's lives, with birth certificates, passports, driving licences, pension-entitlement records, taxpayer numbers and so on. Almost always, these stated a person's sex. Being a man or woman now meant, in part, having pieces of paper that said so. For someone who had changed their body, this offered a way to bolster their claim to a new sex: persuade a bureaucrat to change those pieces of paper.

In America, decentralised birth and marriage records meant inconsistent decisions. In 1955 Tamara Rees, a male transsexual who had undergone surgery in the Netherlands a year after Christine Jorgensen's operation, married a man in a church in Reno. The county clerk declared himself unwilling to look beyond first impressions, saying that 'as long as they come in here with a dress on, they're women'. But four years later, when Jorgensen and her fiancé applied for a marriage licence in New York, her fame invited closer scrutiny. Her attorney pointed to her passport, which gave her sex as female, and a letter from Harry Benjamin stating that she 'must be considered female'. Nonetheless, the city clerk decided that her birth certificate, which she had been unable to change, barred her marriage to a man.

Overall, the trend was towards accommodation. By 1965, ten American states allowed post-operative transsexuals to amend the sex on their birth certificates. Though this was not possible in the UK, in *Conundrum* Morris writes of a bevy of bureaucrats, in the local county council, passport office, register office and department of social security, who smoothly and efficiently updated documents when she returned from Casablanca from 'M' to 'F'.

In the meantime, the ways people thought of social roles such as man and woman, and institutions such as marriage, were becoming more individualistic and atomised. In her fascinating and comprehensive book, *How Sex Changed: A History of Transsexuality in the United States*, published in 2002, Joanne Meyerowitz of Yale University argues that, between Jorgensen's sex change in 1952 and death from bladder cancer in 1989, the *sine qua non* of womanhood in American law and practice changed. As doctors, journalists and lawyers wrote and talked about Jorgensen and other transsexuals, they spun into being a new way of thinking about what it meant to be a woman. No longer was it possession of the type of body that can become pregnant; now it was the ability to have receptive heterosexual sex, twinned with an inner sense of being female, something like a subjective version of John Money's gender roles.

A definition of biological sex as reproductive capacity is, inherently, a communal one. It is about the role the individual plays within its species – whether that role is conceived of as shaped by evolution, ordained by God or something else. John Money's gender roles, too, concerned how individuals fitted into society – which stereotypes their upbringing had fitted them to adhere to. Now the focus had narrowed. What mattered was whether an individual could provide the sexual, not repro-ductive, services that a man expected of his wife – an individual rather than societal contract – and how she felt about herself. Though it was not yet consistently named, 'gender identity' had arrived.

2

SISSY BOYS AND THE WOMAN INSIDE

Why some men want to be women, and why some people don't want you to know

'He got in the girls' line instead of the boys' line at the drinking foun-tain ... He was playing with dolls, playing dress-up ... he loves jewelry ... his favourite characters are Cinderella [and] Snow White ... he talks like a girl, sometimes walks like a girl, acts like a girl ... he's standing in front of the mirror and he took his penis and he folded it under, and he said, "Look, Mommy, I'm a girl."'

These words come from parents' descriptions of their sons in a landmark fifteen-year study that began in the 1960s by Richard Green, an American doctor and lawyer who spent much of his career in gender medicine. At the time, and for many years after, no gender clinic saw children as patients, but Green wanted to answer a question that had intrigued doctors ever since they became aware of men who said that they were really women: had they always been that way? Were there little boys who insisted they were really girls, and if so, did they grow up to be transsexuals? Or, in the phrase that was now starting to be used, was 'gender identity' formed in early childhood, or perhaps even innate?

The title of Green's book, published in 1987, gives his findings away: *The 'Sissy Boy Syndrome' and the Development of Homosexuality*. (He chose his title as a comment on the stigmatisation of effeminacy.) Most of these effeminate little boys, who rejected their maleness and wished ardently to be girls, were not future transsexuals, but future gay men. Later studies have confirmed these findings. This chapter looks at the research into the origins of cross-sex feelings – and some of the reasons why transactivists have sought to bury it.

The adults Green and other gender clinicians saw said they had been highly 'feminine' little boys, and that they had always felt like they were, or should be, members of the opposite sex. But in no field of medicine are patients' reports the last word. Inevitably, and generally unintentionally, they recast their life stories to fit with what they currently believe about their condition. Moreover, studying only current patients misses an equally important part of the story: people who started out with similar characteristics but developed differently.

So Green turned to the gold standard for investigating the origins of a condition: a prospective study, which follows people who seem likely to develop it to see what happens. (The alternative, a retrospective study, starts with people who have the condition and tries to reconstruct how they got there.) He recruited around sixty 'sissy boys' and a similar number of 'controls': ordinarily masculine boys matched for age and socio-economic situation. He interviewed them and their parents every year or two. Of the forty-four in the first group whom he managed to stay in touch with, eighteen were unambiguously homosexual as young adults, fourteen fantasised about or engaged in homosexual activity with some frequency, and just twelve were exclusively, or nearly exclusively, heterosexual. Just one said he felt like a woman.

No research design is without its flaws, and for prospective studies the difficulty is staying in touch with the participants. Some move away and some lose interest – and there is often reason to think that those who stay in touch are atypical. For this study, the drop-out rate was on the high side: nearly a third. But it is hard to believe that many parents sufficiently concerned about their son's cross-sex behaviour to have enrolled in the study would not have bothered to tell the researcher, a decade later, that their son looked set to live life as a woman.

Since then, another dozen studies, in various countries, have looked at children suffering from misery caused by cross-sex feelings – now called gender dysphoria. In every one the majority outgrew their dysphoria, and a majority of those 'desisters' turned out gay in adulthood. The most recent, and best, of these studies, published in March 2021, followed 139 boys seen at a Toronto clinic between 1975 and 2009, around two-thirds of whom satisfied the clinical criteria for a diagnosis of gender dysphoria. It found that more than 90 percent of them later ceased to feel dysphoric and became reconciled with their sex, generally before or early in puberty.

It is not possible to predict with much accuracy which gender-dysphoric children will persist, if permitted to express themselves how they wish but not encouraged to believe that they are members of the opposite sex, and which will desist. The severity of gender dysphoria is not a particularly good indicator. In his final interview, aged seventeen, 'Todd', Green's sole persister, certainly sounds settled in his desire to be a woman. 'I feel like a woman inside', he tells Green. '[Women] just seem better. I don't know – a better life . . . I just feel like a woman.' But in the earlier interviews, he did not stand out as unusually effeminate or dysphoric.

The various later studies and clinical experience suggest that if gender dysphoria persists well into puberty it is more likely to be permanent. But persistence is still by no means certain. Susan Bradley, a child psychiatrist who set up Toronto's first gender clinic for children in 1975, recalls a child she worked with whose dysphoria continued into adolescence. They lost touch for a time. Then she ran into him. He was dressed in smart men's clothes, and told her that he had fallen in love with a young man who loved him back. He now accepted himself as gay, and had abandoned all thought of being a girl.

Green tried hard to persuade the parents of his 'sissy boys' to be accepting. 'We would say: you don't need to be a jock to be a boy,' he told me when I interviewed him in London in 2017, two years before his death. 'You don't need to be a girl to draw pictures. There are other boys like your son. Find [non-feminine, non-macho] activities he likes, such as board games. We would say to the father: "So he's not an athlete. He still deserves a father."'

Even so, Green's book makes upsetting reading in places. These boys clearly knew their parents were embarrassed by them. And despite his advice, some tried to shame the boys out of their 'sissiness'. Three were put through 'reparative therapy' at another clinic: dressed in macho clothes, forced to give up dolls and feign interest in sports, and punished for any hint of effeminacy.

Heartbreakingly, these boys later told Green that their parents had been right to try to fix them. 'I'm glad that they got help, because I don't think lots of parents would do that,' says 'Kyle'. 'They'd be too ashamed or whatever.' It seems doubtful, however, that this 'therapy' had any effect on their sexuality, though it evidently made them feel terrible about themselves. In their final meeting, 'Kyle' tells Green that 'dreams I've had, and stuff like that' have led him to fear that he may be gay, after all. 'Well, they are about other guys . . . I don't want to talk about it. You're the first person that I've ever said any of this stuff to . . . I don't want to be that way.'

34

It now seems very likely that male sexual orientation is, often or nearly always, set early in life and thereafter unchangeable. Some studies suggest a genetic influence; others, that the uterine environment plays a role. The permanence of male sexuality is suggested by the failure of 'conversion therapy' that attempts to turn gay men straight, whether by counselling or by linking sexual arousal by homoerotic material to aversive stimuli, such as electric shocks. And lastly, as Green and many others since have shown, adult male homosexuality is often heralded early in life by 'effeminate' behaviour.

Other evidence already suggested that there was a porous boundary between gay men, on the one hand, and transwomen who were sexually attracted to men, on the other. In the late 1960s, when Green was starting his study, a graduate student at San Francisco State University had spent a month interviewing twenty-one 'MtFs' (male-to-females) in the Tenderloin district, seventeen of whom he classed as transsexuals. All seventeen had previously regarded themselves as gay men. First they had been 'hair fairies' – feminine gay men with backcombed hairdos – and then drag queens, often working as prostitutes. But after meeting transsexuals their self-conception changed and they started to identify as women. Those who underwent surgery often left the Tenderloin. One of the grad student's informants claimed that transsexualism was 'a way of settling down'.

What the two groups have in common is called 'androphilia' – exclusive sexual attraction to males. Paul Vasey, a Canadian psychology professor, studies androphilic males in various non-Western settings. His ongoing research suggests strongly that whether highly feminine boys grow up to identify as gay men, transwomen or something else is largely determined by their culture. The degree to which their gender non-conformity distresses them, whether they will try to suppress it and whether they will seek to modify their bodies all also seem to be largely culturally determined.

Since 2003 Vasey has spent much of his time in Samoa, studying the *fa'afafine*, a 'third gender' consisting of males who were highly effeminate in early youth and often not discouraged in that feminine self-expression as they grew up. Samoan culture regards them as neither men nor women (though still unambiguously male). *Fa'afafine* rarely undergo body modification, and do not typically experience distress because of their sex. 'If a *fa'afafine* went to New Zealand or Australia and had a sex-change operation and returned to Samoa, no one in Samoa would say that individual is now a woman,' says Vasey. 'But traditional, non-Western frameworks for understanding masculine women or feminine men as "third genders" are often warped when viewed through a Western lens, which reinterprets them as transwomen or transmen. It's a type of colonialism.'

Since 2015 Vasey has also studied the *muxes*, a third-gender group of males found among the Zapotec indigenous peoples in Oaxaca, Mexico. He is now carrying out a comparative study of *fa'afafine*, *muxes* and Canadian gay men. His findings suggest that all three groups are 'cultural variants of the same biological trait, namely male androphilia'.

Vasey's earliest work on gender non-conformity in males was a multi-author review of gender dysphoria in children, published in 2000. It concluded that children who experienced distress with their sexed bodies often started out as merely gender-atypical, with the distress developing only as they learned that their feelings and behaviour were unacceptable to others. 'Your framework for understanding these things depends on the cultural context,' he says. 'If you're growing up in Samoa they don't mean you change your body, whereas if you grow up in Canada or England the pool of possible interpretations that you draw on includes, "I'm a transsexual and have to undergo medical intervention and pretty radical surgery." '

Part of the 'gender identity' puzzle was now solved. Androphilic males are often highly gender non-conforming in childhood, and may develop gender dysphoria and a cross-sex identification if their culture is insufficiently accommodating. But they were not the only ones turning up at gender clinics. And for clinicians, it was the others who seemed far more mysterious.

*

It was an 'aha' moment, says Ray Blanchard. In the mid-1980s, the clinical psychologist was working at the Clarke Institute of Psychiatry in Toronto, trying to work out what motivated gender-dysphoric men who wanted cross-sex hormones and surgery. And now he had met 'Philip', a patient whose case history made him feel that suddenly everything was clear.

Understanding Blanchard's moment of revelation requires a closer look at earlier clinicians' observations. For all the sanitised accounts in newspapers and memoirs, they had always understood that cross-sex identification had a great deal to do with sexual desire, and played out differently according to sexual orientation. 'There was never a question throughout the twentieth century whether there are different types of transsexuals,' says Blanchard. 'The question was how best to classify them.'

Blanchard started with two broad groupings: androphilic males and the rest. The first group were the minority – former 'sissy boys' who had persisted in wanting to be girls, highly feminine in their presentation and interests. The rest were quite different, and more varied. Many had wives and children, and conventionally masculine jobs and pastimes. Some reported fantasising during sex that they were women and their female partners were men penetrating them, or that they and their wives were lesbians. Yet others described themselves as bisexual or asexual – lacking in any sexual desire. It was not easy for an observer to see why they might seek to be accepted socially as women, or what they meant when they said they felt like 'women inside'.

The sole cross-sex behaviour that many reported, erotic transvestism, is a common fetish of heterosexual men. A study in Sweden in 2005 found that 2.8 percent of males experienced sexual arousal in response to cross-dressing. For some, it is sufficiently intense and central to their sexual arousal to constitute a 'paraphilia' – an atypical, extreme sexual interest that may be classed as a disorder if it causes serious problems or distress. But male cross-dressers do not usually express cross-sex identification. 'I was looking for the bridge', says Blanchard, 'between wearing women's clothing as a masturbatory aid and wanting to be a woman.'

And then he met 'Philip'. A thirty-eight-year-old with an MBA, Philip suffered gender dysphoria severe enough to have caused episodes of depression. He recalled throwing a penny into a wishing-well when he was six and praying to be turned into a girl. His sexual experiences had been with women, and during them he imagined being a woman too. When he masturbated, he imagined his naked body as a woman's, focusing on the breasts, vagina and soft skin. Sometimes he imagined a man was penetrating the vagina.

Philip said he had cross-dressed once in childhood but never since, because he got nothing from it. His readiness to describe his cross-sex fantasies made it unlikely that he was concealing a history of erotic cross-dressing. And hence Blanchard's 'aha' moment: 'Here you had what, up till that point, had been called transvestism, and there were no clothes.' Women's attire was not the true object of such a man's affections, he concluded: rather, the clothes were the means whereby a man gave life to that object, namely himself in female form. Blanchard turned to Greek to name this sexual desire: 'autogynephilia', which means love of oneself as a woman.

Understanding the life histories and motivations of these newly identified 'autogynephiles' posed several thorny problems. Since they had shown no signs of gender dysphoria or cross-sex identification as children, a prospective study, such as that carried out by Richard Green, was not an option. Complicating matters, by this point gender doctors had realised that their patients were intentionally deceiving them. An informal network had developed, with post-operative transsexuals coaching pre-operative ones in what to say to get approved for surgery: that your earliest memory was of knowing that you were truly a girl, and that you had been certain of that inner truth ever since.

Patients also lied about their sexual desires and experiences. Doctors at many clinics (though not the Clarke) regarded androphilic men as the only suitable candidates for surgery: in a homophobic world, turning gay men into straight (trans) women seemed to make sense. A patient who was sexually interested in women might therefore not admit it. On the other hand, one who seemed *too* interested in men risked being written off as a confused gay man. This double-bind might lead some to deny interest in sex altogether. Another reason this might happen is that men who wish they had a woman's body commonly find their male genitalia disgusting, and may become adept at screening out awareness of the physical signs of arousal.

To get at the truth about autogynephilia despite these obstacles, Blanchard used two techniques. One was phallometry, in which a pressure gauge is used to measure tumescence. Patients listened to stories about presenting as a woman – very dull ones, so as not to excite anyone who did not have an erotic interest in cross-dressing. (Here is a sample: 'You put on your eye shadow, mascara, and lipstick.') Most of the men in Blanchard's second group who had denied an erotic interest in cross-dressing became aroused. The other was a questionnaire developed for gauging motivation to provide socially acceptable answers. The patients who denied erotic cross-dressing, or who claimed to be bisexual or asexual, scored more highly, suggesting that they were more likely to be saying what they thought doctors wanted to hear.

All in all, Blanchard saw no reason to change his initial broad-brush division between androphilic transsexuals and the rest. The self-described bisexuals in the second group, he concluded, were autogynephiles who were attracted to women, but also desired men to validate their feminine identities. Those who described themselves as asexual were concealing their desires, perhaps even from themselves. He later drew finer distinctions within the group of autogynephiles, according to the nature of the fantasies. If these centred on clothing, the man was more likely to be content without medical transition. If they centred on the body, especially on imagined female genitalia, he was more likely to be severely dysphoric, and less likely to be able to find peace without surgery.

None of Blanchard's work was intended to put obstacles in the way of transition. He wanted to understand the clinic's patients, and help them decide what to do. Many were conflicted: concerned for their wives and children, and perhaps their careers. Moreover, autogynephilic desire seemed to compete with ordinary heterosexual desire, and could be temporarily eclipsed by a new partner. A man who had started fantasising about being a woman during adolescence might fall in love, conclude that those fantasies were a phase and marry – only for

them to return years later. If the significance of persistent fantasies of having female genitalia was more widely known, fewer
people would be made miserable by marriages entered in good
faith that ended in misery when the husband transitioned.

In the 1980s and 1990s, when Blanchard was doing his
research, the number of patients seen by gender clinics was tiny.
The sole treatment pathway was physical transition: oestrogen
and vaginoplasty for male patients; testosterone and mastectomy, and perhaps phalloplasty (a risky and complex operation
in which flesh stripped from an arm or thigh is crafted into a
neo-phallus), for female ones. Long delays were common.
When patients were eventually seen, the personal crises that led
to referral were past. And central to assessment was ensuring
that they fully understood the goal of castration and bodily
remodelling. They had to confront a tough question: was their
desire to transition strong enough?

It made for strict gatekeeping. At the Clarke, four-fifths of
patients abandoned the idea of transition before surgery. Some
did not show up for the initial assessment. Others never
returned, perhaps having concluded that living with gender
dysphoria was preferable to proceeding. Even after that, referral
for surgery depended on the 'real-life test': changing name,
pronouns and clothing, and maintaining a cross-sex presentation for two years. A surprising number presented for follow-up
appointments yearly, but never embarked on this trial. Clinicians
could be confident that patients who stayed the course were
unlikely to experience regret. And indeed, research at the Clarke
– and other clinics with similar rules – found that hardly any
did, and most were happier post-surgery.

The clinic would write to employers, asking for sympathy and
flexibility during the real-life test regarding such questions as
which workplace facilities patients would use. Post-surgery, the

thinking went, they would use those intended for their adopted sex. Superficially, their bodies were now similar, and as for any risk of sexual violence from admitting males to female spaces, those males' sexual organs had, after all, been removed.

Such decisions were made ad hoc by clinicians, perhaps without thinking through all possible situations and certainly without consulting women about what some would have seen as unwarranted intrusion. But the main considerations were how rare post-operative transsexuals were – and that there was no suggestion that pre-operative transsexuals would have the right to expose themselves in women's spaces, as later campaigners would demand. 'These anomalies were not the cause for great soul-searching,' says Blanchard. 'It wasn't necessary to square them with every philosophical and ethical consideration everywhere. And thinking back on the patients that we approved for surgery, I don't think they would have wanted to go into a women's shower and show themselves as having a penis.'

*

Blanchard was writing in specialist journals for an audience of a few hundred sexologists. But his typology of transsexualism was not destined to moulder in academic archives. In the 1990s and 2000s it found two popular chroniclers. And what happened next was an early warning of the rise of gender-identity ideology, within which 'transgender' is a political identity understood as entirely separate from sexuality, and the very mention of autogynephilia is taboo.

The first of those popularisers was Anne Lawrence, a transwoman who came across Blanchard's work in 1994, aged forty-four and about to embark on transition. A medical doctor, she read everything she could find about transsexuality, but little resonated with her feelings and experiences. In the description of autogynephilia, however, she experienced the shock of recognition. 'If you had asked, "are you a woman inside?" I would have replied, "I don't think so," ' she says. 'What I always knew is that I wanted to have a woman's body. I hated the penis; I hated the erections; that's what I had to change.'

Lawrence had wanted to transition since at least her teens. She recalls sitting in a university dorm with a utility knife, contemplating self-castration. But she held back from transition because she thought she would not make a sufficiently convincing woman. In her early forties, however, she started seeing Marsha Botzer, a transwoman practising as a gender therapist in Seattle, who assured her that she would pass very well. If anything, the idea of autogynephilia was 'delegitimising in the eyes of the gatekeepers', she says. Moreover, Blanchard's theory made her see what she was embarking on in a more complex light – though ultimately she decided to go ahead anyway. 'It made me realise what an audacious thing it was to do – to rebuild your life around your paraphilia with consciousness and deliberation.'

In 1998 Lawrence published an essay about autogynephilia on her website, entitled 'Men trapped in men's bodies' as a riposte to the trope that transsexuals are women trapped in men's bodies. She then solicited anonymous, first-person accounts from other autogynephiles, and in 2012 published an analysis of several hundred in a book of the same name.

Sexual tastes you do not share are inevitably hard to comprehend. But autogynephilia is especially so, since it is rare and even more rarely spoken of. Lawrence reveals a secret world. She talks about the 'pain, frustration and incomprehension' autogynephiles feel about not having the bodies they want. Many of their fantasies are clearly sexual, even if unusual – for example, imagining being penetrated in a non-existent vagina while placing something in one's anus. But almost anything coded female or feminine, she writes, can cause an 'intense, perplexing, shame-inducing erotic arousal that seems to simultaneously animate and discredit [autogynephiles'] desires to have female bodies'. Her informants recount erotic fantasies of pushing a baby buggy, joining a knitting circle, being called 'ma'am', having bubble-gum-blowing contests with girls, wearing clip-on earrings, taking birth-control pills, having a Pap smear test, and so on and on.

Lawrence considers the mechanism whereby this inwardly directed desire brings a cross-sex identity into being. She draws an analogy with the way the average heterosexual man not only wants sex with women, but has romantic feelings for his beloved and bonds with her. Autogynephiles, she thinks, do not merely desire their inner woman: they are 'men who love women and want to become what they love'. Cross-dressing often loses its intense sexual charge over time, and becomes comfortable and relaxing, just as a happily married man becomes less sexually excited by his wife, but becomes ever more deeply attached to her.

Those who reject Blanchard's theories think he, and by extension Lawrence, fundamentally misunderstand the nature and meaning of autogynephilic fantasies. They argue either that the fantasies are perfectly natural because all women feel sexual about their femaleness, in which case autogynephilia is actually evidence that a male person is really a woman; or, alternatively, that those fantasies are mechanisms for coping with being born in the wrong body, in which case surgery will end them. Could those critics be right?

It is true that a woman may feel aroused when contemplating her body or clothing – for example when putting on lacy underwear or a low-cut dress. Autogynephiles' fantasies are of a different nature. The way they symbolise themselves as women in their imaginations has a 'fetishistic flavour' that is 'qualitatively different from any superficially similar ideation in natal females', Blanchard writes. For example, they report arousal at the simple act of putting on everyday women's clothes. Natal women do not find getting dressed for work an orgasmic experience.

It would indeed be natural that someone whose body did not match their gender identity fantasised about having the right body. But if gender identity is not sexual in origin, then there is no reason those fantasies should be erotic. They also tend to continue post-transition, strengthening the conclusion that they constitute a paraphilia rather than a coping mechanism. Moreover, autogynephiles often eroticise aspects of woman-hood that most women dislike, such as menstruation, undergoing intimate medical examinations, experiencing sexism or wearing uncomfortable clothes. 'Forced feminisation' – some-one making a man cross-dress or undergo sex-reassignment surgery – is a staple of transgender erotica. Quite a few of Lawrence's informants say they would find it shameful to be a woman, and that this turns them on. 'Experiencing the daily humiliation and degradation of being a woman, forced to wear women's clothes and lipstick, is extremely attractive to me,' writes one.

The second person to bring Blanchard's ideas to a wider audi-ence was Michael Bailey, a sexologist at Northwestern University in Chicago. His 2003 book, *The Man Who Would Be Queen*, illus-trated Blanchard's typology with portraits of two (pseudony-mous) transwomen: 'Juanita' and 'Cher'. It is an entertaining romp around the evidence regarding the origins of homosexual-ity and erotic cross-dressing, and makes no bones about relating male transsexuality to both.

Bailey finds Juanita, his example of Blanchard's androphilic type, quite beautiful. Indeed, he says that many of the transsexuals he interviewed were 'more attractive than the average genetic female'. And he writes affectionately about the eccentric and artistically talented Cher, whom he identifies as an autogynephile – though she vehemently disagrees. She tells him about the 'robot man' that 'Chuck' (her name pre-transition) constructed to enact his fantasy of vaginal penetration. It had a 'penis' made of a dildo, and an arm that could be manipulated to stroke his back. A mirror on the ceiling enabled Chuck to view this simulacrum of heterosexual sex, dressed as a woman with the robot man penetrating his anus.

Bailey knew his book would be criticised by activists who disapproved of Blanchard's typology. But the level of vitriol shocked him – as it did Blanchard, who felt 'survivor's guilt' at seeing Bailey targeted, and horror at the diatribes that started to be published about Blanchard himself online. 'That kind of boiling hatred reminded me of when I was a small kid, brought up in a farming community,' he says. 'You would sometimes come across the rotting, stinking corpse of some small dead animal, and it's like a physical blow.'

Bailey's university received complaints alleging that he had broken rules governing research on human subjects, slept with one of those subjects and taken payment to write referral letters for people seeking sex-reassignment surgery – sackable offences, if true. An allegation was made to the state regulator that he was practising psychology without a licence. Rumours were circulated that he had abandoned his family, and that he had a drink problem. His book had been nominated for a 'Lammy', an award for excellence in celebrating or exploring LGBT themes. After protests, the nomination was withdrawn.

Bailey's family was also targeted. Andrea James, a trans-woman working in consumer advocacy in Los Angeles, posted pictures of his children online, with captions saying 'there are two types of children in the Bailey household': those 'who have been sodomised by their father [and those] who have not', and asking whether his young daughter was 'a cock-starved exhibitionist, or a paraphiliac who just gets off on the idea of it'.

'The situation went from disconcerting to disturbing to terrifying,' says Bailey. 'I knew that some people didn't like the ideas I wrote about; I did not know how deranged some people would get or how co-ordinated they would be. And then, from terrifying, it became humiliating. I was national news, with all kinds of accusations, from lying to my research subjects to having sex with them.'

Blanchard and Lawrence hunkered down and let the storm blow over. Now nominally retired, though still publishing, Blanchard says he is 'quite cheerful' about the attacks on him – which continue – though 'traumatised by proxy' by those on Bailey. Lawrence is also retired, though she is considering trying to bring her ideas to a wider audience, perhaps by writing explicitly autogynephilic erotica.

But the campaign against Bailey might have succeeded, had it not been for Alice Dreger, a bioethicist and medical historian who moved in some of the same professional circles. The claims were so numerous, and so widely disseminated, that at first she thought they must contain some truth. After meeting Bailey and hearing about the harassment of his family, she decided she had to be sure. In an essay published in *Archives of Sexual Behavior* in 2008 she debunked them all, using evidence from emails and more than one hundred interviews. The material is enlarged upon in her acclaimed 2015 book, *Galileo's Middle Finger*.

Bailey had been targeted for publicising ideas transactivists wanted buried, Dreger concluded. The aim had been to 'undermine Bailey's reputation, undo any positive praise his book received, and make Bailey as personally miserable as possible'.

She presented copious evidence that three transwomen had orchestrated the campaign: Andrea James; Lynn Conway, a computer scientist; and Deirdre McCloskey, an economist. Strikingly, one had previously acknowledged autogynephilia, and another described what sounded awfully like it in an autobiography. In an email to Lawrence in 1998, James praised the 'Men trapped in men's bodies' essay, described Blanchard's observations as 'quite valid, even brilliant' and said she recognised autogynephilic tendencies in herself. In McCloskey's autobiography, *Crossing*, she writes that her teenage self, Donald, experienced 'a rush of sexual pleasure' when dressing in his mother's underwear, and used to break into neighbours' houses in search of girls' clothes. She also specifies his preference for autogynephilic pornography: 'There are two kinds of cross-dressing magazines, those that portray the men in dresses with private parts showing and those that portray them hidden. [Donald] could never get aroused by the ones with private parts showing. His fantasy was of complete transformation . . .'

But now self-reflection had been flung to the winds. Being transgender was to be understood as a matter of identity, not sexuality; Blanchard, Bailey and Lawrence were contradicting a cherished narrative; and everyone had to pick a side.

Partly, this was because of the 'Great Awokening' – an expression coined by journalist Matthew Yglesias as shorthand for the American Left's shift to an identity-driven style of politics. Activists had started to judge people and ideas, not according to the evidence, says Bailey, but according to a very particular notion of social justice. In their way of thinking, gender is a political identity – an innate characteristic that has nothing to do with sexuality. In the past couple of years he has assigned his grad students an article he and Blanchard co-wrote, entitled 'Gender dysphoria is not one thing'. The students typically find it upsetting and enraging, he says, since it contradicts cherished ideas.

But referring to autogynephilia for any reason other than to deny its existence provokes even greater rage than other sins against 'wokeness'. Blanchard thinks one reason is that it complicates the task of 'selling' transsexualism. 'If a guy decides he's coming to work as a woman from now on, it's one thing for him to say: "I'm coming to terms with the fact that I've always been a woman inside," and quite another to say: "I've moved on from just masturbating in women's clothes to wearing them all the time." '

In *Galileo's Middle Finger*, Dreger offers another insight: since autogynephilia involves a fantasy of truly becoming, or already being, a woman, any reference to it can be experienced as an insult. 'There's a critical difference between autogynephilia and most other sexual orientations: most other orientations aren't erotically disrupted simply by being labelled,' she writes. 'When you call a typical gay man homosexual, you're not disturbing his sexual hopes and desires. By contrast, autogynephilia is perhaps best understood as a love that would really rather we didn't speak its name.'

This explains why such rage is mostly directed at women, even though it is men who commit almost all anti-trans harassment and violence. Blanchard's observations of extremist transactivism in recent years have led him to believe that the leaders are mostly autogynephiles. Their anger results from 'envy of women and resentment at not being accepted by women as one of them', he has tweeted. 'They direct their ire at women because it is women who frustrate their desires. Men are largely irrelevant.'

Consider the favoured insult of the angry youth wing of transactivism: TERF, which stands for 'trans-exclusionary radical feminist'. The first part does not refer to excluding trans people from jobs, housing or other goods: it simply means denying that identifying as a woman makes you one. 'Radical feminism' is feminism understood as a liberation movement to free females from the patriarchy – a man cannot be a radical feminist, only an ally. Only females, therefore, can be TERFs. There is no equivalent insult for males who deny that sex can be changed by self-declaration.

Lawrence adds another piece to the puzzle of transactivist rage. She posits that autogynephilia's inwardly directed nature, and the frustrations attendant on requiring others to validate your cross-sex identity, mean that the condition co-occurs with narcissistic disorders more often than would happen by chance. And narcissists often respond to minor slights with disproportionate rage. It is not hard to find evidence of 'narcissistic personality traits, including a sense of entitlement, grandiosity, and lack of empathy' in the attacks on Bailey, she writes in a 2008 paper entitled 'Shame and narcissistic rage in autogynephilic transsexuals'.

Two processes are essential to creating and maintaining a healthy sense of self, says Lawrence: mirroring (being witnessed empathetically by others) and idealising (feeling a commonality with an admirable other). Autogynephilia can disrupt both. The urge to cross-dress is regarded as shameful, meaning it is concealed and the young autogynephile has no one to empathise with him and approve of the 'woman inside'. And whom can he identify with or look up to when older autogynephiles deny what drives them?

Lawrence urges clinicians and researchers to strive for empathy. 'Virtually all transsexuals are likely to have been shamed and criticized for their gender variance before transition, and . . . are likely to encounter subtle or blatant disrespect, harassment, discrimination, or violence after transition,' she writes. She counsels care in the choice of language: 'it might be helpful to begin to describe autogynephilic transsexuals as persons who want to "become what they love", as an alternative to more stigmatising descriptions.'

Between the studies of effeminate boys and gender-dysphoric men, it had become clear that a male might identify as a woman for more than one reason, and that gender dysphoria and cross-sex identification were related to sexuality in two separate and quite different ways. But the rise of left-wing identity politics and the determination to bury the concept of autogynephilia meant that, as trans people became more common and visible, this complex, nuanced picture of transness was simplified and erased.

The rest of this book is largely concerned with the consequences, which go far beyond the harassment and defamation of anyone who carries out research into the origins of gender dysphoria, or even talks about such research. They fall most heavily on children and on women. But first it is time to look more closely at the ideology that has been substituted for the scientific findings. What, precisely, is a 'gender identity'?

3

MY NAME IS NEO

Gender-identity ideology 101

'You're here because you know something. What you know you can't explain, but you feel it. You've felt it your entire life, that there's something wrong with the world. You don't know what it is, but it's there, like a splinter in your mind, driving you mad.'

With these words the mysterious Morpheus tells Thomas Anderson, aka Neo, the hero of *The Matrix*, that his life is a sham. The film, released in 1999, has been interpreted in many ways, including as religious allegory, a vision of an online future and an expression of teenage alienation. But many trans people regard it as expressing their experiences. Some gender therapists even prescribe it as viewing for their clients' families. It was written, produced and directed by the Wachowski siblings, both of whom were born male and came out as transwomen after its release. In 2020, Lilly, the younger and second to transition, confirmed that it was a 'trans metaphor'. This chapter will use the film to explain gender-identity ideology. Its characters represent the figures that stalk transactivists' discourse, from transphobes to detransitioners, and its premise and plot illuminate their worldview.

For those who have not seen it, a one-paragraph plot summary. Anderson, a computer programmer by day and hacker who goes by the name Neo at night, is intrigued by online references to something called 'the Matrix'. The sinister Agent Smith warns him off investigating further, but when Morpheus offers him the choice between a red pill that will reveal the truth and a blue pill that will leave his life unchanged, Anderson chooses the red pill. The world fractures and melts away. He comes round in a womb-like pod plugged into a grid with countless other humans, and is rescued by the *Nebuchadnezzar*, Morpheus's ship. Morpheus explains that Anderson's life has been a simulation in the Matrix, a program devised by sentient machines after they defeated humans in a war that blotted out the sun. Since that deprived the machines of their power source, they created the Matrix to keep humans passive while their bio-energy was harvested. Morpheus thinks Neo is 'The One', a prophesied leader who will lead a fightback against the machines.

In the trans-allegorical reading, the Matrix is 'cisnormative' society, and people unplugged from it are trans. (The prefix 'trans' means 'on the other side of' in Latin; 'cis', meaning 'on the same side of', is a recent coinage for non-trans.) The red pill represents cross-sex hormones. Anderson's exit from the pod where his body has been imprisoned represents the experience of transition: a second birth. Slimy, gasping and helpless, detached from the tubes that have sustained him, he is ejected from a dream state into the real world.

The Agents, terrifying programs that patrol the Matrix and destroy anyone who recognises it as illusory, represent transphobia. They are self-doubt, hatred of authenticity and acceptance of a vicious system. Morpheus, their chief enemy, represents the power of acceptance and self-actualisation. The Oracle, whom Morpheus brings Neo to visit, represents an older, wiser trans person, or a gender therapist. She tells Neo he is not The One, but only because that is what he must believe in order to do the right thing; later, she tells him he must discover his identity for himself.

Trinity, the toughest and coolest of the *Nebuchadnezzar*'s crew, plays the role allotted in action films to even the most kick-ass woman: she stands by her man. Her belief in Neo revives him after he is killed by Agent Smith. Before she administers the life-giving kiss, she whispers that he cannot be dead because the Oracle told her that she would fall in love with The One. She represents the importance of having one's trans identity validated by others.

The moment when Neo starts to believe in himself offers two trans-allegorical readings. As Agent Smith pummels Neo, he repeatedly refers to him as Mr Anderson – 'deadnaming' him, in the activists' lexicon. Like 'misgendering' – referring to someone by pronouns matching their sex rather than their gender identity – this is deeply wounding. When Neo fights back, he asserts his true identity with the words 'My name is Neo.' (It sounds more dramatic than it looks on the page.) The scene is set in a subway station, and Smith, the avatar of transphobia, almost kills Neo by pushing him under a train. That can be taken to represent campaigners' oft-repeated claim that someone struggling with their gender identity faces a choice between transition and suicide. Lana, the older Wachowski, has spoken of contemplating suicide in a subway station pre-transition.

Cypher is a crew member who has tired of the grim conditions on the *Nebuchadnezzar*. He betrays the ship to an Agent in return for a promise that he will be plugged back into the Matrix (he dies before this can happen). A creepy character who desires Trinity and resents Neo, he is occasionally seen as symbolising 'chasers' – men who desire (genitally intact) transwomen. This is a relatively common male sexual taste (as evident from the number of 'shemales' on Pornhub, and tourists visiting Thailand for the 'ladyboys'). But since it distinguishes between trans-women and natal women, many transwomen reject it as a perversion.

Cypher is better understood as representing detransitioners as they are regarded from within gender-identity ideology. Taking the red pill did not work out for him, and he seeks to blame and take revenge on others. Self-hating and filled with regret, he collaborates with and is used by the forces of transphobia.

Switch, another crew member, is the only character written as explicitly trans. The Wachowskis planned for the part to be played by two actors, male in the real world and female in the Matrix, to represent a programming glitch. Though the studio vetoed the idea, the script and direction were left unaltered – which explains some puzzling details. Alone of all the *Nebuchadnezzar*'s crew, Switch wears white; this was intended as a visual cue that the two actors were the same character. Switch's final words before dying inside the Matrix, in the 'wrong' body, are: 'Not like this. Not like this.' They are a lament for 'trans erasure' in death – the way a trans person is sometimes buried and mourned under their pre-transition identity.

Kid, who appears in the sequels and whose back-story is told in *The Animatrix*, a series of nine shorts, somehow manages to wake up from the Matrix without the aid of a pill. He represents the logical end-point of gender-identity ideology's premise: the non-hormone, non-op trans person, who undergoes no medical or surgical treatment, but identifies out of their sex by nothing more than self-declaration.

The sequels subvert the first film to some extent (they are also heavy going). It turns out that the Matrix has been through many iterations, and that Neo is a program written to bring about each one's destruction and replacement. But this time he rejects his allotted role, and peace is achieved by a synthesis between humans and machines. 'The first movie is sort of classical in its approach,' Lana Wachowski said in 2012. 'The second movie is deconstructionist, and an assault on all of the things you thought to be true in the first movie . . . The third movie is the most ambiguous, because it asks you to participate in the construction of meaning.'

*

The idea underlying all this – and which can be seen in nascent form in Einar Wegener's feeling that he had a 'woman inside' – is 'dualism'. This is the belief that the immaterial psyche and the vessel that houses it are separate and of different kinds. The best-known proponent of this was the seventeenth-century French philosopher and mathematician René Descartes, who saw mind as pre-eminent over matter. In his 1949 book, *The Concept of Mind*, the British philosopher Gilbert Ryle coined a felicitous phrase for the way dualists conceive of a person: as a 'ghost in the machine'. Gender-identity ideology gives the ghost a sex – one that can differ from that of the machine.

What feminists used to mean by 'gender' was something external: a societal structure in which female people were inferior and subordinate to male ones. But within gender-identity ideology, it is an inner essence given public form by self-declaration. No one else can define that essence, and only you can know who you truly are. Rather like being The One, in fact – or in love, as the Oracle says to Neo. 'No one can tell you you're in love, you just know it.'

When *The Matrix* was released, almost no one understood a trans person's avowed cross-sex identity as anything like this. Most people thought – and many still do – that transness meant 'transsexuality': such a deep discomfort with one's sexed body, and strong identification with the opposite sex, that only surgery to reshape the body to the extent possible could bring a measure of peace. Accommodations to allow such people to live 'as if' they were members of the opposite sex were understood as legal and bureaucratic fictions.

The idea of a non-hormone, non-op transwoman – someone who retains a physiologically normal male body but understands themselves to be a woman because that is their 'gender identity', and expects everyone else to agree – would have seemed nonsensical to almost everybody. (Recall that in the allegory this is the type of person represented by Kid, who wakes up from the Matrix without the aid of a red pill.) And yet, in the two decades since the film's release, this very concept of transness has conquered medicine, law, public policy and the media.

This surely could not have happened without the internet, not just because social media enabled its spread, but also because many people now spend more time in virtual worlds than the real one. Someone who rarely engages with nature or exerts themselves physically will be predisposed towards body-denialism. And if you spend a lot of time playing computer games, you will have become accustomed to identifying with avatars who can be altered on a whim.

You will also be predisposed to believe that the mind is a computer program. In his 2015 book, *In Our Own Image*, the artificial-intelligence expert George Zarkadakis discusses the metaphors employed throughout history to explain human intelligence. In ancient sacred texts, humans were created from clay, animated by a spirit breathed into it by a god. In the third century BC, hydraulic engineering inspired the notion of fluid 'humours' that caused ill health when they got out of balance. In the 1600s, clockwork suggested to Descartes and others that bodies were complex automata. From the 1700s, chemistry and

MY NAME IS NEO

electricity led to new metaphors – think of Frankenstein's monster brought to life by lightning. Hermann von Helmholtz compared signals in the brain to telegraph messages.

In our computerised age, mind is imagined as software running on the brain's hardware. Unsurprisingly, this idea has an intuitive appeal for those who believe that a true self may be housed in a body of the wrong sex. Transwoman Martine Rothblatt, a biotech entrepreneur and author of *From Transgender to Transhuman: A Manifesto on the Freedom of Form*, takes it further, arguing that transhumanism, a loose movement that seeks to conquer death, is a natural extension of gender-identity ideology.

Transhumanists envisage a variety of paths to a post-human future, including upgrading bodies and minds with increasingly sophisticated plug-ins, using nanobots to keep disease and ageing at bay, merging human and artificial intelligences, using gene therapies to speed up evolution, and cryonics (freezing heads at the moment of death, in the expectation of future revival). 'We can of course self-replicate our bodies via sexual intercourse (or IVF),' wrote Rothblatt in 2010. 'But we can soon also satisfy that urge to self-replicate by copying just our minds in software.' If this seems reductionist, consider Bina48, a robot Rothblatt commissioned in 2007. A disembodied head with thirty motors under its rubber skin that allow it to make expressions, it was modelled on Bina Rothblatt, the woman Martine married as a young man and has remained married to since transitioning in 1994, and was trained to respond and converse using recordings of her.

This way of thinking about human existence sheds light on one of the many contradictions of gender-identity ideology. If identity is all, and a man or woman may have any type of body, then why bother with medical or surgical transition? And indeed, some cutting-edge activists now regard the very concept of transition as transphobic, since it suggests that a trans person needs to align the outer self with the inner, rather than just declaring who they have always been. Take, for example, an article for Therapy Route, an American website, by Mx Van Levy, a non-binary therapist, entitled 'Why the term transition is transphobic'. The reason presented is that the word 'transition' is 'based on the idea that gender looks a certain way and that people need to change from looking/sounding/acting/and more, a certain way for their identity to be respected . . . The reality is, we are who we are, and our outside appearance does not change who we are on the inside . . . The term transition implies that we were one gender and are now another. But that is not the case. We are and always have been our gender . . . changing how we look on the outside is not a transition.'

For such activists, medical or surgical transition is simply a matter of choice for those trans people for whom it seems meaningful. Altering the body is no part of attaining a new identity, but if the body is a mere meat puppet, why not alter it if you wish?

In fact, mind-as-program works no better than previous dualistic metaphors, as research psychologist Robert Epstein explained in an essay for *Aeon* magazine in 2016. 'Your brain does not process information, retrieve knowledge or store memories,' he writes. Computers operate in an algorithmic fashion on symbolic representations of the world that are stored in memory banks; humans – and other organisms – do not. 'Even if we had the ability to take a snapshot of all the brain's eighty-six billion neurons and then to simulate the state of those neurons in a computer, that vast pattern would mean nothing outside the body of the brain that produced it,' says Epstein.

Which is as good a way as any of saying that gender dysphoria is very real, in the distress it causes and the need for compassion and research into effective treatments, but gender identity conceived of as separate from the body that houses it is not. And indeed, many of those who feel driven to transition are anything but body-denialist: they are painfully aware that their bodies cause them grief, and desperate to accommodate themselves to those bodies. They are among the people most ill-served by an ideology that pretends bodies are inconsequential and easily changed, and that what makes a person who they are is a sexed soul, or a ghost in a machine, or a program running on a computer, or whatever metaphor you prefer. The truth is that we are our bodies, and our bodies are our selves.

*

In the spread of gender-identity ideology, developments in academia played a crucial role. This is not the place for an extended critique of the thinking that evolved on American campuses out of 1960s French philosophy and literary criticism into gender studies, queer theory, critical race theory and the like. I will merely touch on what some have dubbed 'applied postmodernism' and the form of activism, known as 'social justice', that seeks to remake humanity along these ideological lines. And I will lay out the key elements that have enabled trans-sexuality, once understood as a rare anomaly, to be converted into an all-encompassing theory of sex and gender, and body and mind.

Within applied postmodernism, objectivity is essentially impossible. Logic and reason are not ideals to be striven for, but attempts to shore up privilege. Language is taken to shape reality, not describe it. Oppression is brought into existence by discourse. Equality is no longer achieved by replacing unjust laws and practices with new ones that give everyone the chance to thrive, but by individuals defining their own identities, and 'troubling' or 'queering' the definitions of oppressed groups.

A dualistic ideology can easily be accommodated within such a framework. Being a man or woman – or indeed non-binary or gender-fluid – becomes a matter of defining your own gender identity and revealing it to the world by the medium of 'preferred pronouns'. It is a feeble form of dualism, to be sure: the grandeur of Descartes' 'I think, therefore I am' replaced by 'they/them' on a pronoun badge.

The great difficulty for this philosophy is getting other people to accept identities that are entirely subjective and have no physical correlate. In *The Matrix*, that life on the *Nebuchadnezzar* was real, and life within the Matrix a sham, could be established by props and cinematic techniques. Neo enters the Matrix via cables plugged into his spine and skull, and uploads programs into his brain that endow his computer projection with skills and weapons. As his projection roams the Matrix, the shot repeatedly cuts back to his unconscious body on the *Nebuchadnezzar*.

But people in our world – the artificial one in the allegory, remember, populated by mere bodies, not true identities – have no access to a communal realm like the *Nebuchadnezzar* where those identities can be encountered. Declaring pronouns can do only so much to reveal an inner self to everyone else. If you want everyone to accept gender-identity ideology, they must be persuaded that sexed bodies are not material, and that gender identities are.

A wide variety of claims are made in support of these propositions. The way they are deployed is often reminiscent of the 'Gish gallop' – a debating technique named for creationist Duane Gish, who would fire out unrelated falsehoods, half-truths, irrelevancies and misrepresentations in quick succession to overwhelm his debating opponent. These points do not actually add up to an argument in favour of the proposition, but they waste an opponent's time and distract them from making their own argument.

The only way to counter a Gish gallop is to get your rebuttals in first. So here are mine for the four arguments I have most often seen used in favour of the proposition that sex is immaterial.

The first of these is that the very notion of binary sex is an artefact of Western colonialism. Before white people arrived, indigenous peoples were supposedly too wise to think that humans came in just two physical types. The *fa'afafine* of Samoa, the *muxes* of Oaxaca, India's *hijra* and the 'two-spirit' people of some Native American tribal groups are cited. Never mind the racism inherent in claiming that the rest of the world needed Europeans to explain how reproduction worked; such third genders have no bearing at all on these traditional societies' understandings of biological sex. They are, rather, testimony to the rigidity of their sex roles: a way to prevent effeminate, same-sex-attracted males from sullying the class of men. (Female third genders are rarer, but include 'sworn virgins' in traditional, deeply patriarchal Balkan societies, who were granted some male privileges in return for renouncing marriage and child-bearing. They were usually motivated by the desire to inherit property, or to escape an arranged marriage without setting off a blood feud.)

The second, dubbed 'Nemo's Law' by some wit online, is the gender-identity equivalent of Godwin's Law – the tendency in long online discussions for someone eventually to bring up the Nazis. Nemo's Law is the observation that if you mention sexual dimorphism, sooner or later someone will bring up clownfish, which are 'sequential hermaphrodites' born with the potential to mature into either males or females. When the dominant female in a group dies, her mate changes sex to take her place, and the largest non-breeding male becomes fertile. That person will then imply that since clownfish can change sex – or, more generally, that since not all living things are sexually dimorphic and incapable of changing sex – there can be no objective distinction between male and female. But you need a definition of male and female to observe that clownfish can change sex – or that some other living things are hermaphrodites, or reproduce asexually – and you will then be able to see that sex in humans is indeed binary and immutable.

The third is to claim that people with intersex conditions prove that sex is not binary. In her 1993 essay, 'The five sexes', Anne Fausto-Sterling, professor of biology and gender studies at Brown University, argued that five sexes should be recognised: male, female, merm, ferm and herm (the extra ones are, offensively and somewhat absurdly, defined as males with some female aspects, females with some male aspects and people who possess one testicle and one ovary). Then she goes further, describing sex as a 'vast, infinitely malleable continuum that defies the constraints of even five categories'. She gives startling estimates for the prevalence of intersex conditions: 4 percent in the essay; 1.7 percent in *Sexing the Body: Gender Politics and the Construction of Sexuality*, a book published in 2000.

Such figures are nonsense. To get to even 1.7 percent you must include people with developmental anomalies that are so minor they may never become apparent, as well as more serious conditions that still create no difficulty in classifying a person as male or female. The share of people whose chromosomes do not match their body type (the XY karyotype that normally builds a male body together with breasts and a vagina, for example), or whose physiology is so ambiguous that medical investigation is required to class them as male or female, is more than a hundred times lower.

More importantly, the argument is nonsense, too. 'Sexes' are classes of organisms defined by the developmental pathways that evolved to produce gametes: eggs and sperm. As with any part of the body, reproductive organs may develop in anomalous ways, just as some people are born with extra fingers or toes, or missing eyes or legs, but humans are still ten-fingered and ten-toed, binocular and bipedal. For there to be even three sexes there would have to be a third gamete, and there is not.

Fausto-Sterling later said she was writing 'with tongue firmly in cheek'. And yet anyone who has taken gender studies in the past two decades will almost certainly have been assigned her essay, and it is taken inexplicably seriously. So entrenched is the 'five sexes' claim that Googling 'how many sexes are there' turned up 'five' as the top answer until the search algorithm was tweaked in response to complaints.

The fourth argument, which I will consider in most detail, is that sex – not gender – is socially constructed. This is a claim of breath-taking proportions, given everything that is known about the mechanisms of reproduction and humanity's shared evolutionary history with other sexually dimorphic species. Nonetheless, it is now social-justice orthodoxy. It is most closely associated with Judith Butler, the most influential gender theorist of all. She claims that sex and gender are not distinct things, and that sex/gender is socially constructed.

Understanding this is key to understanding the wide difference between what gender activists mean when they talk about transness, and what most ordinary people think they mean. Most people think being trans means a mismatch between someone's sex and their gender identity – and that is what many trans people think, too. But it is not what the activists mean. Indeed, they regard it as 'transphobic', since it suggests the existence of some objective identity other than the one a trans person declares. In this, as in much else, the activists do not by any means speak for all trans people. But it is the activists' version of the ideology that is in the ascendant, and that is being codified into laws.

So what, then, does Butler think transness is? The answer is a mismatch, not between physique and identity, but between a social act imposed on an individual and that individual's self-knowledge. She claims that what medical professionals do when they register a newborn's sex is not observational, but 'performative'. A performative utterance is one that changes social reality. Marriage vows, which turn two single people into a legal couple, are an example. More whimsically, so is the Sorting Hat ceremony in the *Harry Potter* children's series, which turns new Hogwarts pupils into Slytherins, Hufflepuffs, Ravenclaws or Gryffindors.

In Butler's vision, then, medical professionals make children male or female by classifying them, and children are shaped into boys or girls, and later men or women, as they adopt the gender performance associated with their assigned sex/gender. It is now standard in transactivism to refer to people as AMAB or AFAB – assigned male/female at birth. Being trans is what happens when a person's emerging understanding of themselves conflicts with the assignation made by the doctor or midwife – who, in effect, guessed wrong.

Sometimes people who are not close to this subject imagine that the words man and woman can be used to denote social roles, and male and female kept for biological sex. But the 'assigned at birth' argument means that, within gender-identity ideology, transwomen are not only women, but also female. Depending on its owner's identity, a penis may be a female sex organ. Riley J. Dennis, an American transwoman YouTuber (and self-described 'lesbian icon'), talks about 'girldick', which is 'basically like a big clitoris'. Or a transwoman's penis may be described as an 'outie' vagina.

I have tried to explain all this to many people who did not take gender studies or a similar subject during the past decade, and who do not move in left-wing activist circles or spend much time on social media. Universally, they refuse to believe that it is anything more than ivory-tower thought experimentation. And yet it has infected august publications that print solid scientific sense day after day. In 2019 the *New York Times* gave Veronica Ivy (who at the time went by the name Rachel McKinnon), a Canadian philosopher and transwoman who holds a women's cycling world record, an op-ed slot to argue that 'the rules require me to race in the women's category. That's exactly where I belong: I am a woman, after all. I am female as well.' The 1.2 billion years of evolution since sexual dimorphism first appeared would beg to disagree.

And although any issue of *Nature* or *Scientific American* will contain articles that make sense only if you accept the evolved biological basis for sexual dimorphism, both have denied that there are clear criteria for classifying humans as male or female. In an editorial in 2018, *Nature* argued for laws to privilege gender identity over what it referred to as 'sex assigned at birth', citing intersex conditions as 'proof' that sex is a fuzzy concept. In an article in 2017 entitled 'Beyond XX and XY', *Scientific American* claimed that 'the more we learn about sex and gender, the more these attributes appear to exist on a spectrum'. An accompanying graphic illustrated some of the many ways in which the complex cascade of developmental events that lead to functioning male or female reproductive systems can go awry. What it really showed was how remarkable it is, given how much can go wrong, that most people's bodies end up with standard configurations – in the reproductive system, or in any other.

Once the activists are done with demoting sex from an objective characteristic of individuals to a social fiction, it is time for step two: to 'reify' gender identity – that is, to turn it from an abstract idea into something concrete. The main argument put forward is that neuroscientists have found a brain structure that is different in trans people, or shown that trans people's brains look like those of the sex with which they identify.

This is an odd claim to make if you also insist that biological sex is not binary, since you have to know which bodies are male and female before you can group brain scans into male and female and look for the differences. It is equally strange to claim that differences between brains could be a solid basis for classifying people as men and women, but those between genitals could not. Machine-learning algorithms can be taught to classify brain scans as male or female with around ninety-five percent accuracy. But that is far worse than the human eye can do with faces, and worse still than it can do with genitals.

Perhaps the oddest thing about this argument is the way a few small, inconclusive studies have been interpreted as showing that gender identity, rather than gender dysphoria, is 'in the brain'. The neuroscientists who study trans identification are not (usually) claiming to show that trans people have brains of the opposite sex. That is a misrepresentation by activists. Rather, they are attempting to discover the physical correlates of an unusual mental state. And it would hardly be surprising if feelings of dissociation from one's bodily sex are linked with detectable differences in brain scans.

The final step is to impose some structure on this ragbag of arguments for dematerialising sex and reifying gender. It is here that postmodernist techniques come into their own, in particular the 'deconstruction of binaries', as first carried out in the 1960s by French philosopher Jacques Derrida. Binaries are paired categories that encode dominance and subordination. The details of deconstruction vary, but the aim does not: to show that the supposedly dominant category is actually a subset of the supposedly subordinate one.

Over the years, a bewildering variety of binaries have been deconstructed. Theorists have claimed that speech is a form of writing (Derrida's canonical example), presence a form of absence and sanity a form of neurosis. Nowadays the technique is mainly applied to sex and gender within 'queer theory' – a hard-to-define academic field that seeks to upend conventional thinking about what is normative or deviant; innate or socially constructed; stable or mutating. All the arguments described above, from pre-colonial gender fluidity to trans brains, have been deployed to open up the category of Woman and argue that Man can be included within it.

A remarkable example of deconstruction is provided by the definition of 'female' proposed by Andrea Long Chu, an American transwoman and author of *Females: A Concern*, published in 2019. 'Everybody is female, and everybody hates it,' writes Chu. 'Femaleness is a universal sex defined by self-negation . . . I'll define as *female* any psychic operation in which the self is sacrificed to make room for the desires of another . . . [The] barest essentials [of femaleness are] an open mouth, an expectant asshole, blank, blank eyes.'

This definition is obviously influenced by pornography (and Chu has written that 'sissy porn did make me trans'). It is striking that receptive anal sex, which is possible for people of both sexes, is the act that Chu regards as defining females. If you actually are female, it is also highly offensive – and would be incomprehensible, if you did not understand that the aim is to enable males to count as females. Deconstruction is supposed to free the members of a subordinate class from subjugation within a binary – and I suppose it does, in a purely linguistic sense. But it is freedom at a high price: denial that the subordinated class even exists in any clearly defined way.

It is all an immense pity, because there is a concrete sense in which deconstructing binaries could be liberatory. As Simone de Beauvoir explains in her classic *The Second Sex*, published in 1949, patriarchy centres Man and defines Woman only in relation to him. This value-laden binary is reinforced by many others, including subject/object, order/chaos, active/passive, strong/weak, reason/emotion and light/dark. Feminism is the task of centring Woman in her own life, and unpicking these associations. In the binary reason/emotion, for example, emotion is both taken to be inferior to reason because it is Woman's domain, and taken to be Woman's domain because it is inferior to reason. Feminists reject both propositions. A rounded life requires both, and neither need be the domain of one sex or the other.

The two elements of a binary, in other words, can continue to describe the same distinct groups as they always did, while being stripped of the associations and interpretations that situate one group as dominant and the other as subordinate. Such work is essential to imagining a better future, for women and every other group on the wrong side of a binary. But queer theory does none of it. Instead, because of gender-identity ideology, the quest for the liberation of people with female bodies has arrived at an extraordinary position: that they do not even constitute a group that merits a name.

4

CHILD, INTERRUPTED

The catastrophic consequences of an adult
ideology for gender-dysphoric minors

In this chapter, I pick up the story of gender-dysphoric children
started in chapter 2, and look at what the theory of innate gender
identity means for them. When Richard Green and others first
studied them in the 1970s and 1980s, no clinician believed their
feelings actually made them members of the opposite sex, or
dreamed of treating them with drugs or surgery. They simply
sought to predict how those children would feel as adults. And
every study pointed to the same conclusion: they were pretty
likely to grow up gay, and very unlikely to still identify as or want
to be members of the opposite sex. There was no such thing as a
'trans child' in the sense of one who could be identified as
certain, or even highly likely, to grow up to be a trans adult.

But these facts contradict gender-identity ideology. So nowadays, they are ignored. The identity claims of gender-dysphoric
children are taken at face value and even the possibility of desistance is denied. Paradoxically, an ideology that holds that physiologically normal males can be every bit as much women as
people born female, and vice versa, is used to justify children
being put on a path to surgery and sterility. Doubters are treated

as bigots who could not care less if gender-dysphoric children kill themselves, rather than as whistle-blowers looking out for children's interests. This medical scandal, which has been unfolding for years, is now coming to wider notice.

It all started with the best of intentions. In the 1990s, clinicians who accepted that most gender-dysphoric children would desist wondered what could be done to help the minority who wouldn't. There seemed to be no early way to identify them (some studies suggested a correlation between the severity of gender dysphoria and likelihood of persistence, but not enough to predict an individual's path). The only option was to wait and see. But that had downsides, in particular the irreversible changes puberty brings.

These differ for transwomen and transmen because testosterone's effects are so hard to disguise. A transwoman who has gone through male puberty will bear its legacy for life: a deep voice and Adam's apple; marked facial features; facial and body hair; and an enlarged frame with big hands and feet. The legacy of pubertal oestrogen for transmen is less visible, and can be masked fairly successfully by taking testosterone in adulthood (except for breast growth, which can be undone only by mastectomy). But young gender-dysphoric children of both sexes often dread the coming physical changes. Might there be a way to delay them, giving more time to determine who would persist?

So clinicians in Amsterdam decided to put puberty on pause. Starting around age twelve, they injected a small group of children with triptorelin, one of a group of drugs known as 'puberty blockers' because they stop the signals sent by the pituitary gland that orchestrate puberty by triggering oestrogen or testosterone production. The idea was that any desisters would come off blockers when they realised that they no longer wanted to transition, suffer nothing worse than a slight delay to their development and grow up identifying as their own sex (and very likely gay). The persisters, meanwhile, would be spared undesired physical development and, at age sixteen – when they were old enough to consent to irreversible treatment – start cross-sex hormones, develop the secondary sex characteristics of the opposite sex and pass well for the rest of their lives.

But that is not how things played out. Instead, something striking happened. Of the seventy children enrolled in a study between 2000 and 2007, every single one progressed to cross-sex hormones. Almost all had surgery at age eighteen: the removal of any breast tissue that had developed despite the blockers and sometimes phalloplasties (the construction of a neo-penis from tissue harvested from a forearm or thigh) for the females; and castration and vaginoplasty for the males.

These children were all highly gender-dysphoric, and had not desisted by the start of puberty. The clinicians believed they had done a good job of picking out likely persisters, and indeed it is plausible that they had. But recall that every single study on children had found a majority desisting. It beggars belief that clinicians somehow learned to predict exactly which children would persist, exactly when they started using puberty blockers. Far more plausible is that puberty blockers, as well as blocking the physical changes that puberty brings, also blocked the developmental process whereby gender dysphoria often resolves.

That is when clinicians should have paused for thought. But many elsewhere had not even waited to see the study's results. Canadian clinicians started prescribing puberty blockers not long after the Dutch, and the first American clinics started in 2007. The UK clinic that receives all specialist referrals in England and Wales for gender-dysphoric under-eighteens, known as the Tavistock for the mental-health unit within which it sits, was more cautious. But in 2014 it also started prescribing them routinely, under pressure from activists who said British 'trans children' were unfairly denied treatment available elsewhere.

Nobody knows how many children have received puberty blockers by now, since nobody is counting. But the number is certainly in the thousands, and perhaps in the tens of thousands. The US alone, which had just one paediatric gender clinic a decade ago, now has more than fifty offering a full range of services. The drugs are being used for children whose dysphoria is mild or of short duration; who express a cross-sex identity but no distress; or who assert a novel identity such as non-binary or gender-fluid. In the US, they are increasingly prescribed by non-specialists under the misleading rubric of 'informed consent', which means that patients or their parents sign a statement to the effect that they have researched the consequences – in other words, sign away their right to sue.

And everywhere the same pattern is evident: almost every child who takes puberty blockers progresses to cross-sex hormones. A different Dutch clinic says its desistance rate is 3.8 percent; at the Tavistock, it is 1.2 percent. The notion that puberty blockers give time for dysphoria to resolve is simply untenable. Instead, they are part of a treatment pathway that ushers children towards adulthood identifying as a trans person.

Increasingly, children start on this pathway very young. After all, if you believe in innate gender identity, then when a child declares he or she is really of the opposite sex, there is nothing to do but concur. And so they are 'socially transitioned': presented to the world as members of the sex they want to be.

This 'gender-affirmative' approach is championed by the most influential clinicians. One is Diane Ehrensaft, the director of the University of California, San Francisco children's hospital gender clinic, who sits on the board of Gender Spectrum, an activist group in San Francisco. Her book, *The Gender Creative*

Child, is a manual for early transition. At an event in 2016 run by Gender Spectrum, Ehrensaft claimed that a toddler can indicate a trans identity to parents with non-verbal 'gender messages'. One born male may unpop the fasteners on a bodysuit to make it look like a dress; one born female may pull out hairclips. She claims that children know if they are transgender by the second year of life – in fact, 'they probably know before that, but that's pre-verbal'. She has encouraged parents to socially transition children as young as three.

Both social transition and puberty blockers are presented to parents as easily reversible. But in reality, they are the early stages of what physicians call a 'cascade of intervention'. (Readers with children may have heard the expression in the context of epidurals for pain relief during childbirth, which increase the likelihood of other medical and surgical measures.) Very few socially transitioned children return to presenting as their own sex before progressing to medical steps. In 2016 Johanna Olson-Kennedy, the director of the Center for Transyouth Health and Development at Children's Hospital Los Angeles, told Reuters that she had supported over 1,000 children to socially transition, with only one eventually desisting.

Pre-pubescent children easily pass as the opposite sex, and after socially transitioning may give little thought to their true sex for years. When adolescence beckons, they become distressed and agitate for puberty blockers. And, as much clinical experience now shows, that is an almost sure route to cross-sex hormones. So parents who socially transition their children are fast-tracking them to medical and surgical transition, all the while believing that such decisions are many years away.

Pressure is growing to bring forward those irreversible steps. Since children who socially transition are unlikely to desist, the reasoning goes, why make them linger in a child's body while their peers go through puberty? Some clinicians now prescribe cross-sex hormones below the former threshold of sixteen, and a small but increasing number offer surgery. A 2018 paper Olson-Kennedy co-authored mentions mastectomies being performed on transboys (that is, natal girls) as young as thirteen. She has been captured on video (by a parent from 4thWaveNow, a group of parents opposed to gender-identity ideology) brushing off parents' worries about surgery on minors, saying that 'if you want breasts at a later point in your life, you can go and get them'. In 2020 Trinity Neal, a sixteen-year-old male child in Delaware, had genital sex-reassignment surgery paid for by Medicaid.

Gender clinicians who resist affirmation have been side-lined – or worse. The highest-profile casualty is Ken Zucker, who in 1984 became director of Toronto's paediatric gender clinic. He is one of the biggest names in gender medicine: editor of *Archives of Sexual Behavior* and author or co-author of two of the studies from before the gender-affirmation era showing that childhood dysphoria usually resolves. He has assessed at least 1,500 gender-dysphoric children and adolescents. Along with Bradley, he introduced puberty blockers to Canada in 1999. 'By and large, the adolescents we saw weren't motivated to work through their gender dysphoria,' he says. 'They were in a holding pattern. Our view was that it was a tertiary treatment. Less invasive options were not viable because the kids weren't interested. Talk therapy didn't seem to do anything.'

Yet, as the pressure for affirmation became stronger, Zucker was cast as a reactionary for recommending that pre-pubertal children did not transition socially, but were instead supported to become comfortable in their own sex, and progressed to drugs and social transition only in adolescence. There are still clinicians who follow this approach, he says, but they keep a low profile because they don't want to be 'terrorised'.

Zucker's own experience shows they are right to worry. In 2015 the mental-health clinic that housed his unit announced a review. When it arrived ten months later, it accused him of traumatising patients, engaging in 'conversion therapy' to change trans people's identification, and having mocked a young transman he was referring for surgery as a 'hairy little vermin'. He was sacked on the spot and his unit soon closed.

In an article for *New York* magazine, American journalist Jesse Singal debunked the allegations. The 'vermin' story was a case of mistaken identity – as the review's authors should have realised, since the paediatric gender clinic did not do surgery referrals. Others were unverified gossip. Singal concluded that Zucker had been subjected to a 'show trial' because he did not espouse gender affirmation. Three years later, after a lawsuit against his former employer, Zucker was vindicated. The clinic apologised, withdrew its allegations and paid him a substantial settlement. He now works in private practice, but the message had been heard loud and clear: clinicians who urged caution risked their reputation and livelihood.

*

As academia and medical research have become politicised, high-quality research casting doubt on affirmation has been suppressed, and low-quality research in its favour gets fast-tracked to publication. In 2020 the National Institute for Care and Health Excellence (NICE), the official body tasked with assessing the effectiveness of treatment options within Britain's National Health Service, produced reviews of the evidence for prescribing puberty blockers and cross-sex hormones for childhood and adolescent gender dysphoria. It ranked the standard of evidence as 'very low' in every category it considered. Every single study that found any benefit for puberty blockers, it concluded, 'could represent changes that are either of questionable clinical value, or the studies themselves are not reliable and changes could be due to confounding, bias or chance'. Solid evidence of benefits for cross-sex hormones prescribed to teenagers, it said, was similarly non-existent.

One paper, published in January 2020 in *Pediatrics*, a high-impact journal, claims that puberty blockers make it less likely that a person will consider suicide. But an analysis by Michael Biggs of Oxford University published a few months later in *Archives of Sexual Behavior* (the journal edited by Ken Zucker) shows that it is catastrophically flawed.

The analysis is based on data extracted from a low-quality, non-representative online survey. No attempt was made to ensure that respondents were in America, or to stop people responding repeatedly (each response was entered into a prize draw). The survey is known to have elicited nonsensical answers about whether respondents had taken puberty block-ers – most who said they had were already older than sixteen when the drugs were first used in gender medicine in the US. And finally, there was no attempt to adjust for pre-existing differences between those who took blockers (or said they had), and those who said they would have liked to. Clinicians would have been less likely to give the drugs to people with severe mental-health issues, for example, who would then be more likely to contemplate suicide for reasons unrelated to not getting blockers.

Another widely reported paper, also published in 2020, claimed that undergoing 'conversion therapy' aimed at changing someone's gender identity is associated with worse future mental health. It, too, has been subjected to an article-length demolition by other researchers. It is based on the same flawed survey, and so is doomed before the data analysis even starts. But the problems do not stop there.

The paper conflates all sorts of therapeutic interactions – voluntary and coerced; those with diagnostic and therapeutic aims; those where the primary purpose is related to gender identity and those where it is not. Anyone who had detransitioned was excluded – a serious omission, since such people are among those most likely to have been harmed by gender affirmation. The survey provided no information on respondents' initial state of mental health, making it plausible that those who remembered more interactions with therapists were the ones who had worse mental health to begin with. And finally, the main result – that people who reported more interactions also reported worse mental health – is based on a measure of perceptions of distress, which is by no means the same thing.

Despite the lack of evidence, the American Academy of Pediatrics (AAP) claims that gender affirmation is the only ethical treatment for gender-dysphoric children. Its position paper was written by an activist-led sub-committee, and is so far from evidence-based that a paper debunking it point by point ran in the *Journal of Sex and Marital Therapy* in 2019. In order to ensure that the AAP could not later claim ignorance of his critique, the author, James Cantor, a Canadian sexologist, mailed it to the heads of the organisation's main committees. He received three confirmations of receipt, but no responses. 'I largely wrote that paper to be used when someone brings a court case,' he says. 'That was why I wrote it the way I did, down to referring to specific sentences to make it easy to cite.'

The misrepresentations are egregious. 'Remarkably, not only did the AAP statement fail to include any of the actual outcomes literature on such cases, but it also misrepresented the contents of its citations, which repeatedly said the very opposite of what the AAP attributed to them,' Cantor writes. For example, the AAP statement says that conversion therapy for children has proven 'not only unsuccessful but also deleterious'. But the sources it cites refer to sexual orientation, not gender identity, and therapy for adults, not children. The AAP 'told neither the truth nor the whole truth,' he concludes, 'committing sins both of commission and of omission, asserting claims easily falsified by anyone caring to do any factchecking at all.'

The lack of decent research and misrepresentation of findings mean gender affirmation cannot even be described as a risky experiment on children, since 'experiment' implies someone, somewhere, is tracking outcomes and comparing them with other options. But what can be said with some certainty is that it is not so much a treatment for gender dysphoria as a means to ensure that cross-sex identification persists. That must be acknowledged when the costs and benefits are totted up. To return to the analogy with epidurals, medical researchers – and labouring women – do not merely weigh the immediate risk of inserting a needle in the spine against the benefit of avoiding a painful labour. They also consider the fact that an epidural increases the likelihood of the use of instruments to aid delivery and of proceeding to a Caesarean section.

Humans find it hard to think this way, because we are naturally very poor at reasoning with counterfactuals. Many proponents of gender affirmation, for example, are late-transitioning transwomen, for whom the changes they went through in puberty are a source of ongoing unhappiness. But they forget that the majority of children will desist if they are not affirmed, because they did not belong to that majority themselves. And they seem not to realise that even if skipping puberty would have enabled them to pass better, it might have brought them different regrets – or to appreciate how unpleasant it must be for the bulk of trans people, who transitioned in adulthood, to hear that failing to pass is a catastrophic outcome.

The clinicians in Amsterdam checked back with the patients they had studied a couple of years after discharge. Some did not reply, a few had abandoned transition because of poor health – and one had died of necrotising fasciitis, a rare but serious bacterial infection, contracted as a complication of vaginoplasty. But the fifty-five who survived, replied and had completed their transition at least a year earlier seemed to be living productive lives, no longer experienced gender dysphoria and expressed themselves happy with the decision to transition.

That they were not suffused with regret is, of course, a relief. But a year or two is not a long follow-up, and a mortality rate of over one percent for a treatment given to healthy children is sobering. Moreover, children who would otherwise have desisted might have been at least as happy, and would certainly have been spared major surgery and lifelong reliance on artificial hormones. Without a comparison group who did not receive puberty blockers, there is no way to know.

Doctors are usually cautious when treating children, especially when interrupting normal physical development. But very surprisingly, puberty blockers have never been put through clinical trials for use in gender medicine, and are not licensed by their manufacturers for this purpose. Their main uses are to treat hormone-related conditions in adulthood, in particular endometriosis and prostate cancer, and to 'chemically castrate' sex offenders. The two studies that looked at what happened when they were used to delay puberty in animals suggested this caused defects in spatial memory and increased behaviours thought to be analogous to depression in humans.

Their only licensed paediatric use is to treat 'central precocious puberty', a rare condition in which children's bodies mature far earlier than normal. This causes major physical and social issues, but even so, there are concerns that the side effects are unacceptable. The drugs stop calcium being laid down in bones, and studies suggest a significant drop in IQ. American women treated in childhood for precocious puberty are suing the manufacturer of one puberty blocker, Lupron, alleging that it caused brittle bones, mental problems and chronic pain.

Whether blockers cause such direct harms will not be known for years. But there is no doubt about an indirect harm that will be suffered by any children who start taking them young enough to avoid puberty altogether: sterility. Cross-sex hormones cause the secondary sex characteristics of the desired sex to develop – breasts, beards and so on – but only a person's own sex's hormones can cause their ovaries or testicles to mature.

These children may well be sacrificing their future sex life, too. I can find no systematic research into sexual functioning in adults who missed out on puberty, but puberty is when people become fully orgasmic. Dire consequences are suggested by *I Am Jazz*, the long-running American reality-television show starring Jazz Jennings. Jennings was born a boy in 2000, socially transitioned as a pre-schooler, started puberty blockers at age eleven and oestrogen at twelve, and underwent sex-reassignment surgery at eighteen. After a consultation with a surgeon, Jennings says: 'I haven't experienced any sexual sensation. The doctor is saying an orgasm is like a sneeze. I don't even know what she's talking about.'

Many people are unaware of the impact of missing puberty on fertility. They read articles about transmen giving birth, and do not understand that those transmen must have experienced much or all of female puberty before starting testosterone. Or they hear mention of 'fertility preservation' – the extraction and storage of eggs and sperm – before sex-reassignment surgery and do not realise that without at least partial puberty, there will be no eggs or sperm that can be preserved. There is also widespread ignorance about the effects of cross-sex hormones on the fertility of people who transition in adulthood. Buck Angel, a transman who performs in pornographic films, has sought to publicise unpleasant effects of testosterone use in females: vaginal atrophy and agonisingly painful uterine cramps. Transmen who decide to go through female puberty and retain their sex organs to keep open the option of pregnancy may find they soon need a hysterectomy for medical reasons.

For transwomen, yet another downside of blocking puberty is that it keeps the genitals child-sized. This means there is too little skin for standard sex-reassignment procedures. More must be harvested from elsewhere to line the neovaginal cavity – Jazz Jennings's surgeon used intestinal tissue, and had to carry out further operations when the wound reopened.

And finally, the cross-sex hormones to which early social transitioning almost inevitably leads come with their own risks. For transmen, they are associated with higher risks of cardiovascular problems, including high blood pressure, heart attacks and stroke, dementia in later life, liver problems, diabetes and joint problems. Less is known about the impact on transwomen, but low testosterone is known to cause fatigue, brittle bones and high cholesterol levels in biological males, and taking oestrogen is likely to raise their risk of some cancers, including breast cancer.

Even critics of gender affirmation sometimes talk as if the harms all accrue to the children who would otherwise have desisted, while the persisters reap gains. But damage to brains and bones is bad for everyone, as is the loss of fertility and sexual pleasure. Activist groups often campaign against laws requiring sex-reassignment surgery before legal sex change, since such surgery causes sterility. But they support gender affirmation, which they seem not to understand causes sterility too.

All in all, gender affirmation not only locks in persistence but creates trans adults who have lost fertility and sexual function, and exposed themselves to unknown health risks, in return for passing better. And those trade-offs are being made, not by adult trans people in full awareness of the risks, but in childhood, when parents and clinicians decide to socially transition children, or give them puberty blockers, without anyone acknowledging where this is almost certain to lead.

*

Why do parents go along with this? Many simply do not know that, without affirmation, most gender-dysphoric children will desist. The suppression of high-quality research, and the reification of identities within left-wing politics, mean they think they are doing the right thing. Any doubts are quelled by an oft-repeated claim that gender-dysphoric children face a choice of transition or suicide. 'When you have the top clinicians saying that if you don't take the affirmative approach, you're going to kill your kid . . .' says Denise, the founder of 4thWaveNow. 'Well, it's the worst thing that could happen. And to think that you could be responsible for it.'

Horrifying statistics are thrown around without context. Once you search for sources, they fall apart. Take, for example, an endlessly repeated figure of forty-eight percent for the share of young trans people who have attempted suicide. It turns out to be based on the responses of twenty-seven British trans people in a larger survey promoted on LGBT websites. Not only is the number of respondents tiny, but there is no reason to think they are typical (if you want to find out something about a whole population, you must construct a representative sample).

In an article in 2017 for 4thWaveNow's website, Ray Blanchard and Michael Bailey debunked the transition-or-death narrative. Although suicide is somewhat more common among gender-dysphoric people than the general population, they write, it is still very rare. And that elevated risk can be explained by gender dysphoria co-occurring with other mental-health conditions, such as eating disorders and depression. There is no evidence that these are caused by dysphoria, or that transitioning will resolve them and make suicide less likely.

Scrolling through posts in a closed Facebook group for parents taking the gender-affirmative approach with their children, the importance of the transition-or-death narrative is clear to see. If a newcomer expresses doubts, old hands immediately intervene to say they must affirm their child's gender to stop them killing themselves. And another thing becomes apparent: some parents go beyond lovingly accepting their 'trans child' and actively encourage transition, perhaps to boost their liberal credentials, or because they like being their child's saviour, or because they enjoy the excitement and attention a trans child brings. In discussions about gender dysphoria, many say their child has never experienced it, but merely announced when just a toddler that they were the opposite sex. Plenty have two or more trans children. One says she has eight children, without a single 'boring cis child in the whole bunch!'

Such groups function to normalise ideas and behaviour that might otherwise lead parents to doubt the wisdom of the gender-affirmative approach. There are discussions of 'tucking' underpants for transgirls, which squash the genitals between the legs, and 'packers' for transboys (soft prosthetic penises and testicles that give a crotch bulge). 'Best boy bump for the little guys', runs the ad for one; the 'Bitty Bug', a tiny crocheted version, is available from Ravelry, a crafting forum. Reading as an outsider, these parents seem to have collectively lost their minds. But they are following the approach recommended by medical organisations and high-profile gender doctors – some of whom are members of the group.

And if they sometimes seem to be suggest-selling trans identities, they are not the only ones. In another of the recordings made by a parent from 4thWaveNow, Olson-Kennedy describes a highly gender non-conforming eight-year-old she assessed. The child's parents and school were puzzled by her boyish style, but she seemed happy and never said she thought she was a boy – indeed, she insisted she was not. Until Olson-Kennedy came up with a homely analogy – pop tarts. 'You know how they come in that foil packet?' she said to the child, in her re-telling. 'Well, what if there was a strawberry pop tart in a foil packet, in a box that said, "cinnamon pop tarts"? Is it a strawberry pop tart, or a cinnamon pop tart?' The little girl replied 'strawberry', paused, turned to her mother and said: 'I think I'm a boy and the girl is covering me up.'

An under-acknowledged reason some parents take the gender-affirmative approach is that they cannot bear gender non-conformity or homosexuality, and instinctively understand the link between the two. In 2019, after some staff at the Tavistock raised concerns that children were being fast-tracked to transition, an internal review passed to *Newsnight*, the BBC's flagship investigative programme, concluded that parents who preferred their child to be trans and straight, rather than 'cis' and gay, played a significant role in some referrals. Two clinicians said there was a dark joke among staff that soon 'there would be no gay people left.'

If you move in liberal circles, it may seem incredible that there are people who loathe and despise effeminacy in men and butchness in women. I am afraid you are living in a bubble. There is simply no doubt that some parents' extreme discomfort, even homophobia, about childhood gender non-conformity influences their decisions about transition. Some of them are quite open about it.

In an interview in 2017 with *Good Housekeeping* magazine, Kimberly Shappley, a conservative Christian mother living in Texas, tells the story of her gender non-conforming child. From the moment he was born, she explains, 'everything about Kai [a male child christened Joseph] was geared toward femininity.' Joseph would fashion t-shirts into skirts, or drape them to pretend he had long hair. Shappley gave him crew cuts and forced him to wear camouflage and superhero designs. To no avail. By the time he was two, 'family members were flat-out asking me if this kid was gay. It made me nervous, and I was constantly worried about what people would think of me.'

In *Trans in America: Texas Strong*, an Emmy award-winning short film released the same year, Shappley explains that having a gay son 'could not happen, and would not happen. We started praying fervently, and praying turned into Googling conversion therapy, and how can we implement these techniques at home to make [Joseph] not be like this. Putting [Joseph] in timeout for acting like a girl, putting her in timeout for stealing girl toys, spanking her – really spanking her – every time she would say "No, I'm a girl."' Eventually, guided by a therapist and a child psychiatrist who persuaded her of the wrong-body narrative, Shappley allowed her child to transition aged four. She finds the result far less disturbing: 'I now have a happy, healthy, outgoing, loving, beautiful, sweet little girl who loves Jesus and loves her brothers.'

A final, remarkable aspect of this link between homophobia and transition is that organisations that purport to campaign for gay rights seem blind to it. *Trans in America: Texas Strong* was produced by the American Civil Liberties Union (ACLU). When Pakistan's government decided recently to start funding sex-change surgery for gay males – a decision inspired by the mullahs' belief that homosexual desire indicates that you have a brain of the opposite sex – *Pink News*, a British website founded to cover issues relevant to gay people, described Pakistan as 'making history with this move for trans rights'. This is despite ample evidence that some gay men in Pakistan, and in Iran, which has similar policies, undergo such surgery unwillingly rather than risk the penalties for gay sex. These include beatings, imprisonment and even execution. A growing number of gay people are waking up to the link, however. I have heard gender affirmation described as 'postmodern gay conversion therapy'.

As I write, the gender-affirmation bandwagon is rolling on in the US. In many states, laws are being considered or have been passed that ban any other approach. Activists have exploited legislators' ignorance about the likely course of childhood gender dysphoria, and their praiseworthy desire to avoid a repeat of the failed and cruel attempts to 'straighten out' gay people. These laws are so sweeping that a therapist who seeks to explore what might lie behind a child's declaration of a cross-sex identity, or who merely tells parents that desistance is common and suggests they delay social transitioning, risks being struck off or even prosecuted.

Similar laws are being proposed and passed in other countries, including Australia, Canada and the UK. But in the UK, a pushback against paediatric transitioning is finally under way. A judicial review in late 2020 was the first time that senior judges anywhere were asked to consider whether children can truly consent to the gender-affirmative pathway, in particular to puberty blockers. Encouragingly, their answer was no.

The review was requested by Keira Bell, a twenty-three-year-old former patient of the Tavistock, and 'Mrs A', the mother of an autistic sixteen-year-old girl who was on the clinic's waiting list. Bell's trans identification had its origins in her early teens, when her mother commented on her masculine style and asked if she was lesbian. 'I was definitely having trouble figuring out my sexuality,' she says. 'And my father was very religious. Maybe I internalised homophobia.'

Watching YouTube videos by older butch lesbians segued into watching transition videos. 'Once I discovered about transitioning, I developed tunnel vision,' she says. Her family doctor referred her to mental-health services, which referred her on to the Tavistock, where she had her first appointment at age fifteen. 'It felt very brief: a basic history of my development, and relationships and family; what type of friendship groups I had. It was all based on stereotypes.' The huge problems in her life – being raped as a child, her mother's alcoholism and the chaos and violence that brought to the flat where the two lived, her anxiety and depression, that she was a school drop-out – were barely touched upon.

At her fifth appointment Bell was prescribed puberty blockers (at such a late point in adolescence most sex differentiation has already happened, but not all). 'All I remember is the endocrinologist saying that I would experience menopause-like symptoms and they were fully reversible,' she says. A year later she was put on testosterone and referred to the adult gender service, which, after two appointments, referred her for a double mastectomy. She continued taking testosterone for several years. 'I think I subconsciously hoped I would end up no different than a male, even down to my bones.'

Bell and Mrs A contended that minors cannot be considered competent to consent to treatment that will alter the rest of their lives in ways that they simply cannot comprehend. If puberty blockers are considered in isolation, as the Tavistock insisted they should be, then even a very young child may be intellectually mature enough to consent to them. But the judges accepted the evidence presented by Bell's team that puberty blockers should be considered as part of a single treatment pathway that leads to sterility and sexual dysfunction. They ruled that under-thirteens were not mature enough to understand what that would mean, and under-sixteens probably weren't either. (In March 2021 a separate legal hearing resulted in a ruling that parents could consent to puberty blockers on their child's behalf – not something the Tavistock had wished to allow, since there are neither objective markers for gender dysphoria nor a strong evidence base for outcomes, as there are for other conditions, where parental consent is acceptable. And at the time of writing, an appeal against the Bell ruling by the clinic was due to be heard.)

For anyone who has undergone fertility treatment (as I have), the Tavistock's cavalier approach to its patients' future fertility was shocking. The court heard that in 2019 it had prescribed puberty blockers to three ten-year-olds, all female. The endocrinologist's barrister said there had been no need to discuss fertility with these children, since they could come off the blockers at around age fifteen if they wished, in order to allow their ovaries to mature enough for eggs to be harvested and frozen. They could then decide whether to proceed with transition. There was no mention of the misery involved in taking such a step, or the low success rates of egg-freezing and thawing – or of where a uterus might be found to carry a baby, since it is a safe bet that these children's futures hold testosterone and hysterectomy.

Bell now wishes she had come across radical-feminist ideas earlier – 'that stereotypes don't mean anything, that it doesn't matter if you're masculine, that it's your biology that makes you a woman, and there are other women like you'. The Tavistock's approach was the opposite of what she needed, she says. 'There was never anyone telling me to love myself and that I was fine the way I was. It was just, "change yourself and you'll be better."'

5

MISS GENDERING

Why teenage girls are identifying out of the prospect of womanhood

Keira Bell not only forced clinicians to rethink their treatment of gender-dysphoric minors; she also provided an example of how that group is changing. Until the past decade, hardly any teenage girls sought treatment for gender dysphoria; now, they predominate in clinics around the world. British figures are typical. In 1989, when the Tavistock clinic opened, there were two referrals, both young boys. By 2020, there were 2,378 referrals, almost three-quarters of them girls, and most of those teenagers. Their treatment according to the gender-affirmative model is compounding a medical scandal.

Moreover, as anyone familiar with schools in liberal towns and cities will know, many more girls are identifying out of their sex without ever coming to the attention of gender doctors. Some identify as boys; others as non-binary, gender-fluid, demi-boys or suchlike. They ask to be referred to as 'he/him' or 'they/them', or by novel pronouns such as 'xie/xir' – in other words, as anything but female. This chapter looks at what is driving girls to abandon their sex. The story has three strands: female sexuality, modern feminism and, finally, something this group is particularly prone to – social contagion.

The first strand, sexuality, is less complicated than in males. In the late 1980s, Ray Blanchard turned his attention from male transitioners to the minority of his clinic's patients who were female. Almost all were same-sex attracted and had always been masculine in presentation and interests. These female equivalents of 'androphilic' transwomen would have been butch lesbians if they had stayed living as women. Very occasionally, he saw the female equivalent of a male autogynephile: a gender-conforming, heterosexual woman who found the thought or image of herself as a gay man sexually arousing. Such 'auto-homoerotics' were extremely rare, however.

All this fits well with some of the best-attested findings in all of sexology. Early gender non-conformity and adult same-sex orientation are strongly correlated in females, just as in males; and paraphilias are an almost exclusively male phenomenon (for sources, see the further reading section for this chapter).

To explain the role of modern feminism and gender-identity ideology in driving female teenagers to transition, I will start with the story of a woman who chose to live as a man more than two centuries ago – and how the interpretation of that story has changed in the past few years. She is Margaret Bulkley, the daughter of an Irish shopkeeper born around 1789. Aged twenty, she took the name of her dead uncle, James Barry, assumed a male identity and used a legacy from him to train as a doctor in Edinburgh. She seems to have planned to move to Venezuela once qualified, because women could practise medicine there. But when those plans fell through, she faced a choice: abandon medicine and accept the narrow sphere open to women of the day; or live and work as Barry permanently.

In 2016 Michael du Preez, a retired surgeon, and Jeremy Dronfeld, a novelist, wrote a well-received account in *Dr James Barry: A Woman Ahead of Her Time*. It portrayed a feminist heroine with a wildly adventurous life. Barry rose to senior rank in the army as a surgeon and served twelve years in the Cape Colony, where he – she – probably had an affair with the governor. Not until after Barry's death was Bulkley's subterfuge revealed.

The next person to tackle Barry's life was the novelist E.J. Levy. Her fictionalised account, *The Cape Doctor*, was also planned as the tale of a daring and resourceful woman – a 'heroine for our time, for all time', she said when her publishing deal was announced in 2019. This time, the reception was far less positive. One-star reviews immediately appeared on Goodreads: 'author refuses to acknowledge the fact that Barry was trans and continues disrespecting him by using the pronoun "she"'; 'only cares about erasing and harming the trans community'; 'a horribly disrespectful take'; 'transphobic trash'. A petition demanded that the publishers drop the book. The planned publication date came and went. As this book went to press – and presumably after a rewrite – it was due to appear in June 2021.

The two books' differing receptions allow us to date to between 2016 and 2019 the moment when gender identity eclipsed biological sex among the intelligentsia. Barry was now understood, not as someone who had lived as a man, or even become a man, but as someone who had always been a man: a man wrongly thought to be female at birth. The male persona first presented in Edinburgh was the precise opposite of a disguise: it was a truth revealed.

The changing interpretation of Bulkley's life highlights the malign consequences of the new ideology for the still-unfinished fight for equality for women. Within that ideology, women who aspire to agency and power no longer add weight to arguments for equal rights and freedoms, but instead become men. Women are then the type of people who are content with supporting roles. In the earlier version, a resourceful woman challenged the oppression of her sex; in the new one a transman opts out of that oppression while leaving it untouched.

Selina Todd, a professor of modern history at Oxford University, draws two broad points from the history of women who cross-dress, present as men or act in 'mannish' ways. The first is that their various motives – sexual and economic ones, as well as a desire for personal freedoms – often intermingle. The second is that even a woman who has all these motives for identifying as a man may choose not to do so – if the state of feminism in her time gives her good reason. If her era offers a convincing analysis of the sex-based oppression of women as a group, she is less likely to identify as a man, and more likely to stay and fight for more freedoms for all women.

To illustrate, Todd points first to Lillias Barker, alias Colonel Barker, whose cross-sex identification combined all the elements Todd identifies. After a spell in the Women's Auxiliary Air Force during the First World War, Barker had a short-lived marriage and then a relationship with a man by whom she had two children. That broke up in 1923, around the same time as her father lost his fortune. She started to dress as a man and invented a military back-story, and then an aristocratic one. She lived with various women. Her career as 'Colonel Barker' ended when she was examined by doctors in a men's prison after going bankrupt. Writing later, she gave pragmatic and financial reasons for living as a man: 'I could not use my knowledge of horses, dogs and farm work [as a woman] and I simply had to become a man – I had to!' And yet, says Todd, 'any queer-history module a British undergraduate takes will have "Colonel Barker" as a transman.'

Todd's second illustration – of women who stay and fight for their sex – concerns a new type of 'masculine woman' who emerged as the Suffragettes gained momentum. 'Some were dressing in ways that were considered manly,' she says. 'And as far as we can tell, the reason was simply that they hated the impediments of femininity. They were saying: "I want to do serious work; I want short hair; I don't want skirts."' Many understood their personal decisions to opt out of restrictions on women's clothing and societal roles as part of the campaign to gain more freedoms for all women.

I will have more to say about modern feminism and gender-identity ideology in future chapters. For the moment, I will merely observe that it is an indictment of both that the first generation of girls to be taught that womanhood can be identified out of are doing so in large numbers.

The final, and most disturbing, element of the story of trans-identifying female teenagers was first brought to wider notice by an American physician and public-health specialist, Lisa Littman. Around 2015 she noticed one teenager in her community after another announcing that they were trans on social media. 'The first couple, I thought "that's great, I'm so glad they're comfortable and can express this,"' she says. 'Then the third, the fourth, the fifth, the sixth, all from the same group ... I thought, this is not making sense statistically. My inner epidemiologist said: "hmmm".'

Littman searched, and found prevalence estimates of 1 in 30,000–100,000 for trans identification (since revised upwards) and no mention of clusters. So she started looking for discussions about trans issues on Tumblr and Reddit – and was appalled to find a 'horrific environment of teenagers giving each other terrible advice. Saying, "your parents and doctors are idiots." They were reinforcing and validating talking points to shut down the conversation.'

She then found online groups of parents concerned about their children's sudden trans identification, such as 4thWave-Now in the US and Transgender Trend in the UK. Of course, what seems sudden to a parent may not be so to a teenager – but this does not explain why this sort of surprise has become common only recently, or disproportionately with females. Often these children had friends who simultaneously identified as trans; many had been diagnosed with mental-health problems. But doctors and therapists seemed completely uninterested when parents raised such issues. 'Naturally,' says Littman, 'I thought this was something that needed to be studied and recorded.'

The standard approach when a physician thinks they may have stumbled upon a previously unobserved phenomenon is simply to look for more cases. It is too early to produce a representative sample in order to estimate prevalence or test treatments, so the aim is merely to come up with hypotheses for further investigation. Littman posted information about participating in a study on three websites where parents critical of gender affirmation shared accounts of their children's dysphoria starting in adolescence, asking for it to be shared with anyone who might be eligible.

Most of the 256 parents who completed Littman's anonymised ninety-question survey reported that their children had announced they were trans after spending more time online, after several friends had done so, or both. Almost two-thirds of these parents' children had previously been diagnosed with at least one psychiatric or developmental condition; many had self-harmed. Littman hypothesised that 'social and peer contagion' had played a role, and that adolescent cross-sex identification might sometimes be a distraction from emotional pain, like taking drugs, cutting, bingeing or starving. And she coined a name for the phenomenon: rapid-onset gender dysphoria (ROGD).

When Littman's findings were published in August 2018, she became the latest victim of hostility towards anyone who contradicts the innate gender-identity narrative. Brown University, where she worked, was bombarded with claims that her research was biased, shoddy and harmful to trans people, and demands for her sacking. Ehrensaft, the San Francisco gender therapist, compared Littman's research technique to 'recruiting from Klan or alt-right sites to demonstrate that blacks really are an inferior race'. Under pressure, the journal that published her paper conducted a post-publication review. Minor changes were made to the presentation, but the findings remained unchanged.

*

Susan Bradley, the former head of Toronto's first paediatric gender clinic, continues to study and write in the field, though retired. What she is seeing now is very different to what she saw in the 1980s, she says – and her thinking about what drives cross-sex identification in children has changed. 'I now think that all, or nearly all, have some autistic traits,' she says. Among the traits common to young people with autistic-spectrum disorders is rigid thinking, which can lead to discomfort with nuance and anyone who seems not to fit into the usual categories. If such children prefer clothing or activities associated with the opposite sex, or are experiencing the early stirrings of same-sex attraction, they may conclude that they have been misclassified.

Also common in people with autistic traits is lack of insight into one's feelings, in particular low self-esteem caused by perceived rejection by peers. Such children may latch onto a concrete explanation for their misery: that they were 'born in the wrong body'. When they research online and discover trans-identification, they feel accepted for the first time. They are also concrete, rather than abstract, learners, says Bradley, making it difficult for a therapist to uncover what lies behind the claim of a trans identity. 'They don't like to be asked to self-reflect, because from their perspective you're trying to dissuade them.'

Sasha Ayad, a counsellor in Houston, Texas, witnessed the emergence of the new teenage cohort up close. In 2014, she worked with a 'very quirky' teenage girl with autistic traits who was spending all her time online. One day the teenager said to Ayad: 'I don't think I'm a girl.' As they talked more, it became obvious that everything she said was lifted wholesale from the internet. 'I worked on helping her accept her uniqueness,' says Ayad. 'And a year later, she said to me: remember that thing we used to talk about – I don't have that problem any more. I think it was because I had no friends. I wanted friends online.'

A couple of years later Ayad had shifted to private practice, and the number of girls with gender-identity issues had increased hugely. She soon realised that the environment had changed in ways that made her job much harder. No one had affirmed that first child's boyhood, and they had worked things through without the world proclaiming that yes, the child really was a boy. 'It's like if you took girls with eating disorders and gave them a belief system that validated their body hatred,' says Ayad. 'I'm not dealing with a child and their dysphoria; I'm dealing with a child, their dysphoria and their religion.'

Many of Ayad's clients arrived at their trans identities by strikingly similar routes. An anxious, lonely girl enters puberty and has unpleasant experiences in which being female plays a part – sexualised harassment and bullying, say, or being rejected by a crush. She falls out with a friend, becomes withdrawn and turns to social media for an explanation of why she feels so bad. New, virtual friends ask how she identifies and what her pronouns are. This prompts further searches. Quite quickly, her thinking becomes reorganised around a concept she had not heard of a few months earlier. 'With enough time and rumination,' says Ayad, 'anyone distressed can end up thinking that they're trans.'

Then the child comes out – at first only online. By the time she tells her parents, she has been immersed in these new ideas for months, and primed by her internet cheerleaders to interpret their shock and confusion as transphobia. 'All of this is happening on a backdrop of zero real-life relationships,' says Ayad. 'A kid is this and that identity – and they've never even held hands with another human being.'

Littman has recently started a study of detransitioners – people who abandon transition and return to identifying as their own sex. They rarely show up in any statistics, because few inform the health-care professionals they regard as having damaged them, believing that to do so would be pointless, even traumatic. Detransition may be more common among the new cohort Littman identified, but until her findings are published, there is no way to be sure. So let me tell you the stories of three detransitioners: Lara (not her real name), Helena and Kay. Each seems to me to have been trying to identify out of womanhood rather than into manhood. And their motives are better understood as created by gender-identity ideology than as described by it.

Lara, a twenty-four-year-old European lesbian, was a gender non-conforming child who favoured cropped hair and boys' shirts, and disliked feminine beauty rituals. In school, she was teased about her boyish appearance. She came out to friends as same-sex attracted at fourteen. The label 'lesbian' revolted her, since she associated the word with pornography sniggered over by male classmates, depicting two women and aimed at straight men. She fell in love, but had to play second fiddle to a boy her girlfriend was also seeing. She spent hours in her bedroom writing fiction in online groups with girls she had never met. She identified with her male characters: romantic heroes of the sort she longed to be. She fantasised she had a twin brother who could do everything she longed to do, but felt unable to.

Aged fifteen, Lara developed bulimia, spending months in hospital and relapsing whenever she went home. When she was eighteen, her desire to pare away at her hated female body led her to a fateful online search: was it possible to have your breasts removed without a medical reason? One search led to another, and within a week she had become convinced that her misery was caused by having been wrongly 'assigned female at birth'. Suddenly everything made sense: her misery and loneliness; her compulsion to starve away her curves; her distaste for the label 'lesbian'; her girlfriend's preference for a boy; the fantasies of being male.

She found a therapist who dealt with gender issues. Rather than exploring why a shy young lesbian might feel uncomfortable in her body, he said that transition would solve her problems, including her eating disorder. He put her straight on testosterone. Her voice broke and her muscles bulked up. She sprouted facial hair, and gained confidence. She changed her name to Emil and the sex on her birth certificate and other official documents to male.

Aged twenty, Emil had a bilateral mastectomy. It was supposed to end his gender dysphoria; instead, it merely shifted the focus to his female genitals. Dressed, in public, he 'passed'; naked, in front of the bedroom mirror, he felt like a fake. So he pressed onwards. At twenty-one his uterus and ovaries were removed. Nobody warned him that a radical hysterectomy is a major procedure, followed by months of pain and weakness. Everyone expected him to celebrate.

The doctor who removed his female reproductive organs had given him the names of two surgeons who carried out phalloplasty. One showed him video clips of an operation. He found them horrifying. And he still had not recovered from the hysterectomy. Searching for support online, he found forums for women who had undergone the procedure because of endometriosis or cancer. He felt a connection with these women, who understood what he had been through. And then a simple but radical question occurred to him: how could an operation that can be done only on women possibly turn someone into a man?

And, with that reframing, the past five years stopped making any sense to him. Almost as quickly as Lara's thinking had reorganised around the tenets of gender-identity ideology, Emil abandoned them.

Nowadays, Lara regards herself as a woman, and female, words she takes as synonymous. Her physical presence is ambiguous. She has a tenor voice, an Adam's apple and short hair brushed onto her forehead. She shaves her chin. But she is dainty: the testosterone came too late to broaden her shoulders or jaw, or to enlarge her feet or hands. She struggles to eat healthily, though she has managed to stay out of hospital for some years. She is easily read as female, but is in some respects reminiscent of a gentle, shy, teenage boy. She berates herself as a fool for having fallen for what she now regards as a 'crazy, cultish' ideology – though you do not have to talk to her for long to realise that she has thought more deeply about many subjects than most people her age.

Eating disorders and the internet also played a part in Helena's transition. The twenty-two-year-old from Ohio joined Tumblr at thirteen and, as her adolescence became more miserable, discovered fandoms dedicated to starvation and self-harm. She gorged on arty shots of razors slicing forearms, hollow bellies and protruding ribcages, accompanied by expressions of angst and exhortations to starve. In 2015 Tumblr finally banned such materials. But by then Helena was cutting and making herself vomit – and, moreover, had found social justice Tumblr, where to be white, straight and 'cis' makes you evil. 'You're told you are responsible for black transwomen dying in the streets; their throats are being slit because of you,' says Helena. 'Now that I look back, I know this is not how life works, but at the time I felt awful.'

She felt slightly better when she convinced herself she was bisexual – an entirely theoretical affair. But she also started to read about gender-identity ideology. 'The more I immersed myself, the more I picked up on things I related to,' she says. 'A big one was females who identified as trans and non-binary saying, "I used to think my problem was that I was fat, but actually I have gender dysphoria."' She started to identify as gender-fluid between 'demigirl' and 'bigender' and demanded that people refer to her by the neo-pronouns 'xie/xir'. She developed intense fantasies about being lanky, broad-shouldered and flat-chested. The near-farcical mismatch with her actual physique – petite, curvy and very pretty – created dysphoria, which convinced her she was a transboy.

A school counsellor drew up a plan for her to save money for transition, gave her addresses of gender clinics and discussed coming out to her mother in a sensitive, low-key way. It didn't work out like that. In Helena's re-telling, she blurted it out in the car: 'I've had gender dysphoria my entire life, but I didn't have the words for it. I'm a boy, my pronouns are he/him and my name is "insert cringe trans name here".' Her mother did not take it well. They had a huge row in a grocery store – Helena said her mother was a 'horrible transphobe', and her mother said Helena was 'delusional' and had been 'propagandised by liberals'.

A few weeks after her eighteenth birthday, Helena said she was staying over with a friend and drove eight hours to a Planned Parenthood clinic in Chicago that ran on 'informed consent' lines. After a brief chat, a nurse showed her how to inject testosterone and gave her a prescription for more. When she left for college two days later, she did so as a boy.

The first semester was a honeymoon. Helena started a relationship with another transboy (who has since also desisted). They lived in the trans house on campus, where Helena 'embraced [her] new trans family'. Then things started to go downhill. Her mental health deteriorated and she suffered episodes of rage that she now attributes to mega-doses of testosterone – the clinic had prescribed four times the usual starting dose, which Helena did not realise at the time and still cannot account for. She started self-harming again, and skipping class, and drinking and taking recreational drugs. She dropped out before she was kicked out.

'I was supposed to be this cute Tumblr transboy living his truth,' she says. 'Instead I had transformed from a little girl with short hair into this testosterone-addled thing.' When she finally admitted that she regretted transition, her therapist said she was making no sense; that the only cure for dysphoria was transition. Then Helena read about Littman's research. 'And I thought: that happened to me!' Re-identifying as a woman was a great relief, and she is grateful she never progressed to surgery. But she worries about how her time on testosterone will affect her future health. And the psychological issues are far greater. 'I feel like a cult survivor, a thousand percent. That cult robbed me of my adolescence.'

It is remarkable that a feminine girl like Helena could become convinced she was really a boy. But eating disorders and gender dysphoria both involve feelings of bodily dis-ease, and you do not have to spend long on social media to find girls who hate their curves and regard testosterone as a cure-all. My third story is an even starker illustration of how far gender-identity ideology has progressed, and of the ineffable nature of the inner self it posits.

Kay, who lives in Melbourne, is twenty-four. She was seventeen when she stumbled into gender Tumblr. 'All these posts asking whether you've "questioned your gender", and if not why not?' she says. She spent days in online searches for 'How do you know what your gender is?' and 'What does gender feel like?' She learned that gender 'has nothing to do with your biology, appearance, interests or hobbies, sexuality, colour preferences, clothing preferences, the way you present . . . so I was like: "well, what is it then?" All I got was stuff along the lines of: "Only you can decide."'

At that point, many people would have given up. But Kay is unusually logical – she is doing a degree in mathematics – and prone, she admits, to rumination and rigid thinking. So she came to a rational yet outlandish conclusion: that she was one of the rare people who lacked a gender altogether. Her 'agender' identity did not match her 'sex assigned at birth', which made her trans.

She came out to a few friends, wore flannel shirts and sometimes men's trousers, and considered using men's toilets to strike a blow against cisnormativity, but chickened out. Online, however, where she used 'they/them' pronouns, being under the trans umbrella was rather pleasant. As a bisexual woman of colour, she already had some credibility; being trans gave her more. 'Oppressed labels get you fawned over on Tumblr,' she says. 'You get more leeway to think and maybe have dissenting – not too dissenting – views. If you're just a cis straight white girl you're nobody, and nobody cares about you or your opinion.'

About eighteen months later a friend said 'something TERFy' to Kay. She cannot even remember what, but that started her on another bout of rumination. This time she worked back from the absurdity of her 'agender' status to conclude that gender-identity ideology was nonsense and that her trans identification had been cut out of whole cloth. It was a relief 'coming back to reality and thinking for myself and not having to repeat lies', she says. But the whole episode 'wasted a shitload of time'.

Kay's story is undramatic compared with Lara's. But I think it is still telling. Schools across the Anglosphere now promote the sort of self-examination that led to her trans identification. Moreover, respect for declared identities is now mandatory in most schools, universities and workplaces. Had Kay wanted to, she could have insisted that everyone around her used 'they/them' pronouns. Anyone who forgot that this ordinary young woman did not identify as such could have been in big trouble with HR.

But the main thing I thought when Kay told me her story was: 'Here's the shoeshine boy.' Supposedly, shortly before the 1929 stock market crash that started the Great Depression, a shoeshine boy offered stock tips to Joe Kennedy (JFK's father), and the story is often cited by market-watchers when they think that a bubble inflated by unsophisticated retail investors is about to pop. Similarly, trans identification has moved outwards from the highly gender non-conforming and dysphoric, through the troubled and unhappy, to those who are a little intense and spend a lot of time online. With luck, Kay is a sign that the bubble of trans identification among teenage girls is about to burst.

*

Lisa Marchiano, a Jungian therapist based in Philadelphia, is in an informal group, along with Ayad, of therapists who support each other in counselling families with trans-identified teenagers. When she first heard of the phenomenon, she interpreted it through a Jungian lens. Jung wrote about the 'animus', or masculine side of women, and 'anima', or feminine side of men. 'The idea that teenagers were playing with this seemed wonderful to me,' she says. And then one of her adult patients told her that these girls were getting mastectomies. 'That completely changed the way I saw it. Jungians know that to concretise something symbolic is a very bad idea.'

Marchiano had studied history at university and initially trained as a social worker. So she was ideally placed to recognise what was happening to teenagers as what Jung called a 'psychic epidemic'. As historians of medicine know, diagnoses vary from place to place and time to time, and many medical conditions are not 'out there' waiting to be spotted by doctors, but are shaped by them and the wider culture.

Edward Shorter, a historian of mental illness, coined the term 'symptom pool' for the medical presentations regarded as legitimate in a given culture. When a doctor sees a patient with psychosomatic symptoms – ones that are physical, but produced by mental states – these are moulded by patient and doctor together into a recognised illness. 'Mental-health syndromes are always a kind of fiction, shaped by culture and expectations,' says Marchiano. 'Our emotional lives, and the ways they can become disrupted, are protean.'

A new medical paradigm, therefore, may do something more profound than give doctors a new way to understand what they see: it can change what they see. Sometimes, a new condition is born – and sometimes it gains sudden popularity. The history of medicine is scattered with psychosomatic diseases that appeared, spread like wildfire and died away as medical thinking changed again.

One sign a new condition may fall into this category is that it mainly affects teenage girls and young women. They are more likely than other demographics to indulge in 'co-rumination':

repetitive discussion and speculation within a peer group. That can lead to internalising problems, and thence to anxiety, depression and self-harm. Girls are also often more empathetic than boys, and better at reading moods, which means emotions spread faster in a female peer group than in a male one. That is why self-harm and eating disorders can run through female friends, and why historical episodes of mass hysteria, such as fainting fits, uncontrollable laughter or crying, and outbreaks of paralysis or tremors, have so often occurred in convents and girls' schools.

Judging by the historical record, when a psychic epidemic hits, doctors often feel moved to centre interventions on the female reproductive system. Take the 'reflex doctrine' of the nineteenth century, which held that a disturbance in any part of the body could cause malfunction in any other, by a 'reflex action' of the nerves travelling via the spine. Doctors regarded the female sex organs as particularly prone to exerting these malign influences, and removed them to treat an astonishing array of conditions: paralysis, fits and ailments of the heart, thyroid, stomach, skin, ears and eyes. When Marchiano realised that girls who said they felt like boys were being given drugs and surgeries that would leave them sterile, at first she thought she must be misunderstanding something. 'And then I thought: no, Lisa, this happens all the time, and it's happening again.'

In *Man into Woman* Einar Wegener briefly wonders where the healthy ovaries that are to be transplanted into his abdomen are to come from. The answer, almost certainly, is that the unnamed – and probably unwitting – donor had been diagnosed with a reflex ailment. Indeed, Wegener's own symptoms seem to have been shaped by reflex theory. In the 1920s, as the 'woman inside' was becoming real to him, he suffered from monthly nosebleeds. Some reflex theorists believed in 'vicarious nasal menstruation':

that bleeding from the nose might replace the monthly shedding of the womb's lining. Since nobody believes in reflex theory any more, no males turn up at gender clinics today saying that their nosebleeds follow a monthly cycle.

The most striking parallels with the sudden, marked increase in trans identification by teenagers are two linked diagnoses that flared up towards the end of the twentieth century: multiple-personality disorder (MPD; now called dissociative identity disorder) and recovered-memory syndrome. The theory behind both was that a child might respond to trauma or abuse by 'splitting', their psyches fragmenting so that the memory could be locked away. Therapists used hypnosis, free association and sometimes psychoactive drugs to bring the split personalities, or 'alters', to the surface, recover the forgotten memories, integrate the personalities and – supposedly – relieve the patient of all symptoms.

In *Creating Hysteria: Women and Multiple Personality Disorder*, published in 1999, journalist Joan Acocella describes how a disease so rare that most doctors never came across it turned into an epidemic.

In 1944 a literature search turned up seventy-six cases of multiple-personality disorder in the previous two centuries. Then, in 1957, two therapists published *The Three Faces of Eve*, the story of a mild-mannered housewife, 'Eve White', whose alter ego, 'Eve Black', partied, drank and slept around at weekends – only to wake up as Eve White on Monday mornings, with no memory of what she had done. The therapists claimed to have integrated the pair into a third, rounded personality, 'Jane'. The book and a film of the same name were roaring successes. So was *Sybil*, also a book and then a film, in which Sibyl's mental problems are attributed to childhood abuse.

More books followed, and more films, TV programmes and interviews. Seminars, conferences and academic papers trained therapists to make the diagnosis. Acocella estimates that, between 1985 and 1995, forty thousand Americans were formally diagnosed with MPD and several million more came to believe that they had repressed memories of childhood abuse.

This would not have seemed so plausible, had it not been for an uncomfortable truth. During the 1970s and 1980s the feminist movement had brought the phenomenon of child-abuse within families out of the shadows. But anyone who dared whisper that some of the stories coming out of therapists' offices might not be entirely true was accused of protecting perpetrators and betraying victims.

Until the Satanic Panic. As patients and therapists vied to outdo each other, the recovered memories became increasingly outlandish. By the late 1990s some patients were describing lurid abuse by vast networks of Satanists: dungeons where children were raped and murdered; Black Masses featuring forced abortions; child-trafficking on an industrial scale. At this point, even some believers were given pause. A few accusations made it to court – and were proven beyond doubt to be false.

That was a turning-point. Lawsuits in which supposed victims sued alleged abusers gave way to malpractice suits against therapists. State governments barred evidence obtained under hypnosis from court. Health insurers stopped reimbursing treatment. Some therapists were stripped of their licences. In 1998, *Dissociation*, the house journal of the recovered-memory movement, stopped publishing. Though dissociative identity disorder is diagnosed more frequently than it used to be, it is once again quite rare.

There are many parallels between MPD and gender dysphoria. In both, a few therapists account for a large share of diagnoses. The literature about both encourages patients to cut themselves off from doubters. Both offer people with nebulous malaise a striking label that makes them feel special – and promise the sort of complete cure that is unusual in mental health. The research base for treatments in both cases is of abysmal quality. And both depend on unfalsifiable theories.

Even the discourses are strikingly similar. Compare the catchphrases: 'If you think you might be trans, you probably are,' and 'No one else can tell you your gender identity,' with these quotations from *The Courage to Heal*, a self-help book about recovered-memory syndrome published in 1988: 'If you think you were abused and your life shows the symptoms, then you were,' and 'The patient sometimes knows more about the disorder than the therapist.'

The idea that a child could suffer horrific assaults, immediately bury the memories deep in their psyche, remember nothing of what had just happened and grow up to be deeply psychologically damaged by this dissociation is now a commonplace of popular culture, despite the total lack of evidence that such a thing can happen. It – like the idea that a child can have a 'true self' of the opposite sex to their body – would seem absurd in nearly every place and time. Such conditions are known as 'culture-bound syndromes'. Those documented by anthropologists include *pa-leng*, an obsessive fear of becoming too cold found in some parts of Asia, and *koro*, a Malay word for a man's belief that his genitals are shrinking and vanishing. Naturally, such syndromes are easier to spot when the culture is not yours.

Our hyper-connected world makes it easier than ever for culture-bound syndromes to break their bounds. In his excellent book, *Crazy Like Us: The Globalisation of the American Psyche*, journalist Ethan Watters argues that this is particularly likely to happen with American culture-bound syndromes, because of the country's cultural dominance. One of his case studies is the arrival of Western-style anorexia in Hong Kong.

The few self-starving young women seen by doctors in the territory before the mid-1990s did not have distorted body images or a pathological fear of being fat, but spoke instead of a feeling of bloating, a blockage in the throat, or simply a total lack of appetite. Then, in 1994, a teenage girl who had stopped eating some months earlier collapsed and died on a busy street. Journalists seeking to explain the unprecedented event turned to international sources – and unintentionally presented to Hong Kong's teenage girls a possibility hitherto undreamt of: that distress and self-hatred could be expressed by self-starvation. Sing Lee, a doctor who had been perhaps Hong Kong's sole specialist in self-starvation, went from seeing two or three cases a year to two or three cases a week.

Today's trans-identified female teenagers are the last piece in the puzzle of cross-sex identities: why they develop and in whom. The role played by fashion in social contagions suggests that their numbers will not rise forever, and indeed may soon start to fall – especially if lawsuits start coming, as they did with recovered-memory syndrome and multiple-personality disorder. But already this new psychogenic illness has broken the bounds of American culture, and gone global.

6

BACK IN THE BOX

How gender-identity ideology harms all children

'For as long as I can remember, my favourite colour has been pink,' starts the children's book *I Am Jazz*, by Jazz Jennings. Jazz's favourite activities are mostly girly: dancing, singing, backflips, drawing, swimming, putting on make-up and pretending to be a pop star. Jazz's parents are so puzzled that they consult a doctor, who explains that they are mistaken in thinking they have a son: Jazz 'has a girl brain but a boy body. This is called transgender.'

I Am Jazz and similar books are widely recommended by many activist groups for reading in schools. The stereotypes they promote teach children ideas about what is proper for boys and girls that feminists had thought consigned to the dustbin of history. This is just one of the ways in which gender-identity ideology harms all children, not merely those who end up identifying out of their sex.

As queer theory conquered campuses, and the simplistic 'wrong body' version conquered popular culture, writing about transkids proliferated: storybooks for children, novels for teenagers and workbooks for readers of every age. Memeified versions circulate on social media. All express the same contradiction. Gender identity is an innate, ineffable sense, unrelated to body type, behaviour and presentation. But that inner truth is manifested by stereotypes.

It is rare to read an account of a transkid that doesn't mention clothing, hair and toys. 'I didn't like playing with dolls, or wearing dresses, and I hated having long hair,' says transboy Kit in *Can I Tell You About Gender Diversity?* In *Introducing Teddy: A Gentle Story About Gender and Friendship*, Teddy becomes a girl by turning his bow tie into a hair bow. When Jazz is allowed to wear 'girl clothes . . . being Jazz felt much more like being ME'.

One of the cross-sex traits presented as indicating that a child may be trans is same-sex attraction. When the protagonist of *George*, a book for young teenagers, thinks about kissing a boy, 'the idea made her tingle' (female pronouns are used for George, even before he identifies as Melissa). 'He's such a freaking girl anyway,' says a classmate. These books never make the connection between homophobic bullying and identifying out of one's sex. A generation ago, progressives campaigned for schools to crack down on taunts about gay boys being girls; now, the bullies are presented as right.

I have never seen a story that explained a child's alienation from their sex except in terms of discordant gender identity. There is no acknowledgement that a gender non-conforming child may internalise parental disapproval. A girl whose mother dreamed of a princess and got a rugby player, or a boy whose father dreamed of a prop forward and got a ballet dancer, may grow up feeling profoundly wrong unless the parents abandon their dreams and embrace the child they have.

Conditions commonly seen with gender dysphoria, such as eating disorders and autism, do not get a look-in. I have never seen a book about, say, a weight-obsessed pubescent girl who wants to rid herself of her developing curves with testosterone and surgery, until an understanding parent or teacher helps her accept herself as she is. I would love to read a young-adult author's take on a boy like those Richard Green studied: a proto-gay child who believed he was meant to be a girl, until puberty reconciled him with his sex.

The importance of gendered performance in fiction about transkids raises a question: if adults stopped fussing about the 'right' clothes and activities for boys and girls, then how, in practical terms, could a child express a trans identity? If no behaviours or norms were off-limits to one sex or the other, how could a child feel, or indicate to the world, that they were not actually members of their sex? And another question: why have teachers, authors and publishers accepted this repackaging of tired sex stereotypes? The answer lies in the contradiction at the heart of gender-identity ideology. For all that gender is supposedly *revealed* by stereotyped appearances and actions, it is *defined* as an inner knowing. This helps conceal how regressive it is.

Gender-as-stereotypes is generally called 'gender expression', and gender-as-feeling, 'gender identity'. But the latter is explained in terms of the former. Consider the 'genderbread person', an outline figure that adorns classrooms all over the English-speaking world. It is labelled with identity (in the brain), attraction (in the heart), sex (in the groin) and expression (all over).

In one popular version, the text describes sex as a mish-mash of secondary sex characteristics and guesswork by medical staff: 'the physical traits you're born with or develop that we think of as "sex characteristics", as well as the sex you are assigned at birth'. Gender identity is defined circularly: 'how you, in your head, experience and define your gender, based on how much you align (or don't align) with what you understand the options for gender to be'. Attraction is 'how you find yourself feeling drawn (or not drawn) to some other people, in sexual, romantic, and/or other ways (often categorised within gender)'. The only concretely defined characteristic is gender expression: 'how you present gender (through your actions, clothing, and demeanour, to name a few), and how those presentations are viewed based on social expectations'.

This is all terribly confusing. But the key to understanding it is to notice that those 'social expectations' are the only objective input. And every parent, teacher and child knows what they are: pink and princesses for girls; blue and superheroes for boys. From here, children can classify their gender expressions, which delineate what they 'understand the options for gender to be'. They can then 'experience and define' their gender identities. And now the regressive truth is revealed: as if by magic, sex stereotypes have been plucked from the wider culture and installed in children's heads.

Accompanying teaching materials often seem about to make an excellent point, only to miss it spectacularly. You nod along to descriptions of restrictive gender norms, hoping for the right conclusion: that nobody need conform if they do not want to, and that there is nothing wrong with boys playing with dolls or girls playing with trucks. You long to hear that girls (or boys) are people with female (or male) bodies who behave however they damn well please; instead you hear that girls (or boys) are people who behave in feminine (or masculine) ways. You hear, in other words, that the way people perform stereotypes makes them who they are – and that bodies that don't match those stereotypes need to be changed.

In 2018 a British teacher recorded a training session on gender by Mermaids, a British charity that campaigns for early paediatric transitioning. The group's favoured teaching aid is a 'gender spectrum' with Barbie at one end and G.I. Joe at the other, and 'jelly baby' outline figures in between, morphing from pig-tailed and curvy to stocky and broad-shouldered. The trainer claims that, in many non-Western cultures, it is understood that people may not be at the end of the gender spectrum associated with their sex assigned at birth. 'If they are growing up and if they recognise that some of their jelly babies are further down towards the female [end of the] spectrum,' she says, 'they may take on a female name and female clothing, live and work as a woman within the tribe, and vice versa to varying degrees.' In other words, what makes children girls or boys is where they fall on a scale from Barbie to G.I. Joe. It is extraordinary that, nowadays, this counts as progressive.

'All Of Us', an Australian course for twelve- and thirteen-year-olds, has a module in which children list behaviours typical of boys and girls. For boys, the lesson plan gives examples such as building things, liking action films and playing with toy cars. For girls, it lists cooking, dancing, shopping, wearing make-up and gossiping. You read it hoping that teachers are expected to follow up by saying that there is no need for either boys or girls to limit themselves like this. Sadly, they are told to say that a transgender person is one whose sex assigned at birth 'does not match the gender they identify as', and show a video about Nevo, a transboy who is 'undergoing a transition, medically and socially, to make his external appearance more masculine and to make his life better reflect how he feels inside. This is also known as affirming one's gender identity.'

Bish, a British sex-education website for teenagers, says that 'you get to choose your gender identity, whether you are a he/she/they or zie and you get to choose how you want to do your own gender.' It recommends placing yourself on several 'gender scales'. Listed under 'looks masculine' are rational, tough, takes charge, independent, headstrong, active and outgoing; under 'looks feminine' are emotional, soft, takes part, sharer, sensitive, passive and shy. It notes that these are what men and women are 'supposed to be like'. Indeed, and if it endorsed smashing those stereotypes to your heart's content, I would applaud. Instead, it invites you to work out where you are on each scale, and from that decide whether you are a boy or girl, or something in between.

Susan Matthews, a researcher at Birkbeck, University of London, has studied the most recent development in gender pedagogy: the gender-identity workbook. Titles such as *How to Understand Your Gender*, *The Gender Quest Workbook*, *The Gender Identity Workbook for Kids* and *Who Are You?* present becoming your best self as a matter of language. And absurdly adult language in those aimed at children, too. *Who Are You?*, which is supposedly for pre-schoolers, offers 'just a few words people use: trans, genderqueer, non-binary, genderfluid, transgender, gender neutral, agender, neutrois, bigender, third gender, two-spirit'. It says that gender is 'much more than the body you were born with', and that kids 'know who they are by how they feel inside'. But what gender is, and what those feelings might be, is never explained.

Readers are encouraged to try on gender identities in search of one that fits. The process is presented as arduous. *The Gender Identity Workbook for Kids* – aimed at seven-year-olds – advises readers to 'try asking your gender to take a rest. Go ahead, write a note to let your gender know you need some time to enjoy or deal with something else.' Matthews likens this work to religious examination of conscience: 'a new form of the spiritual diary, the daily stock-taking in which the individual counted sins and named sexual faults'. Defining 'boy' and 'girl' according to body type, then, is not merely bigoted, but sinful, and defining them as based on ineffable feelings outwardly manifested in clothing and toy preference is not merely progressive, but virtuous.

Most children will survive this stuff without becoming alienated from their physical reality. Even so, it does all children harm. It confuses them about their bodies, and suggests that gender non-conformity marks people as not genuine members of their sex. Boys learn that they shouldn't cry or share; girls, that they should be vain airheads. Slip up, and others may conclude that you are not a 'real' boy or girl.

*

It should not be surprising that a belief system positioning bodies as trivial in comparison with identities is bad for children. Their bodies and identities are still developing, and they are not mature enough to make irreversible decisions. Society has long understood that some parents are not fit to care for their children, in which case others must step in, but also that most parents are the people who know their children best and care most about them. Since gender identity is supposedly innate and unknowable to anyone else, however, parents are now displaced from their role as guardians of their children's safety and future well-being.

As embodied creatures, we are connected by ties that have deep evolutionary significance. The categories of man and woman underpin those of father and mother, and the relationship of each to their children. If such categories are to become a matter of self-declaration, then those ties must be dissolved. Families become meaningless and individuals create themselves. To return to the allegory of *The Matrix*, consider the question of Neo's mother. In the 'real' world, he has none: his body was grown in a pod and his identity self-constructed in adulthood. The never-mentioned woman who thinks she gave birth to Thomas Anderson inside the Matrix is deluded, and she and Neo are nothing to each other. It is striking how many trans people describe themselves online as 'self-made woman' or 'self-made man'.

As I wrote this book, many parents whose children asserted trans identities told me their stories in confidence. They were not bigots, though all have suffered from being described that way. They simply saw children they had known from birth struggle to cope with homophobia and societal narratives about gender non-conformity. There was no one unbiased those parents could turn to for advice, and the stories they and their children read in the media were entirely one-sided.

One told me that her teenage daughter, whom she had tried to guide away from transition, had gone ahead, left home and cut off contact. She later desisted, but did not get back in touch. Another spoke of a male teenager who was happier for having rejected 'toxic masculinity' by identifying as a woman, but also about the 'agonies of anxiety' she and her husband suffer when they think about the long-term consequences of an obsession they think is highly unlikely to last. A third talked with deep grief of the homophobic bullying and name-calling at school, and uncritical media coverage of trans issues, that she believes convinced her gay son that he must be a girl. She refused to consent to any medical steps, but her child is now nineteen and can make his own choices.

A fourth regards herself as having dodged a bullet. Her daughter, who was finishing junior school, had started repeating gender catchphrases and seemed increasingly miserable. When the mother discovered by chance that the child was flirting with coming out as non-binary – and that an astonishing share of the pupils at the secondary school she and her husband had been considering were trans-identified – they immediately looked elsewhere. Without encouragement from classmates, their daughter's confusion came to nothing, and she seems to have stopped questioning whether she is actually a girl.

These parents say that their attempts to protect their children are actively frustrated by everyone else. It is now common for schools to accept children's announcements of new identities without question, and even to change children's sex in school records without informing parents. I have heard from parents who discovered that pupils were told to use one name and set of pronouns for their child – except when the parents were around, when they should switch back to birth name and pronouns – and others who were told that if they continued to 'misgender' their child, social services would intervene.

All this happens in a suffocating silence. Mainstream media outlets focus on the heart-warming narrative of children discovering their true identities, and supportive parents who accept that revelation. Parents who do not feel this way mostly do not want to go public, even if they can find a forum, in case it harms their relationship with their child.

The stories of detransitioners, which are the most dangerous for the gender-identity narrative, are also silenced. They find each other online: on Twitter, where they use the lizard emoji to signal their detrans status, or on the detrans subreddit (though as I write transactivists have taken it over by claiming that it was a hate forum). Seen from within gender-identity ideology, they are apostates. Some of the abuse I have seen heaped on them is truly shocking. They are accused of faking their stories to incite transphobia, or of being in the pay of the American evangelical Right. Or they are told that they screwed up, and should now shut up and stop causing trouble for 'real' trans people.

Irreversible Damage, a book about female detransitioners by journalist Abigail Shrier published in 2020, is the first time their stories have been widely heard. Shrier struggled to get the book published and advertised. The first publisher to consider buying it backed out after staff threatened a walk-out. Amazon refused to accept ads for it, and when a parents' group started to crowd-fund billboards advertising it, the crowdfunding platform pulled the plug after transactivists complained. (There is, however, clearly an appetite for a non-airbrushed take on paediatric transitioning. Shrier's book has sold extremely well.)

Many detransitioners find telling their story impossibly painful. It takes courage to speak truth that others do not want to hear – especially when you used to be one of those trying to shout the truth-tellers down. They often feel deep shame, says Lisa Marchiano, the Jungian therapist. Some I have spoken with recall with remorse their own attacks on people who spoke against paediatric transitioning. Others regret having encouraged others to transition when, with hindsight, they were all caught up in the same craze. Many feel like fools for being so sure they wanted something and then realising they were wrong.

Recovery requires them to forgive themselves. Just how hard that is depends in part on how far they went before desisting. Someone who took cross-sex hormones for a year or two may struggle to recover their footing in reality. But someone who regrets having their reproductive organs removed must process the worst sort of grief: that caused by an irreparable loss you eagerly brought upon yourself. Not only are they sterile, but they have lost body parts that matter for general health. A woman who has undergone hysterectomy is more likely to suffer a range of health problems, from heart disease to urinary incontinence. One without ovaries will have to take artificial oestrogen to stave off menopause. 'Knowing you made a choice that really damaged your health, and you did it when you were barely twenty,' says Marchiano: 'that is a very difficult thing to come to terms with.'

Even as detransitioners and sceptical parents have to be sought out and befriended before they will tell their stories, gender-identity ideology's most ardent adherents are given platforms everywhere. Susie Green, the chief executive of Mermaids, took her child to Thailand for sex-reassignment surgery at age sixteen – two years below the legal age in the UK. And yet Green is frequently asked to comment on stories with a trans angle. The careers of Jazz Jennings – and her parents – were launched in 2007, when Jazz was six and the family appeared in a documentary presented by Barbara Walters. The family have been on television ever since. Kai Shappley (the Texan child whose mother would not accept a gay son) is now an actor, and played a transgirl in the 2020 Netflix reboot of *The Baby-Sitters Club*.

This celebration of one group, and denigration and silencing of the other, surely has an impact on whether children seek to transition, and also on whether they eventually desist. Coming-out school assemblies, and teachers explaining how special and brave the trans child is, help lock children into trans identities they might otherwise have abandoned. (This is not to deny that trans children will face bullying. The two evils do not cancel out.)

When I spoke with Richard Green before his death, *National Geographic* had recently published an issue with transgender children on the cover. Green was certain that such publicity was a terrible idea. The 'tremendous personal investment' of both child and family in the trans identity would make desistance much harder, he said. The sceptical parents I have interviewed would love to be proved wrong; to see their transitioned child blossom. But parents who have turned their children into their public activism are all in. They can never allow themselves to entertain the possibility that setting their child on the path to trans adulthood might have been an error.

Child transition is an issue in an increasing number of divorce battles. Most do not come to public notice (I heard about the trend from medical professionals who have been called as expert witnesses). But in 2019 one was reported worldwide: that of a seven-year-old male child in Texas whose mother insisted she had a daughter named Luna, and father, that he had a son named James.

The case was a Rorschach test for America's polarised media: which parent was the hero and which the villain depended on the politics of the outlet. The mother persuaded a court to grant her custody and order the father to dress the child in girl's clothes and use female pronouns. Then the father gained joint custody, after providing evidence that the child showed no interest in presenting as a girl during custodial visits. The mother appealed, and won, and, at the time of going to press, the child is known as Luna, a girl whose father has no say in her care.

However this story plays out, its poisonous twists cannot be good for the child's mental health or relationship with the warring parents. But it is cast in the shade by what happens in Canada, where gender-identity ideology is entrenched in law and the government grants itself sweeping powers to intrude on family life. There, parents may find that, set against their child's, their opinions are irrelevant.

In 2013 the Jacksons (not their real name; a Canadian court order prohibits its publication) separated. Their daughter Max became distressed and depressed. In 2016, aged twelve, she was referred to the school counsellor. Unbeknownst to her parents at the time, she mentioned feeling a commonality with the transboy protagonist of a film she had seen online. The counsellor concluded that Max was trans, arranged for a change of name and pronouns in school records, and referred Max to a psychologist, who recommended testosterone and made a further referral to a paediatric endocrinologist.

A consent form was sent to the Jacksons; the father refused to sign. 'I wasn't even looking at the trans part of it,' he says. What jumped out were the disclaimers: that this was an experimental treatment; that no one knew the long-term effects of taking cross-sex hormones so young; and that sterility was near-certain. He reasoned that his daughter could do as she chose when she reached eighteen. Until then, protecting her was his job.

But under British Columbia's Infants Act, a child of any age has the right to medical treatment that is opposed by parents if the doctor thinks it is in the child's best interests, and that the child is 'mature enough' to decide. In 2019, the supreme court of British Columbia ruled that Max could consent to medical transition independently of the father's wishes (his ex-wife was no longer opposed). His refusal to refer to his child as a boy, and continued opposition to transition, were ruled 'family violence', and he was banned from speaking to the press. But after a period of silence he started to speak to media outlets, some of which named him and the doctors involved in the case. In March 2021 he was arrested, and a month later was sentenced to six months in prison for criminal contempt of court. 'The initial bad actors are the teachers and school counsellors who secretly put young girls on the path to gender clinics,' says Carey Linde, a lawyer who has represented the father in most of the hearings. 'And then Canadian law allows doctors to provide experimental treatments without parents even knowing.'

You can judge how easy it is to find a doctor in Canada willing to certify that puberty blockers and cross-sex hormones are in a child's best interests from the recording of an event at Vancouver Public Library in February 2019. In it, Wallace Wong, a child psychologist, can be heard saying that his paediatric gender clinic sees around five hundred children who are in public care. His caseload is around one thousand, he says, and his youngest client not yet three. He advises parents to accelerate children's transition by exaggerating their gender dysphoria, and claiming that if transition is prevented, they will kill themselves. 'Pull a stunt,' he says. 'Suicide, every time – they will give you what you need.'

*

The final harm to children I want to discuss concerns safeguarding. As the belief that biological sex is over-writeable by self-declared gender identity takes hold, institutions are abandoning the protocols set up to avoid a repeat of child-abuse scandals in the Catholic Church, Boy Scouts, residential homes, boarding schools and many other institutions. Guidelines written by trans lobby groups and adopted by schools, sporting federations, social clubs and so on mean that toilets, changing rooms and dormitories are now segregated according to the sex that children – and adults – say they are. Parents are left in the dark.

In 2018, Helen Watts was expelled from the UK Girl Guides for objecting to the organisation deciding to allow males to become members and group leaders, provided they identified as girls or women. The new rules say there is no need to inform girls or parents if males will be sharing sleeping accommodation or washing facilities. Watts wonders whether Girl Guides has considered the consequences for personal care (her questions have gone unanswered). 'How would you, or your five-year-old, feel about her being cleaned up after a toileting accident by a male who identifies as a woman, and you're not even supposed to know?' she asks.

Watts also objects to leaders being told that conversations about gender identity can be confidential. 'I understand the need for discretion and sensitivity,' she says. 'But that should apply just as much to the girls, whose interests Girl Guides is supposed to represent. Girl Guides is potentially putting teenage girls and boys in the same accommodation and not tell-ing parents. All leaders have safeguarding training, and we learn never to agree to keep a secret. We're keeping information from parents that might alter their decisions. It undermines trust, and builds a barrier between children and parents. It's gaslighting on a massive scale.'

Such concerns have nothing to do with believing trans people are unusually likely to be predators. Safeguarding procedures need to cover everyone, no matter their gender identity. 'I know of a Guide leader who had to bring her four-year-old son on a weekend camping trip, and there had to be rules for where he was to shower and sleep,' says Watts. 'Including male children along with female ones is a risk you have to assess and manage – unless they say the magic words, "I'm a girl." '

Child-safeguarding rules are largely about nipping problems in the bud and preventing honest mistakes. But they are also intended to prevent rare, catastrophic institutional failures. The history of institutional child-abuse has shown how predators can 'groom' people and organisations to accept behaviour that should have raised red flags. The only defence against such grooming is to apply child-safeguarding rules to everyone, always, with no exceptions, and to regard child safeguarding as an obligation of every adult. That is why I am writing the next few paragraphs, though I know from experience how ready people are to misinterpret and dismiss fears about harms to chil-dren as malicious mud-slinging.

Let me be clear: in what I am about to say there is an analogy, and it is *not* between transactivists and paedophiles, but between some transactivists and campaigners for gay rights post-1968 – who were naive, self-centred and blind to children's welfare, and therefore easily manipulated by paedophiles. (The further read-ing section for this chapter lists copious sources for a claim that may seem inflammatory, but on which the historical record is crystal clear.) My point is that transactivism can be exploited by those who would harm children – *not* that trans people, or trans-activists, want to harm children, or do not care if others do.

In the late 1960s, some European liberals thought that breaking down sexual taboos was a task that had to be started young. In German kindergartens run along radical-left lines, teachers encouraged children to fondle them, view pornography and simulate sexual intercourse. Contemporaneous accounts show that parents often felt qualms, which they suppressed because of what they had been told about how children should naturally behave. What happened was child-abuse, though motivated by political conviction rather than sexual desire. But it did not take long before paedophiles saw their chance.

The leaders of the sexual revolution were men whose aims were to legalise homosexuality – and, in some cases, to smash the heterosexual family unit. Few if any wanted to endanger children; they simply did not give children enough thought. Left-wing organisations tolerated groups such as the UK's Paedophile Information Exchange (PIE), which had links with the Labour Party and the civil-rights group now called Liberty. In Germany, a political organisation called the Study and Work Group on Paedophilia made remarkable advances. In 1980, a youth group affiliated with the liberal Free Democratic Party adopted pro-paedophilia positions, as did the Green Party, formed the same year.

Paedophiles gained such a hearing on the Left partly by persuading Leftists that their enemies' enemies were automatic-ally friends. In this case, the enemies were Conservatives, Catholics, evangelicals and fascists, all of whom opposed both gay activists and paedophiles. On the Left, that made speaking out about paedophile infiltration nearly impossible.

In 1979, Eileen Fairweather, a tyro journalist, was writing for *Spare Rib*, a feminist magazine. She was assigned to read the book *Paedophilia: The Radical Case*, which argued for lowering the age of consent to four. The author, Tom O'Carroll, was an early member of PIE who was later imprisoned for child-abuse. Fairweather recalls 'anguished, earnest' discussions about what to write. 'I did draft something, arguing that the existing age of consent was not "patriarchal", but protected children,' she says. 'But I never even dared show it to anyone.' Paedophiles had so thoroughly infiltrated the gay movement by that time that if you dared criticise those calling for 'child sexual liberation' you were branded anti-gay. Fairweather says she sees 'the same intimidation and paralysis of intelligence' today, caused by the fear of being called transphobic.

In the 1990s, Fairweather won press awards for her work uncovering paedophile rings in British children's homes and schools. She became an acknowledged expert on how paedophiles exploit 'institutional weaknesses and political correctness'. It is therefore concerning that gender-identity ideology raises red flags for her, in particular the advice to teachers to keep secrets from parents and discourage children from speaking up about concerns regarding sharing their private spaces with children of the opposite sex.

The worry is *not*, I repeat, that trans people are unusually likely to be child-abusers. Gay people aren't, either, and yet their movement was infiltrated by those who were – with two baleful consequences. Children were harmed who could have been kept safe and, even today, homophobes conflate homosexuality and paedophilia. Anyone who cares for the welfare of either children or trans people should want to avoid history repeating itself.

7

SHE WHO MUST NOT BE NAMED

How gender-identity ideology erases women

The body-denialism at the heart of gender-identity ideology is harmful for all humans, since we are in fact embodied creatures. But it is especially harmful for women, since female bodies impose costs and make demands in ways that male ones don't. It is female bodies that bear almost all the burden of reproduction, and ignoring that fact doesn't change it; it merely muddles thinking about how to arrange society to accommodate reproduction while ensuring that women can live full, self-actualised lives. And it is also especially tempting for women, because throughout history women have been objectified and reduced to their bodies, with men as subject, occupying the realms of mind and intellect. 'The body has been made so problematic for women that it has often seemed easier to shrug it off and travel as a disembodied spirit,' wrote Adrienne Rich in 1976 in *Of Woman Born*, her book about motherhood.

Any feminism worthy of the name must offer a strong analysis of how society can accommodate and support motherhood. But it must go beyond that: many women are not mothers, and mothers are many other things as well. This is a

difficult balancing act, and no doubt both feminism as a movement, and individual feminists, have toppled off on both sides
many times. But what is happening now is an error of quite a
different order.

The idea that being a man or woman is a matter of declaration
offers women several false promises. One is that you can identify out of the exigencies of a female body, and by doing so gain
access to male privilege. Alternatively, you can enjoy the benefits of being a desirable young woman in a society dominated by
men – but later avoid the poisonous combination of ageism and
misogyny that positions post-menopausal women as such a
society's most disposable people, since it is now understood
that the mind is what matters. Body-denialism also offers women
a way to suppress the shame and rage that they can feel at being
physically weaker than men, and vulnerable to rape. It is teenage
girls and young women who are most susceptible to believing all
this, as the messiest realities of female lives – pregnancy, wanted
and unwanted; childbirth; infertility; menopause – are, for the
most part, still in their future.

Jane Clare Jones is a British feminist philosopher and editor
of *The Radical Notion*, a quarterly magazine (the title references a famous definition of feminism as 'the radical notion
that women are people'). It is no coincidence, she says, that
gender-identity ideology has been vigorously critiqued on
Mumsnet, a British website set up in 2000 for new mothers.
The site's core users – women who have recently given birth –
are well-placed to see the absurdity of positioning bodies as
inconsequential and easily refashioned. They are also at the
stage of life when women lose any illusion that discrimination
on the grounds of female sex – not womanly identification –
no longer happens. It is obvious that being female matters
socially and politically when you are contemplating the lack of

good part-time jobs, the prospect of the 'mummy track' and the cost of decent childcare.

Mainstream feminism's shift towards concerning itself with self-defined women, rather than females, was only possible because of other changes in the movement. The so-called second wave, which started in the early 1960s and ran for about a quarter-century, had extended women's demands for equality beyond voting and property rights to other systemic injustices, such as unequal pay, and to structural issues that affected women more than men, such as the lack of maternity leave and childcare. This was also when women created the first domestic-violence and rape-crisis services for women and children victimised by men.

But from the 1990s or so, liberal or 'third wave' feminism de-emphasised such structural and communal issues, instead centring choice and agency – for example arguing that some women might like to work in pornography or prostitution, and that this could be empowering. Second-wave feminists, who mostly regarded these as harmful for all women and almost always coerced, were dismissed as 'sex negative' – or simply prudes. Around the same time, intersectionality came to the fore. The term was coined in 1989 by Kimberlé Crenshaw, an American legal scholar who pointed out that discrimination against black women was not merely the sum of racism as experienced by black men and sexism as experienced by white women: the intersecting oppressions mutually reinforced and created distinct hardships. She and others charged that feminism had focused too much on white women, and needed to broaden out.

Perhaps second-wave feminists had spent too little time thinking about the ways in which women differ, and too much thinking about women as victims rather than agents. And the central observation of intersectionality is certainly correct and important: people are members of many identity groups that are salient in modern societies, and those often interact in ways that unidimensional analyses miss. But these developments also paved the way for feminism to lose its focus on females.

Males are easier to include in a movement centred on personal choice than in a movement centred on an analysis of male oppression and exploitation of females. And with the rise of identitarianism on the Left, intersectionality became distorted. In activist discourse, it often came to seem that people were nothing but collections of identity labels, and that everyone who shared a given set experienced the world in the same way. An insight that should have added nuance and richness to analyses of women's sex-based oppression led to fragmentation, and made it easier to ignore that oppression. And when women were discussed as a single, biologically delineated group, the incoherence of including males – or transwomen – had been glaring. Now, with every mention of a woman preceded by a list of adjectives establishing her intersectional position, 'trans' could be added without sticking out like a sore thumb.

The embrace of gender-identity ideology was part of mainstream feminism's shift away from seeking to improve the lives of ordinary women and towards a self-congratulatory, performative, postmodernist style with its origins on campus. To quote 'The professor of parody', a celebrated essay eviscerating Judith Butler by the philosopher Martha Nussbaum, published in 1999: 'Something more insidious than provincialism has come to prominence in the American academy. It is the virtually complete turning from the material side of life, toward a type of verbal and symbolic politics that makes only the flimsiest of connections with the real situation of real women . . . Feminist thinkers of the new symbolic type would appear to believe that the way to do feminist politics is to use words in a subversive way, in academic publications of lofty obscurity and disdainful abstractness. These symbolic gestures, it is believed, are themselves a form of political resistance; and so one need not engage with messy things such as legislatures and movements in order to act daringly.'

Consider the consequences for the feminist movement of accepting the activist mantra that 'transwomen are women' – or the logically equivalent proposition that 'a woman is anyone who says they're one'. I have seen these restated in many ways, sometimes quite poetically. To give just a couple of examples: women are 'an imagined community that honours the female, enacts the feminine and exceeds the limitations of a sexist society' (American transwoman Susan Stryker, writing in *Time* magazine); and women are 'multifaceted, intergenerational, international . . . limitless, formless . . . women are the world' (UN Women, quoting another transwoman, American-Antiguan model Aaron Philip).

At drive-by speed, this sort of stuff may seem flattering, even liberating. After all, who wants to be nothing more than a sex object or walking uterus? But defining women as the people whose bodies developed along the female reproductive pathway is limiting only if you regard female embodiment as limiting. These redefinitions are the antithesis of the 'radical notion that women are people'. They define womanhood as stereotypes enacted by people of different body types; rather than a body type that need not in any way limit the behaviour of the people who possess it. Moreover, they are vacuous – with dire consequences for any feminist manifesto.

I have read many attempts to give trans-inclusionary definitions of woman some objective basis, and all fail. Some rely on weak analogies; others try so hard to include transwomen that they end up excluding some natal women (on grounds other than not identifying as women). For more details, see the further reading section for this chapter. But above all, in every case they fail to do what their proponents want, namely to include within womanhood all the males who want to be included.

This isn't really so surprising. The only thing that these self-identified women have in common is that they are male. The central doctrine of gender-identity ideology – that your gender identity is what you say it is – necessarily precludes any objective delineation. If you cannot see this, it is because you do in fact know what a woman is, and did not notice yourself calling on that knowledge as you read those flowery statements. Try 'a squawm is anyone who identifies as a squawm,' or 'every lazap is a lazap.' Now, can you say what a squawm or a lazap is?

As the class of women is rendered vacuous, feminism is, too. The language gives it away: how could you possibly target a policy on 'multifaceted, intergenerational, international' beings? Certainly not anything as down-to-earth as cheap contraception, paid maternity leave, longer sentences for rapists or tougher rules on bias in hiring. When women are limitless and formless, they can have no political demands.

In particular, feminism can no longer address issues related to female embodiment – or even articulate them. Consider the annual Women's Marches that started in January 2017. They were inspired by the election of Donald Trump, a man who has been accused of rape and recorded boasting of committing sexual assault. Many of those at the first march brandished banners expressing female solidarity, such as 'sisterhood is powerful', and wore 'pussy hats' made from hot-pink yarn to reference Trump's brags about grabbing women 'by the pussy'. And yet, by the second march a year later, these had been deemed insufficiently inclusive of transwomen.

In a slew of critical articles, pussy hats were described as 'exclusionary', 'reductive' and expressive of 'biological essentialism'. One critic dubbed them 'the confederate flag of the women's movement'. In an article for *Grazia* magazine, British transwoman Munroe Bergdorf said they were a 'well-intentioned yet misguided symbol of women's equality'. Organisers in Pensacola, Florida said that 'not every woman has a vagina, and not every person who has a vagina is a woman', and asked marchers to leave their hats at home. A movement that started as a roar of anger about the consequences for female people of male sexual entitlement and violence could no longer even name the problem.

*

Even as the class of 'women' becomes 'some males and some females, with no objective traits in common', female bodies continue to exist. But when they need to be mentioned, there is no word for them. The result is that the very people who berate opponents of gender-identity ideology for 'reducing people to their genitals' insist that females are referred to as body parts and reproductive functions.

Governments, companies, charities and media outlets now talk of 'people who menstruate', 'pregnant people', 'abortion seekers' and 'birthing parents', where they would once simply have said 'women'. Here are a few indicative examples. The UK's National Health Service explains that 'the concept of virginity for people with vaginas has a complicated history'. *Teen Vogue* offers a 'no-nonsense, 101 guide to masturbation for vagina owners'. Information campaigns from cancer charities tell 'anyone with a cervix' to get regular Pap smear tests. An ad for Tampax enjoins the world to 'celebrate the diversity of all people who bleed'. La Leche League USA says it 'supports all breastfeeding, chestfeeding, and human milk feeding families'. An

American charity bemoans the frequency with which 'black birthing bodies' die in the delivery room.

This language carves women up into pieces to be used for sexual and reproductive services. It is reminiscent of porn sites, where visitors are invited to search according to body part and activity of interest, or the surrogacy industry, where children are bought in bits – eggs from an ovary-haver, gestational services from a uterus owner and nutrition from a human milk feeder. Women become orifices, providers of genetic material, vessels for growing offspring and milch cows.

This is not just dehumanising: it also obscures the fact that these body parts and functions come as a package. The same type of person ovulates, menstruates, gestates, gives birth and requires abortions, and possesses the physical features that heterosexual men desire to look at, touch and penetrate. It is the type of person who has been oppressed throughout history, precisely because men want to dominate and control the possessors of this type of body. Dividing women up like this attenuates their power as a constituency – at any one time, it is different women who are menstruating, pregnant, breast-feeding and post-menopausal, for example. How much harder it would have been to argue for the vote for women, or for paid maternity leave, or to end the exemption that allowed men to rape their wives at will, if the only way to refer to the beneficiaries of such changes had been to list bodily secretions and sexual organs.

If the stated reasons for such language, namely to be inclusive of transmen when talking about female issues, were sincere, then we would see similar linguistic manoeuvres in order not to exclude transwomen when talking about males. There would be guides to masturbation for 'penis owners', and articles and advertising campaigns aimed at testicle havers, semen producers and the like. 'Anyone with a prostate' would be told to get it checked. But no such language is used. Factsheets about prostate cancer start by saying: 'Only men have a prostate.' When I googled 'testicle havers', I was asked if I meant 'testicle shavers'.

The asymmetry is flagrant. Take MedicineNet, an American website. The entry for 'female' reads: 'The traditional definition of female was "an individual of the sex that bears young" or "that produces ova or eggs". However, things are not so simple today. Female can be defined by physical appearance, by chromosome constitution (see Female chromosome complement), or by gender identification.' None of this obfuscation is deemed necessary for 'male', to which the same dictionary devotes just five words: 'The sex that produces spermatozoa.'

It is impossible to avoid the conclusion that trans-inclusive language is inclusive in one direction only. It aims at removing all obstacles to using the words 'woman' and 'female' for any male who wants them, without requiring any special accommodation for females who wish to identify into maleness or manhood.

Another revealing comparison is between gender self-identification, which is social-justice dogma, and racial self-identification, which is taboo. This is, on the face of it, odd, since arguing that Black includes White would be much easier than arguing that Woman includes Man. (To be clear, I am not making this argument, but I am not the one saying that males can identify into womanhood.) After all, everyone is ultimately of African heritage. And racial boundaries genuinely are blurred. There are almost as many mixtures of heritage as there are people, and any examination of racist classifications, such as apartheid or the Jim Crow laws, quickly reveals that they are to some extent arbitrary (as well, of course, as unjust).

And yet in 2015, when Rachel Dolezal, a black-identifying American woman who was a chapter president for the National Association for the Advancement of Colored People, was revealed to have lied to conceal her entirely white European heritage, she became a hate figure worldwide. She was forced to resign from the NAACP and dismissed from her university job teaching 'The Black Woman's Struggle' and 'Intro to Africana Studies'. Despite the evident sincerity of her identification with Blackness, she was accused of adopting it as a 'costume', and called a 'race faker' and, in the words of *Vanity Fair*, a liar 'bold and brazen enough to claim ownership over a painful and complicated history she wasn't born to'.

The taboo extends even to comparing the treatment of the two binaries. In 2017 *Hypatia*, a feminist journal, published 'In Defense of Transracialism', by Rebecca Tuvel, a philosopher at Rhodes College in Memphis. For drawing parallels with trans-gender identities to argue that transracial identities like Dolezal's should not be dismissed out of hand, she was subjected to modern academia's version of a witch-hunt. She was sent hate mail and accused of 'epistemic violence'. She was pressured to retract her article, hearing from several senior people in her field that she had jeopardised her chances of making tenure. *Hypatia* received an open letter signed by hundreds of her peers, misrepresenting her words and demanding the article's retraction. Though it was not retracted, *Hypatia*'s board of associate editors released a lengthy and grovelling apology for having published it.

At an academic level, the differing treatment of sex, gender and sexuality categories on the one hand, and racial categories on the other, is because they have been theorised in different fields. The first group comes under queer theory, where liberation means category-busting. A male person who identifies as a woman is striking a blow against 'cisheteronormativity' – the

SHE WHO MUST NOT BE NAMED

assumption that being non-trans and straight is the norm. In critical race theory, however, all white people are taken to hold privileged positions in a societal network of power, and whiteness is inherently racist. People cannot be permitted to identify out of their racial groups, since that would enable white people to identify out of acknowledging their racism and atoning for it with anti-racist work.

The difference is not mere historical contingency, however. I do not think that if postmodernist academia had developed differently, it would be acceptable for white people to identify as black, but not for males to identify as women. The simple truth is that there is a significant constituency in favour of gender self-identification that does not exist for racial self-identification – males who want to be categorised as women more than they want anything else, and have the power to make it happen.

The women most harmed are a highly marginalised subgroup: lesbians. Without a meaningful definition of sex, there can be no meaningful definition of sexual orientation. And so, according to activists, the words gay, straight and so on now refer to attractions towards gender identities, not sexes. The Canadian transwoman Veronica Ivy has said that the only morally acceptable orientation is pansexual (capable of attraction to people of any sex or gender identity), and that having a 'genital preference' (that is, being attracted only to people of one sex or the other) is transphobic. Many trans people pushed back against that. But it is the logical conclusion of insisting that identity-based definitions override bodily ones, since people of any identity may have any configuration of primary and secondary sex characteristics and, for the activists, it is transphobic not to accept people as the gender they claim.

This sort of thing has little impact on straight people, because they are the great majority. Nor does it much affect gay males, since females, however they identify, are not normally in a position to harass males into accepting them as sexual partners. Overwhelmingly, it is lesbians whose sexual boundaries come under pressure.

If a woman says her dating pool is female-only, she is understood as denying that transwomen are women. Even if she reframes her sexual orientation as a 'preference' and tries to argue that she gets to choose whom to sleep with according to whichever criteria work for her, this is still not good enough. 'Your dating preferences are discriminatory,' says Riley J. Dennis, the transwoman YouTuber. 'Because these dating preferences are ultimately harmful to people who don't fit into your box of what a conventionally attractive person looks like, it makes people feel isolated, alone, and unwanted to hear that they are universally unattractive to people.'

Lucy Masoud, a lesbian who worked in the London Fire Brigade for twelve years and is now a barrister, has a long history of activism in support of trans people. As a union official, she persuaded the Fire Brigade to allow paid time off for doctors' appointments and surgery during gender reassignment. In 2020, she was newly single. She joined Tinder, Plenty of Fish and Hinge, as well as some lesbian-specific dating apps, such as HER. Although she set her profile to 'woman seeking women', every third or fourth match was a transwoman, she says. Then Hinge, which asks users to answer quirky questions or finish sentences, presented Masoud with: 'All I ask is that you . . .' She completed it with: 'be on time, don't moan about me getting overly involved in *Love Island* and that you're a biological female.' That got her permanently banned for 'transphobia'.

In 1999 Masoud was working for an accommodation agency in Soho, London. Her then-girlfriend worked in the gay bar next door – the Admiral Duncan, which a neo-Nazi nail-bombed that year, killing three people and injuring seventy, her girlfriend among them. 'We were both caught up in the bomb, and it ruined our lives for a bit,' she says. 'But the gay community rose up. I remember signs plastered all over Soho saying "You can't bomb us back into the closet." What did my girlfriend get blown out of a pub for, if twenty years later we are less able to be open about our sexuality than we were back then?'

*

In its erasure of sex categories, gender-identity ideology seeks to change not just the present, but the past, too. Any woman who, by force, luck or guile, succeeded in transcending societal strictures on her sex is now at risk of being retroactively transitioned. Boudicca and Joan of Arc are both often described as transmen. So is the Pharaoh Hatshepsut (who 'was assigned female at birth but intermittently dressed and ruled as a King', according to Amnesty UK). In 2019 the *Washington Post* removed mention of Jennie Hodgers, who cross-dressed in order to fight in the American Civil War, from a podcast entitled 'Women who won wars'. In an apology, it said Hodgers's inclusion had not been 'in keeping with *Washington Post* style, which states that people should be referred to by their current identity'.

Lesbian icons are now routinely described as transmen, among them Radclyffe Hall, the author of *The Well of Loneliness*, a tragic story of Sapphic love, and Stormé DeLarverie, a professional drag king who was in the thick of the Stonewall riots that launched the modern gay-rights movement. Even fictional characters are not safe. George of Enid Blyton's *Famous Five* books, a girl who hates dresses and long hair, and loves sailing and climbing; Jo of *Little Women*, who whistles, walks with her hands behind her back and promises her father to be the 'man of the house' while he is away at war; and Yentl, who cross-dresses to be allowed to study the Talmud: all are now often 'reinterpreted' as transmen.

Gender-identity ideology's demand that the past be over-written to suit the present is particularly painful for a small but vulnerable group of women: those whose husbands transition in mid-life. Their spouses are now understood, not as becoming women, but as telling the world that they were always women. Their wives are expected to accept that they entered same-sex marriages: that they are lesbians, and always were.

It is easy to hear from women who have accepted their own life stories being recast in this way: they get interviewed in major publications and given book deals. For an example of the genre, see *Love Lives Here* by Amanda Jetté Knox, a Canadian woman whose husband of twenty-two years came out to her as a trans-woman in 2014, just a few months after one of their children came out as a transgirl. (The child now identifies as non-binary.) Knox now regards herself as a lesbian who was hiding that truth from herself until her spouse's revelation. *Love Lives Here* was longlisted for several Canadian literary awards.

It is much harder to hear from women who insist on telling their own life stories from their point of view. One of the few to make it into print is Christine Benvenuto. Both she and her ex, now called Joy Ladin, have published memoirs of Ladin's transition. The two versions had strikingly different receptions.

Through the Door of Life: A Jewish Journey Between Genders, by Ladin, was a National Jewish Book Award finalist and winner of a prize from *The Forward*, a Jewish-American news-media organisation. *Sex Changes: A Memoir of Gender, Marriage, and Moving On*, published the following year, lost Benvenuto friends and almost ended her writing career.

There were calls for her book to be censored, and she was forwarded emails sent by people close to her ex, trying to orchestrate pile-ons and ensure that she was never published again, says Benvenuto. 'At the time I was not familiar with online hate and misinformation campaigns. I've since come to understand how often these tactics are employed in misogynistic attacks against women.' Most people the couple had known expressed a 'strong and blind sympathy' for her ex, while being devoid of any consideration for her, or even her children. Those who did express sympathy were too afraid to do so openly. 'A number of times people approached me in public and whispered – yes, literally – their support, told me they considered me very brave, and so on, clearly nervous about being overheard.'

You might have thought it would be possible to express sympathy for both spouses in such marriages – those who understand and accept their own desires very late, and those who feel that as a loss, even betrayal, and refuse to pretend otherwise. But the stories of unhappy female partners of male mid-life transitioners have become what social scientists call 'forbidden narratives': so disruptive to dominant ideologies that they are suppressed.

Women who refuse to be silenced must seek refuge in online anonymity. One is 'Tinsel Angel', who lives in the north of England. She met her ex-husband in a nightclub two decades ago. Before she moved in with him he told her that he used to cross-dress, but hadn't since he met her. They married three years after meeting, and had a child a year later. Then followed several years when he cross-dressed but tried to keep it secret, and repeatedly promised to stop. 'It made him unattractive to me at a visceral level,' she says. 'There was a pattern of lies being discovered, compromises being made and broken, boundaries being put in place and overstepped.'

One New Year's Eve, her husband said that his resolution was to 'do more girl stuff'. Tinsel insisted that he visit their family doctor, who referred him to a gender clinic. The year in limbo before full assessment was 'hideous, terrible, horrible'. When he was finally seen, he received a diagnosis of gender dysphoria and decided to present as a woman full-time. 'That was my red line,' says Tinsel. She left soon afterwards.

'If I told someone who didn't know me well why my marriage ended, they would say, "that must have been very difficult for him,"' she says. A couple of years later, she came across the expression 'trans widow'. 'It's very descriptive. He's not dead, but his identity is dead. Actually, it's worse: you're supposed to pretend it never existed. I have heard widows say, "my husband and I adored each other, and I have wonderful memories that nothing can take away from me." Whereas everything I look back on is lies.'

In 2017 Tinsel started a thread on Mumsnet and discovered other women whose marriages had ended when their husbands transitioned. Their experiences were very similar, she realised – and in many ways echoed those of women whose husbands subjected them to physical or emotional abuse. Women whose husbands are transitioning frequently have their sanity questioned, their memories discounted and their judgment undermined, says Tinsel. Another similarity was boundary-pushing: promises are made, for example not to cross-dress in front of the children, only to be broken. A third was emotional manipulation. '[My husband] insisted that everything he did, and the decisions he made, were the consequences of his identity, and if he had not done those things he would have killed himself,' says Tinsel. 'That's a tactic often employed by manipulators: give me what I want or I'll kill myself.'

Tinsel now writes about trans widows for feminist websites, and publishes their stories online under pseudonyms. 'I want women in the situation I was in to have some idea how things might pan out,' she says. 'I want them to feel that their boundaries are justifiable, and that if the men they're with keep crossing those boundaries it's okay to leave. In any conversation about this, you end up talking about the men and why they do it. I try to change the conversation to the women and the impact on them.'

8

WE JUST NEED TO PEE

Why female-only spaces matter
so much for women

In 2018, Shelah Poyer, a beautician in Vancouver, started to earn extra money by seeing clients at home. She accepted only women as clients, for reasons of safety and because some services, like Brazilian waxing, cannot be performed on men. So when she received a message on Facebook Marketplace from Jonathan Yaniv, whose profile picture was as male as the name, she replied: Not for men, sorry! 'I'm a woman,' Yaniv replied. 'I transitioned last year.'

Poyer was nonplussed. Truth be told, she didn't feel any better about having a male who identified as a woman in her home than about any other male. And she didn't know what she was being asked to do. 'I wanted to ask about surgery, but how to ask without being offensive?' she says. Waxing male genitalia is a specialised service (testicles have thinner and looser skin than vulvas, and treating them similarly would cause tearing). She stopped responding, but the messages kept coming, and then phone calls to her salon. Now she was spooked.

She blocked Yaniv on Facebook, and her boyfriend sent the importunate would-be client an angry message. Then she heard that a discrimination complaint had been made to British Columbia's human-rights tribunal. For three months she heard no more. Then came another letter, demanding C\$2,500 and an apology, and saying that if she did not comply, there would be a hearing.

Sex has long been a protected characteristic in British Columbia's Code of Human Rights, and gender identity and expression were added in 2016. It was impossible to predict which way a case would go. Like all of Canada's human-rights tribunals, British Columbia's is charged not only with adjudicating complaints, but with seeking to advance anti-discrimination law. It has wide latitude in choosing cases. Devyn Cousineau, the member dealing with Yaniv's complaints, described waxing as 'critical gender-affirming care for transgender women'. The complaints raised 'a novel issue around the rights and obligations of transgender women and service providers', she said.

Poyer felt worried, but also incensed. Didn't women have human rights too, she asked herself? She knew she was not prejudiced; she simply didn't want strange males in her home, stripping off and demanding that she handle their genitals. Their identities were beside the point. Safety was also an issue. 'I should be able to decide who is in my house and around my little daughter,' she says. 'If you have someone who looks like a man and says, "actually I'm a woman," I'm not going to just invite that person into my house.'

A friend suggested she contact the Justice Centre for Constitutional Freedoms (JCCF), a libertarian legal-advocacy group. It had been looking for a case to challenge the inclusion of subjective identities within the province's human-rights code. It accepted Poyer pro bono. The case manager, Jay Cameron, planned two lines of defence. The first was that Poyer did not offer waxing services for male genitals, so turning Yaniv away was not discrimination. The second was that women's human rights included the right to set boundaries, in particular to offer services of an intimate nature to females only. Cameron lined up witnesses, including a specialist in 'Brozilians' (the waxing of male genitals) who would tell the tribunal how this involved specific training and products – and how her male clients often became aroused and sought sexual services, making it vital that she worked from a salon, not from home.

Cameron also sought to overturn the tribunal's unusual decision to ban publication of the complainant's name for privacy reasons. Cameron showed that Yaniv was 'out' about being trans – including in online posts asking for advice about how to behave in women's public toilets and changing rooms. Here is a sample: Yaniv asking if it was okay to show a ten-year-old who had asked for a tampon how to insert it; Yaniv asking whether, when you saw a naked ten-year-old with a tampon string hanging down, it would be okay to ask to borrow a tampon; Yaniv exulting about being on a ferry with children on a school trip.

Yaniv claimed the account had been hacked, and withdrew the complaint. Victory, then – though Poyer had lost money as well as sleep, since she had decided to stick to referrals, rather than risk further attempts by males to use human-rights law to force their way into her home. But Yaniv had continued to try to seek Brazilian waxes. A dozen similar complaints were pending. The JCCF reached out to the victims.

In late 2019, the tribunal heard evidence regarding seven of them. The hearing frequently descended into farce. Yaniv claimed under oath to possess both male and female genitalia; drew an analogy between denying males access to intimate services granted to females and racism; and made racist remarks about the respondents, most of whom were immigrants. Women who had read about the case on Twitter turned up to offer the respondents moral support. As they tweeted, the audience grew. Yaniv tweeted, too – enabling Cameron to get the ban on naming the litigant lifted. Eventually some of Canada's relentlessly politically correct media started to report the story, having ignored the clash of rights as long as they could.

In the end Yaniv lost and had to pay C\$2,000 each to the respondents. For Canadian women, the ruling was a mixed bag. Cameron had hoped the tribunal would accept that religious freedoms, protected in the national human-rights charter, meant his clients could turn away male clients for any services (several gave evidence that they could not be in close proximity to unrelated males). But Cousineau decided that those rights had not been tested, because Yaniv had been motivated by racism and the desire for compensation. At least she accepted that male genitals were not the same as female ones, however, and ruled that a person must 'actively and specifically consent' to handle a 'stranger's genitals for a prolonged period of time'. Overall, says Cameron, 'it was a very significant ruling. To paraphrase, whether you identify one way or another, when you take your pants off, that's reality.'

The saga of Yaniv v. Canadian women is not over. Another complaint is pending, against a beauty pageant that rejected Yaniv as a contestant. It cites its entry rules, which exclude pre-operative transwomen. Yaniv is seeking damages and a ruling that an organisation 'cannot refuse a service to someone just because that person has male genitalia'. Such a ruling could probably be used to try again to force unwilling women into providing intimate services to possessors of such genitalia.

Another waxing complaint is also possible. Since the defeat in Vancouver, Yaniv has made several such complaints, only to withdraw them. One involved leg-waxing, and a beautician who works from a salon and whose religious beliefs preclude close contact with unrelated males. In such a case, safety would not be at issue. Nor would the tribunal have to decide whether it is going to force an unwilling woman to handle a penis and testicles and pretend they are a vulva.

Sooner or later, one of Canada's human-rights tribunals is going to have to face up to a question that strikes at the heart of liberalism and multiculturalism: whose beliefs take precedence? Will it rule that a woman must accept the womanhood of a male person, if that male person asserts it? Or will it support a woman whose beliefs or conscience dictate that the male person's assertion of womanhood, no matter how sincere or longstanding, does not change his sex?

*

Transactivists generally dismiss fears that females will be harmed if males who identify as women access female single-sex spaces and services. Transwomen are merely going about their business, they say, and any concern is prejudiced, even prurient – in the cutesy catchphrase that has spread from the US to other countries: 'We just need to pee.' They reject real-life examples, even ones as egregious as Yaniv, as not really trans, or as indicating nothing about trans people in general. Some accept that trans people may be predatory – but say that women do not cease to be women because they are nasty. These are all logical fallacies.

Saying that Yaniv is not really trans is the fallacy known as 'No True Scotsman'. This is an attempt to defend a false claim by dismissing counterexamples. Someone claims that Scots people all put salt on their porridge; but you know your Scottish uncle Angus takes sugar. Instead of admitting that Angus disproves the statement, your interlocutor insists that no *true* Scotsman would take sugar. But gender-identity ideology admits of no grounds for dismissing an identity claim.

153

It is surely true that Yaniv is unrepresentative. But someone does not have to be representative to cause harm. Yaniv is a 'reductio ad absurdum', the ridiculous end-point of a series of logical deductions that requires you to discard your assumptions. If you start from the position that transwomen are literally women, then, inexorably, you must conclude that male people can force a woman like Shelah Poyer to treat their genitalia as if they were female. Most transwomen won't do this, but Yaniv shows that some will. If you cannot see how this infringes women's rights, you are reading the wrong book.

Finally, the claim that Yaniv's nastiness does not justify expulsion from womanhood 'begs the question'. This expression is often misused to mean 'raises the question', but actually means 'assumes that which is to be proven'. You beg the question when your argument adds no supporting evidence, but merely repeats the starting proposition in different words – for example, arguing that God exists by pointing out that it says so in the Bible. It begs the question to say Yaniv should be treated as a woman because even nasty, predatory transwomen are still women: whether or not they are women is what is at issue.

When used as a riposte like this, 'transwomen are women' is not an argument, but a statement of political positioning that functions like a profession of religious faith. It signals that the speaker is au fait with social-justice ideology, and is therefore both up to date and progressive. And by putting a full stop to any further discussion, it functions as what Robert Jay Lifton, author of the 1961 book *Thought Reform and the Psychology of Totalism: A Study of 'Brainwashing' in Communist China*, called a 'thought-terminating cliché'. In totalitarian regimes, he wrote, these 'brief, highly reductive, definitive-sounding phrases ... become the start and finish of any ideological analysis'.

Assessing the impact of gender-identity ideology on women takes more than repeating a mantra. And in fact it no longer has much to do with trans people at all. You may think the old-style gender clinicians acted wrongly when they gave their patients letters explaining that they were undergoing medical transition that they could show if challenged in single-sex facilities. But at least those letters were not handed out on demand. Gender-identity ideology removes all grounds for challenging any male in women's spaces. Signs on the campus of one British university spell it out: 'If you're in a public bathroom and you think a stranger's gender doesn't match the sign on the door, follow these steps: 1. Don't worry about it, they know better than you.'

In other words, single-sex spaces are now in name only. To decide whether that matters you need to understand why they even exist. The reasons fall under three headings: risk reduction, comfort and an opportunity for women to be somewhere that their needs are centred.

Risk reduction may seem obvious. But queer theorists deny it. In the past decade influential academics have claimed that single-sex spaces were unknown in the Western world before a ball in Paris in 1739, and did not become widespread until the Industrial Revolution, when the sexes mingled in factories. They position single-sex spaces as elitist, sexist and paternalistic; desired solely to signal gentility and maintain prudishness.

In a paper entitled 'How bathrooms really became separated by sex', W. Burlette Carter, a professor emerita of law at George Washington University, demolishes these alternative histories. She demonstrates that sex separation in communal toilets, baths and the like has been common since antiquity, and that a key purpose has always been to protect girls and women from sexual assault and harassment. These dangers were endemic, not a figment of genteel women's and patriarchal men's imaginations.

The United Nations, and charities such as ActionAid and Save the Children, campaign for single-sex toilets in schools in developing countries, recognising that without them girls are at risk of assault and more likely to drop out.

Excluding all males from places where women are at heightened risk of assault is a broad-brush measure. Justifying it does not require that all males are violent, merely that almost everyone who assaults women is male, and it is impossible for women to tell which males pose a risk. Nor is it paternalistic to acknowledge that women are more vulnerable to sexual and violent assault, and that men are overwhelmingly likely to be the perpetrators.

Crime statistics tell the story clearly. In the UK, victimisation surveys show that more than a fifth of females, and just four percent of males, have experienced sexual assault. The UK locks up a high share of its population for a developed country (though a far lower share than the US). But its sex ratio is pretty typical. Of a total of 88,000 prisoners, just 4,000 are female. Moreover, a smaller share of those women have committed violent offences, and almost none have committed sexual ones. Sex offenders make up nineteen percent of the 84,000 male prisoners, and just four percent of the 4,000 female ones. Putting it all together, women are around five times more likely than men to be the victim of a sexual crime, and men are one hundred times more likely to be the perpetrator of one.

The usual response is to say that statistics about men do not apply to transwomen, and that transwomen are at risk if they are forced to use men's spaces. But under gender self-identification, transwomen are not objectively distinct from other male people, so there is no way to calculate robust statistics about them. The little evidence that exists shows that at least some of the males who identify as women are very dangerous indeed. Of the 125 transgender prisoners known to be in English prisons in late 2017, sixty were transwomen who had committed sexual offences, a share far higher than in the general male prison population, let alone in the female one.

So either transwomen are more likely than other males to be sexual predators, or – more probable in my view – gender self-identification provides sexual predators with a marvellous loophole. Whichever is true, allowing males to self-identify into women's spaces makes women less safe. As for the danger to transwomen from using male spaces, raising this is a backhanded acknowledgement of the purpose of female spaces. Arguing that vulnerable males must be allowed to identify out of male spaces because males are so dangerous undermines any argument that males should be admitted to female spaces on demand.

Risk reduction is only one reason for separation by sex. In many situations, most people simply feel more comfortable without anyone of the opposite sex around. Precisely which ones varies from culture to culture. In Finland, mixed-sex groups of friends and relatives sauna naked; in Ireland it is usual to hide behind a towel even in a single-sex changing room. But in all places and times, some occasions that would otherwise be uncomfortable are not perceived to be so if everyone present is of the same sex.

Arguments about what makes people uncomfortable make a lot of people feel – well, uncomfortable. Discomfort may be a code word for bigotry. Men used to defend gentlemen's clubs by saying that admitting women would stop them relaxing – that women were thereby excluded from deal-making was, no doubt, an unintended and regrettable consequence. And presumably white supremacists feel uncomfortable in the presence of black people. But these examples show how silly it is to characterise women's desire to exclude men from their private spaces as bigotry. Women do not run the world, and their changing rooms are not where they plot to keep men down. Nor is their desire to undress away from the male gaze caused by anti-male prejudice.

A comparison is often made with white American women who wanted to keep their spaces white-only in the Jim Crow-era South. But those women were not uncomfortable with admitting black women in the way that women are uncomfortable with admitting men; rather, they were prejudiced against black people in the way white people of both sexes were in that place and time. In any analogy between oppression based on sex and race, women should be compared with black people, not white people. Males entering women's spaces are nothing like black people claiming their place in society; they are like white people denying black people spaces where they can shelter from the minority of white people who wish to do them harm.

The prefix 'cis' is used to obscure this. By positioning everyone else as privileged in comparison with trans people, it enables a linguistic inversion of the power differential between males and females: cis women supposedly oppress transwomen. The absurdity becomes obvious when you switch from gender identity to sex. Males who identify as women may be vulnerable in male spaces; in female spaces they are anything but.

Some high-profile men have taken up the cause of gender self-identification with vigour. Though they profess deep concern regarding transwomen's safety in men's spaces, they have none for female people who can no longer keep men out of theirs. Such a man is the most profound type of misogynist: the type that, perhaps unconsciously, sees women as supporting actresses in men's lives. When a woman's words or actions reveal that she regards herself as the lead character in her own story, he is outraged by her stepping out of what he regards as her proper place – the background. It is also worth noting that his empathy with transwomen is the clearest possible evidence that he does not truly see them as women. If he did, he would not care about their well-being at all.

One consequence of opening women's spaces to males is to recast two common male sex crimes as rights. Exhibitionism – non-consensually displaying one's genitals – is so common that many women will tell you that the first time they saw a penis was when a stranger flashed at them. Voyeurism – non-consensually viewing someone in a state of undress – is known to be a precursor to contact sex crimes. Entering a changing room constitutes consent to see and be seen by the other occupants while undressed. Women grant that consent on the basis that those occupants will be female; gender self-identification removes that basis while denying that it does so. It therefore turns facilities intended for women into places where males can commit exhibitionism and voyeurism with impunity.

The logical impossibility of giving female people privacy in single-sex spaces at the same time as allowing males to enter on demand may mean service providers give up and make all facilities formally mixed-sex. That would be to women's detriment. Those who continue to use such facilities will be less safe. In 2018 the *Sunday Times*, a British newspaper, published data showing that ninety percent of cases of sexual assaults and harassment in public swimming pools occurred in the minority of changing rooms that were designated unisex. And a measure that is often billed as inclusionary will mean that those whose religion forbids the mingling of the sexes, or who are simply bashful, will have to self-exclude.

*

That option is not available to some of the world's most vulnerable women: those behind bars. In Canada, the UK, the US and

TRANS

several other countries, a growing number of male convicts – including rapists and murderers – are held in the female estate. Increasingly, the only criterion for a transfer is stated gender identity.

Several countries started to hold post-operative transwomen in women's prisons in the 1980s. The thinking seems to have been that they were at risk of sexual assault in men's prisons; what female prisoners thought was not a consideration. Then came a step-by-step process, starting with the argument that prisoners had a right to the same health care as everyone else, including sex-reassignment surgery for those diagnosed with gender dysphoria. But being in a men's prison made it impossible to satisfy the 'real-life test', and so the next argument was that refusal to permit transfer pre-surgery constituted denial of health care. The final step was to argue that stated gender identity ought to be enough.

In Canada, for example, the number of male inmates in women's prisons increased after 2000, when Synthia Kavanagh (Richard Chaperon), a pre-operative transsexual who had stabbed and beaten her roommate to death in 1985, won a human-rights case forcing the prison service to provide hormones and sex-reassignment surgery to inmates diagnosed with gender dysphoria. Transfers really picked up after 2017, when the prime minister, Justin Trudeau, committed to housing all prisoners according to how they identified.

The national media have barely reported the consequences. When April Halley, a resident of Newfoundland, heard from fellow feminists on Twitter that males were held in Canadian women's prisons, she didn't believe it, since she thought it could never have happened without public debate. When she discovered it was true, she decided to find out how many. So she asked the Correctional Service of Canada (CSC), which said it had no records. A follow-up call elicited the response that such figures were impossible to provide, since gender was 'too fluid to track'. When she complained to the information commissioner, she was told that her request for the number of males held in the female estate was 'not very clear'. Only when another Twitter user sent her a presentation by an employee of the CSC, which referred to transwomen in women's prisons, was her complaint upheld.

More than a year after her first request, Halley finally received what the CSC insists is the only relevant data it holds. Eight Canadian convicts have been transferred from men's prisons to federal women's prisons, including five murderers and two other serious violent offenders. That figure includes neither males placed directly in women's prisons because their identity claims were accepted before incarceration, nor post-operative trans-women, whom the CSC classes as female. And there are no figures for provincial prisons, where shorter sentences are served.

Halley's research suggests that the first person transferred to a federal prison under the new rules was Fallon (Jean-Paul) Aubee, a contract killer sentenced to life for the murder in 1992 of a witness to a gangland killing. She also found that Tara (Patrick) Pearsall, a serial rapist who posed as a paramedic in order to sexually assault young women, had been transferred to a provincial women's prison two years earlier. Pearsall had told fellow inmates in a men's prison that the point of identifying as trans was to do easier time.

And Halley found press coverage about two post-operative transwomen held in women's jails. One, classified by the CSC as female, is Tara Desousa (Adam Laboucan), whose crimes included a rape of a three-month-old baby so brutal that the victim required reconstructive surgery, and who has admitted to killing a three-year-old when aged eleven. Desousa is now held in a prison with a mother-and-baby unit. Another is Madilyn (Matthew) Harks, who committed at least two hundred sexual crimes against at least sixty victims, including girls of four and five. After being released from a women's prison Harks, who has been diagnosed by psychiatrists as having an 'all-encompassing preoccupation in sexually abusing young girls', was admitted to a women's half-way house, again with a mother-and-child unit.

'The reality is that some of the most concerning offenders have been through sex-reassignment surgery,' says Halley. And indeed, the only research into long-term outcomes for post-operative transsexuals, in Sweden, concluded that transwomen 'retained a male pattern regarding criminality'. One of the women locked up with Harks has lodged a complaint with the CSC, alleging that Harks sexually harassed her. Any inmate who complained about Harks was branded transphobic, she says, so most stayed silent rather than risk loss of privileges and delayed parole. The woman, who is indigenous, suffered abuse in child-hood and says that Harks's behaviour gave her flashbacks. 'The CSC was really dismissive,' says Halley, who has seen the complaint and the CSC's initial response. 'They suggested she speak to a tribal elder about her trauma.'

Heather Mason, who served five terms in Canadian provin-cial and federal prisons for drugs and trafficking offences, is now campaigning to raise awareness of gender self-identification in prisons. She knows of many more dangerous males held in women's prisons, and points out that no one in authority is even counting them, let alone tracking the harm done to female pris-oners. She has personal experience of the issues, having been held alongside several transwomen, and remains in touch with many women still behind bars.

The transfer policy is hopelessly naive about the motives of males who identify as women, Mason says. Those who committed child-abuse or rape are often shunned and mistreated in men's prisons. Some see identifying as a woman as their way out. Transfers to women's prisons are therefore skewed towards precisely those males who are most dangerous to women and children – the latter being particularly concerning because several women's prisons in Canada have low-security, homelike sections where mothers can care for young children.

Holding these dangerous criminals is bound to change the way women's prisons are run to the detriment of women. Security will have to be tighter and prisoners' movements more restricted. Some guards will have to be armed, which is not standard in the women's estate in Canada. Rehabilitation programmes will be affected, too. Male and female offending patterns differ, and women's programmes focus on self-esteem and setting boundaries. They are inappropriate for violent, predatory males. 'These murderers, rapists and child-abusers are being taught to assert themselves,' says Mason, rolling her eyes.

The UK has tried, largely unsuccessfully, to be more cautious. In 2011 the government said that transwomen in possession of a gender-recognition certificate (GRC), which changes their legal sex to female, should be accommodated in women's prisons if possible, but that others should remain in the jail consonant with their sex.

That line proved hard to hold. In 2015 Tara Hudson (Raymond David) was sentenced to twelve weeks for knocking a barman's teeth out in a brawl. Hudson, a self-described 'shemale' escort whose personal ads boasted of 'BIG bouncy 34E boobs' and a '7-inch surprise', did not have a GRC and was sent to a men's prison. A social-media campaign to get her transferred, making much of her Barbie-like appearance and omitting the anatomical details – and the eight previous convictions for violent offences – garnered more than 150,000 signatures and caught the eye of several members of parliament. A week later, Hudson was transferred.

Around the same time, two transwomen held in men's prisons committed suicide. The mother of one said she had not objected to being held in a men's prison; the other, however, had complained of harassment by officers and prisoners. The prison service and government were caught on the back foot. New guidelines were rushed out, saying that all trans people should be held in prisons that matched their self-declared identity, unless there were overriding safety concerns.

It did not take long before this approach caused problems, too. In 2018 Karen White (Stephen Wood), a convicted child-abuser, was remanded in custody awaiting trial for assault. White applied for, and was granted, a transfer to a women's prison – and promptly sexually assaulted several other inmates. Worse has no doubt happened in Canadian prisons. But the UK, unlike Canada, has newspapers willing to publish stories that contradict the gender-identity narrative. While White was being held on remand, a woman who had never reported being raped by Stephen Wood came forward, and investigators discovered another alleged rape victim. White is now serving a life sentence (in a men's prison) for those rapes and the assaults on female prisoners.

The press coverage brought to wider attention the physical realities of a government policy that few members of the public would have thought about in detail. It included photos of White (unshaven, sans wig and make-up) and quotes from the trial ('her penis was erect and sticking out of the top of her trousers'). It brought home that being trans no longer means what most people think: going through such extreme medical and surgical procedures that one is virtually indistinguishable from a member of the opposite sex.

Once politicians order a prison service to accommodate males as if they were females, they put it in an impossible position. It may be told to assess risk – but rape and domestic violence are so wildly under-reported that any risk assessment is necessarily incomplete. The UK prison service checked Stephen Wood's criminal record, and naturally did not find the rapes that had never been reported.

One oft-cited justification for those transfers is that transwomen are unsafe in men's prisons. But are they? According to the UK prisons inspectorate, eleven sexual assaults on transwomen in male prisons were reported in 2019. It estimates that one male prisoner in fifty identifies as a woman. (Most are held in the male estate, where trans status means privileges such as single-occupancy cells and privacy in showers.) That would suggest that around 0.6 percent of transwomen in prison report an assault each year. The Howard League, a campaigning British charity, estimates that one percent of all male prisoners in the UK have been raped, and five percent have been coerced into sex – but those are cumulative, not annual, figures, and also include very many unreported incidents. Estimates in the US, where prison violence is endemic, are much higher.

Overall, it is hard to say how vulnerable transwomen are in men's prisons. Those whose presentation is notably feminine are probably at elevated risk of sexual assault – but they are hardly the only males for whom that is true. Men who are young, gay or known to have abused children are also frequently targeted, and no one suggests moving them to women's prisons, although it would undoubtedly make them safer.

The Karen White case came as no surprise to Rhona Hotchkiss, a prison governor from Scotland who retired a few months after White was sentenced, in March 2019. No longer bound by public-service confidentiality, she decided to speak out about the disaster unfolding under the Scottish Prison Service (SPS), which was earlier and more enthusiastic than its English counterpart regarding transfers of transwomen to women's jails.

In 2010, Hotchkiss became deputy governor of a men's prison. Soon after, a transwoman arrived. 'In my naivety, I was appalled,' she says. 'At the time I described myself as a trans ally. As a gay person, I saw them as another oppressed minority.' She arranged for transfer to a women's prison, and didn't give the matter further thought. Then she became governor of Cornton Vale, Scotland's only dedicated prison for women (some are held on separate wings of other institutions). During her time there, Cornton Vale received several male prisoners. The first one opened her eyes.

While in the male estate, this prisoner had identified as a woman and been granted a transfer; after some time in Cornton Vale he re-identified as a man. Frustrated at the delay while the SPS debated what to do, he threatened to rape other prisoners and staff. Eventually a return transfer to the male estate was arranged – only for the prisoner to identify as a woman again. The experience shook Hotchkiss. 'I thought: what woman threatens to rape other people? I also thought: why should we take people's word for this? We don't for anything else.' After release, the prisoner committed suicide. 'It was a tragedy, a deeply disturbed person,' says Hotchkiss. 'And instead of having their genuine psychological issues dealt with, they were left to say that it's because I can't be a woman . . . a man . . . a woman . . .'

Then Andrew Burns (Tiffany Scott) sought transfer to Cornton Vale. He is one of only one hundred or so prisoners in Scotland classified as so dangerous that his sentence is indefinite. He has held dirty protests, assaulted prison officers, slashed a cellmate's face with a razor and bitten open his own veins to spray staff with blood. Three officers guard him when he is outside his cell, and when he was brought from prison to court for sentencing, it was locked down and prison staff wore full protective gear. In the end the transfer was denied because Scott was deemed too dangerous to be moved anywhere – but under gender self-identification, which the Scottish government has promised to introduce with no exceptions, it would have gone ahead.

In 2017 Hotchkiss moved to Greenock, which holds men and women on separate wings. On the women's wing there were three transwomen. The other prisoners would try to avoid the showers if any of the transwomen were in them, says Hotchkiss, though they were reluctant to complain for fear of being set down as troublemakers. And they were scared to talk to, or even about, the transwomen, for fear of tripping up and referring to them as men or using male pronouns (none looks in the slightest like a woman).

What prompted her to speak out, she says, was the impact on female inmates. One woman who had beaten addiction and turned her life around was found with drugs in her cell. 'She said she had got into an argument with one of the trans prisoners, who had lost control and punched the wall,' says Hotchkiss. ' "All I saw was a violent man intimidating me," she said. "I went straight off and found someone who could supply me with drugs." '

Of all the transwomen prisoners she met, Hotchkiss reckons only one was sincere, though deeply disturbed. The others, in her opinion, were motivated by desire to do easier time, gain access to victims or screw up the system. 'If people have genuine dysphoria, if they have transitioned, then create another unit for them,' she says. 'Women are not human shields. You don't make transwomen safer by making women less safe – and there's a growing body of evidence that women are not safe when you put males inside with them. Most women in prison have been victims of male violence, some from childhood. Why are we re-traumatising them?'

The far greater number of male prisoners, and their far greater propensity for violent and sexual crimes, mean that not very many males will need to seek transfer before women's prisons are overwhelmed. If the UK prisons inspectorate is right, and two percent of male prisoners identify as women, that is a figure greater than half the total number of female prisoners. And if transwomen's offending pattern is male-typical, and the share imprisoned for sex crimes is five times as high as for women, you arrive at a startling conclusion. Of all the sex offenders behind bars (in men's or women's prisons) who identify as women, well over two-thirds are male.

*

Rarely acknowledged in discussions about single-sex spaces is that, until recently, most were for men. The best schools and all universities; well-paid jobs; sporting competitions; political institutions: all were male-only. Some of women's anger at the recent pretence that it is impossible to distinguish between males and females stems from knowing that, when it was women who were excluded, there was no uncertainty. When you are of the sex barred from identifying into the other's privileges, you may not feel accommodating when self-identification in the other direction is cast as a human right.

Especially when you suspect that it is motivated by the desire for validation that Ray Blanchard and others spy in much trans-activism. A notable example concerns Michfest, a music festival for 'women-born-women' that ran in Michigan from 1976 to 2015. In 1991 a transwoman, Nancy Burkholder, was challenged by festival-goers, and left after confirming she was male. In the next few years, other transwomen were also told to leave. In *The Michigan Womyn's Music Festival: An Amazon Matrix of Meaning*, Laurie Kendall of the University of Maryland documents repeated occasions on which pre-operative transwomen attended the festival in defiance of the ban and provoked confrontation, for example by using the communal open-air showers – to put it bluntly, exposing their penises non-consensually in a lesbian-centred space. Kendall describes these as power plays 'perpetrated for their shock value and violation of womyn's spaces and women-born-women bodies'.

From 1994 an activist group, Camp Trans, protested near Michfest every year. It pressed performers to boycott the festival, and was supported by civil-rights groups such as the ACLU and the Gay & Lesbian Alliance Against Defamation (now simply GLAAD). 'We are pretty *over* spending a lot of our time and energy having an event of seven thousand womyn be focused on three or four guys,' Lisa Vogel, one of Michfest's founders, told a reporter. 'Men feel like they get to be whatever they want, even if it's a lesbian.' But by 2015 the pressure had become too much and Michfest closed.

In 2017 Ben, a young Canadian lesbian, went to Michigan Framily Reunion, an event on private land with a similar philosophy and ethos to Michfest. In her early teens Ben identified as a transman, though she never took hormones or had surgery. Her re-identification as a woman, at age twenty, came two years after her realisation that she was sexually attracted to women and her discovery of radical feminism. The Framily Reunion played a big part. 'All these women with cargo shorts and hairy legs and Birkenstocks and no bras!' she exclaims (this is a good description of Ben, these days). 'It was the first time I had met butch lesbians *en masse*. I looked at them and thought: I'm literally just a dyke like they are.'

Ben marvelled at carefree little girls playing tag with no shirts on. 'I remember thinking if I had come here when I was their age, I might not have ended up the way I did. I would have been more fortified in my femaleness,' she says. At first her hatred of her body meant she skipped washing – the showers were communal, as at Michfest – but on the final day she plucked up courage, walked around without her shirt, and showered. 'It was an act of ownership over my body,' she says. 'I felt a safety I had never felt before. A space just for us, where we're the ones that matter.'

Female-only spaces can also be transformative for survivors of sexual or intimate-partner violence. This insight has shaped rape-crisis and domestic-violence services since they were first set up – not just in residential settings, but in support groups, where participants speak frankly about their lives. But under pressure from transactivists, most are switching to gender self-ID.

Judith Green is one of the founders of Woman's Place UK (WPUK), a group of women with a background in labour activism who in 2017 converted their socialist reading group to an emergency campaign against the British government's proposal to allow legal sex to be changed by filling in a form. (The name was inspired by a 1970s slogan, 'a woman's place is in her union'.) She was motivated by hearing about a women's conference five years earlier, which received harassment because it planned a female-only workshop for victims of sexual abuse. 'I felt absolutely enraged that women's boundaries were being so encroached on,' says Green.

She then discovered, to her horror, that the support network that had helped her heal from her own childhood sexual abuse had stopped offering female-only groups. She got in touch and asked where they would refer a woman who wanted female-only services. 'They said they weren't aware of any such services.

They might as well have said: "if you're a bigoted rape survivor, please fuck off." '

People sometimes seem to think Green wants transwomen who are victims of sexual violence to be denied support ('of course I don't – I just think that female victims who want female-only groups should be able to have them'). Or they argue that some transwomen pass so well that they can be included in female spaces because no one will ever know they were born male. But admitting only those who pass perfectly would put staff in an invidious position, Green points out. And what it means to pass in a support group for female survivors of male sexual violence is completely different from what it means to pass on the street. In a support group, someone born male would have to either be open about that or invent a false life history, thus betraying the other participants' trust.

Aurora New Dawn, a British charity that supports victims of male violence, whatever their sex and however they identify, is one of a dwindling number that advocate publicly for female-only groups and services for those who want them. Its chief executive, Shonagh Dillon, has written a doctoral thesis on the silencing of feminist critiques of gender self-identification. She reveals evidence of widespread discomfort about trans inclusion within the women's sector and explains why that discomfort is so rarely expressed.

In 2018 Stonewall, a large British charity that was founded to campaign for gay people but now dedicates itself to transactivism, published research claiming that those working in settings such as women's shelters supported gender self-identification, and that all difficulties could be resolved with risk assessment plus 'sensitivity and common sense'. Dillon was suspicious. After she had retweeted WPUK's concerns about gender self-ID, a transactivist had barraged Aurora New Dawn's funders, the national charities regulator and the End Violence Against Women coalition with demands that they reconsider their support for the charity. If simply suggesting that women should be permitted to discuss gender self-ID was enough to threaten a woman's employment and her employer's funding, could the apparent lack of concern be taken at face value?

For her thesis, Dillon interviewed thirty-one participants from both sides of the debate, pretty evenly split between avowed supporters and opponents of self-ID. But as Dillon asked them to consider specific scenarios, six of the pro-self-ID group ended up saying that they supported single-sex spaces. Only one continued to insist on self-ID, even to the point of insisting that victims of male violence who experienced flash-backs when in enclosed spaces with people they perceived as male needed 'educating' out of their trauma and bigotry. Overall, twenty-seven of Dillon's thirty-one interviewees said it was important to provide female-only space for victims of male violence. All but one of those who had worked directly with victims said they felt unable to speak about the issue for fear of losing funding.

To see how much pressure female-only services can come under, consider Vancouver Rape Relief and Women's Shelter (VRRWS), a feminist collective that works towards ending male violence against women. In 1995 Kimberly Nixon, a post-operative transwoman, was turned away from a training session for volunteer peer counsellors. Nixon took a discrimination complaint to British Columbia's human-rights tribunal. Only twelve years later, when the Canadian Supreme Court declined to hear an appeal by Nixon against a provincial court's ruling in VRRWS's favour, was the case finally ended.

It was a decisive victory for VRRWS, and its peer counsellors and shelter remain female-only. But it marked the organisation as the sworn enemy of Vancouver's transactivists. In 2019 they convinced the city council to stop funding the collective's outreach work. It is routinely insulted and slandered, both online and in mainstream media. One morning in 2019 members arrived at the city-centre property where it runs events to find 'Kill TERFs, Trans Power' and 'Fuck TERFs' scrawled on the windows. The same year, a dead rat was nailed to the door.

The right to organise as women-only is essential to the collective's work, says Karla Gjini, one of its members. The peer-counselling and support groups use consciousness-raising techniques through which women help each other understand the pervasiveness of sexism and its impact on their lives. 'What we are doing here is based not just on our biology, but on how we are treated in the world because we are born female,' she says. She regards attacks by transactivists as just another form of misogyny. 'There's always backlash when women set boundaries and stand their ground.'

9

FOLDING LIKE DECKCHAIRS

How gender self-identification threatens to destroy women's sports

In 2019, the BBC published a heart-warming piece on its website about Kelly Morgan, a rugby player who – as the title of the piece had it – 'play[s] with a smile on my face'. Anyone who read on would have learnt some more striking facts. Morgan, who plays for Port Harlequin Ladies Club in Wales, had broken the coach's ankle during a game of touch rugby – though he seemed remarkably sanguine about it, quipping that Morgan would be a 'good, good player for the next few years, as long as we can stop her injuring players in training'. The risks Morgan posed to other players were a matter of humour to the club's captain, too. She laughingly recalled Morgan folding a player on an opposing team 'like a deckchair'.

The reason Morgan – born Nicholas Gareth Morgan, and a fixture on East Wales boys' teams as a teenager until being injured – could play for a women's team was that World Rugby, like most sporting authorities, had followed the lead of the International Olympic Committee (IOC) in allowing males to compete as women once they had suppressed their testosterone for a year. Morgan, who had started on oestrogen eighteen months before the BBC piece, was therefore entitled to compete as a woman.

The BBC article was read with alarm by rugby's medical and scientific experts – and referees, who bear some legal responsibility for keeping the game safe. As they shared their concerns, top administrators started to worry that they had sleepwalked behind the IOC into an indefensible position. As Heyneke Meyer, a former coach of the South African team, once said: 'Ballroom dancing is a contact sport; rugby is a collision sport.' Those collisions can lead to brain injuries and, occasionally, broken necks – and courts have held referees and administrators liable. If the consequences of trans inclusion went beyond female players being folded like deckchairs and on to neck-snapping, pleading that everyone else was doing it too would hardly cut it in court.

The issues posed by allowing males to compete as females had already started to become visible. One example is Laurel Hubbard, a forty-two-year-old New Zealander who competed in men's weightlifting when younger with modest success. In 2019 Hubbard won gold in the women's division at the Pacific Games, defeating two teenage Samoans. 'This *fa'afafine*, or male, should never have been allowed by the Pacific Games Council President to lift with the women,' said the Samoan prime minister (who can hardly be accused of prejudice against gender nonconforming people: he is patron of the Samoan Fa'afafine Association). 'It's not easy for the female athletes to train all year long to compete, and yet we allow these stupid things to happen. The reality is that gold medal belongs to Samoa.'

To understand how sports got here, you must first understand how competitions came to be sex-segregated. For a long time they were all male-only. A few women engaged in genteel sporting pastimes: Mary Queen of Scots played golf, and in nineteenth-century England horse-riding and croquet were popular with ladies. At the second modern Olympic Games, in 1900, women competed for the first time – 22 athletes out of 997, in just croquet, golf, sailing and tennis.

But competitions women could enter remained few and far between. In 1967, when Kathrine Switzer ran in the Boston Marathon, she was breaking the rules. Two miles from the starting line an official spotted her and tried to drag her off the course. Though she pulled away and finished, she was disqualified. It was another four years before the event admitted women. (Switzer went on to great things, winning the women's gold medal at the New York Marathon in 1974.)

By the 1972 Munich Olympics, the number of female athletes had passed 1,000, and there were women's versions of most events. That they needed to compete separately was obvious to everyone: men's and women's bodies differ in ways that are almost all in male athletes' favour. Since – incredibly – this is now contested, I will spend some time explaining the science.

As a female mammal passes into adulthood, her body readies itself for pregnancy, birth and lactation. For female humans, all this is a big deal. Arduous pregnancies and babies' long helpless period mean that women's bodies evolved to store fat. At least ten percent of the bodyweight of an elite female athlete is fat; for an elite male, that share can fall as low as five percent. The extra fat is worse than useless for women's sporting performance, since it has to be lugged around.

Another sporting handicap comes from what evolutionary theorists call the 'obstetrical dilemma'. As humans evolved big brains and an upright gait, these shifts put opposing pressures on the size and shape of the pelvic girdle. Too wide, and women would barely be able to waddle; too narrow, and childbirth would be impossible. Both big brains and standing upright have evolutionary advantages, enabling us to communicate and plan, and carry tools and weapons. The female pelvis is where much of the price is paid.

The evolutionary compromise is that human babies are born notably immature compared with other primates. But even expelling babies so early is agonisingly painful for mothers, and risky all round. That women's pelvic girdles are not wider suggests that any further adaptations would come at too high a cost. As it is, women's hips are less stable than men's, and their gait is less efficient. Power is transmitted less effectively through the hip, knee and ankle. Wider hips also compromise carrying and throwing. Women's greater flexibility means less energy can be stored in tendons.

Adult men, too, are shaped by evolutionary pressures, in particular from humanity's long prehistory of hunting and fighting (this is visible in the evolutionary record, though you will not hear about it in a gender-studies course). They are not only taller and larger than women, but have wider shoulders and narrower hips, bigger muscles that can contract more quickly and powerfully, bigger hearts and lungs, higher blood-oxygenation capacity and stronger bones.

Taken together, these differences are very large. The average adult man has 41 percent more non-fat body mass (blood, bones, muscles and so on) than the average woman, 50 percent more muscle mass in his legs and 75 percent more in his arms. His legs are 65 percent stronger, and his upper body is 90 percent stronger. The overwhelming upper-body advantage is nowhere near accounted for by differences in size – as can be seen in weightlifting competitions, where competitors are banded by weight, and the male world champion in each category lifts around 30 percent more than the female one.

None of these strength, shape or size differences is so great that there is no overlap (though punching power comes close: in a recent test of untrained men and women, the men's average force was 162 percent greater than the women's, and the weakest man in that study could punch harder than the strongest woman). This sometimes leads people to argue that athletes should be divided by weight or height, or in some other formally sex-neutral way. The point of sporting competitions is to reveal and reward exceptional performance, after all, which may come from many sources other than physiology: training, dedication, mental attitude or even genetic mutations. Some women are stronger and faster than most men; many people have physiques that mean they are not contenders. None of this is fair.

The trouble is that the sporting advantage bestowed on the male half of humanity swamps all others. Consider Michael Phelps, who possesses practically every gift with which a swimmer can be endowed. He has physiological, metabolic, biomechanical and neuromuscular attributes that set him apart, including an extraordinary wingspan, double-jointed ankles and enormous feet. These have enabled him to win more than twice as many Olympic golds as any other athlete.

And yet a female Michael Phelps – a woman who was equally endowed with all the attributes of an elite swimmer except for a Y chromosome – would lose to relatively unexceptional men. Without female-only competitions, she could not demonstrate that she was a phenomenon. In all but a few sports where athleticism counts for little (such as dressage) or flexibility and artistry are central (gymnastics; ice-skating), in mixed-sex competitions it would not matter how exceptional a female was. Prodigies of nature such as Serena Williams, Shelly-Ann Fraser-Pryce and Katie Ledecky would be bumped, not only from the podium, but from the competition.

The magnitude of the male advantage is obvious in sport statistics. The website boysvswomen.com compares the 2016 women's Olympic finalists with the same year's finalists in American boys' high-school competitions. In running, where the male advantage is relatively small, at every distance up to 800 metres the woman who won Olympic gold ran slower than the boys' qualifying time. The slowest boy to make the finals in the 400-metre hurdles finished faster than every female Olympian, despite having to clear higher hurdles. In the high jump and pole vault, boys would have taken all the medals, and the same in shot put, even though the boys throw a heavier weight. In the long jump no woman would have qualified for the boys' competition. In swimming, for almost every stroke and distance, no female Olympian would have made it into the boys' finals.

When you compare women with adult men, and go global, the picture is starker. Every year, in pretty much every athletic event, men break the women's world record thousands of times. The fastest time ever run by Allyson Felix, the women's 400-metre Olympic champion, is beaten more than 15,000 times each year by men and boys. In sports where several advantages are compounded, the differences widen into a gulf. In tennis, the fastest recorded serve by a man is 163 miles per hour; by a woman, 137. The most aces hit in a men's tennis match is 113; in a women's match, it's 31. And these statistics barely begin to capture the differences in game-play.

In 1998, Serena and Venus Williams threw down a challenge: that either of them could beat any male tennis player ranked 200th or below. Karsten Braasch, then ranked 203rd, took them up on it. He prepared with 'a leisurely round of golf in the morning followed by a couple of shandies', he wrote afterwards. He beat Serena in a single set 6–1, and then Venus 6–2. In 2020, when Andy Murray suggested an exhibition match against her, Serena refused, saying: 'I would lose 6–0, 6–0 in five to six minutes, maybe ten minutes . . . the men are a lot faster and they serve harder; they hit harder. It's just a different game.'

I am not dwelling on all this to suggest that women are inferior to men. Evolved differences do not make one sex better than the other, just different. Females cannot make themselves as fast and strong as males by trying harder – any more than males can become pregnant by effort of will. Growing another person inside you, and giving birth, are the most extraordinary physical feats humans are capable of. But it is undeniable that those humans designed by evolution to perform these feats pay a price in athletic performance.

Male and female categories are not the only ones intended to ensure that excellence within one category is not swamped by another's overwhelming advantage. And yet it is only with sex that there is any suggestion of letting athletes self-identify. Some adults are weaker than some teenagers, and yet no one argues that adults should be allowed to compete as under-eighteens. Some heavy people are slow and flabby, but no one argues that heavyweights should be allowed to box against flyweights. The point of age- or weight-restricted competition is to reward the best young or light contestants, not to give ordinary adults or heavyweights an easy ride.

But it is not possible to get the date on your birth certificate, or the numbers on your pre-competition weigh-in, changed. For many decades now, bureaucrats have been willing to provide a few people with documents saying they are members of the opposite sex. No one was thinking about the impact on women's sports – and yet there was an impact, all the same.

Take Richard Raskind, the son of emigrant Russian doctors raised in affluence in Manhattan. After excelling in sports at his private school he went to Yale, where he captained the tennis team. He became a successful surgeon, married a model, gained a pilot's licence in his spare time and, by his mid-thirties, was one of the best players on America's pro tennis circuit. In a profile in 2019 in *Sports Illustrated*, Billie Jean King, one of Raskind's oldest friends, said: 'You talk about it, Dick Raskind had it.'

You probably haven't heard of Raskind – because in 1975, aged forty-one, he underwent sex-reassignment surgery and took the name Renée, French for 'reborn', paired with Richards, a link with the past. Richards's doctor advised her to give up competitive tennis if she did not want her powerful forehand to blow her cover. But Raskind had not been accustomed to the word 'no'. Richards was not going to accept it either.

She began to enter women's competitions. As her doctor had predicted, it was obvious that she was not female. The US Tennis Association let her know that if she tried to compete as a woman at the highest level, she would be required to undergo sex-testing. She kept playing. At a competition in South Orange, New Jersey, twenty-five women withdrew in protest. As far as Richards was concerned, that was too bad. By then she was forty-two and past her prime, she told *Sports Illustrated*. (The journalist didn't think to ask why she hadn't played against other males of a similar age.)

Then Richards sued the US Tennis Association to be allowed to enter the US Open as a woman without undergoing a sex test she knew she would fail. She did so 'for selfish reasons', she told another reporter in 2015. 'I did it because it was my right to do it . . . I thought I was entitled.' In 1977 the case reached the New York Supreme Court. Richards provided two pieces of evidence: supportive letters from Billie Jean King and her surgeon. For the judge, these were enough. He pooh-poohed the US Tennis

Association's claim that Richards would be the first of many – against the backdrop of the Cold War, it feared an army of surgically altered Soviet males. He ruled that when a 'successful physician, a husband and father, finds it necessary for his own mental sanity to undergo a sex reassignment, the unfounded fears and misconceptions of defendants must give way to the overwhelming medical evidence that this person is now female.'

Two weeks later, the tournament started. Richards was knocked out in the first round by Virginia Wade, who had won Wimbledon a few weeks earlier. Richards did, however, make it to the doubles final, where she and her partner lost to Martina Navratilova and Betty Stöve. The judge's ruling had been unfair – as Richards admitted to *Slate* in 2012, long after it mattered. 'Maybe in the last analysis, maybe not even I should have been allowed to play on the women's tour . . . if I'd had surgery at the age of 22, and then at 24 went on the tour, no genetic woman in the world would have been able to come close to me. And so I've reconsidered my opinion.' Still, the fear that women would become runners-up in their own competitions seemed unfounded. And that, for many years, is how things remained.

*

From the earliest days of women's competitions, sports administrators had been more concerned by a different risk: infiltration by men disguised as women. That was rare, if it happened at all. But a review paper in the *British Journal of Sports Medicine* in 1991 describes how several early women athletes turned out, when their careers were over, to have been male – a few even went on to father children. The article concluded there had usually been some ambiguity of sex at birth, meaning that someone registered as a girl experienced partial or complete male puberty.

One of the earliest cases was Dutch track athlete Foekje Dillema, who died in 2007. In 1950 her national record for the women's 200 metres was erased, and she was expelled for life by the Royal Dutch Athletics Federation after it concluded that she was not a woman. 'Sex tests' at the time consisted of a physical examination, and no records of Dillema's remain. But another paper in the same journal in 2012 solves the mystery. Researchers did DNA testing on items Dillema had owned, and found that she had a very rare condition: 46,XX/46,XY mosaicism, in which someone is born with cells of both sexes. Such a person may have testes, ovaries, or 'ovotestes', which combine both sorts of tissue. The researchers concluded that Dillema probably had ovotestes with a preponderance of ovarian material. During puberty, the testicular material would have caused some virilisation.

Dillema was one of the first women to fall foul of efforts to keep men out of women's sports. Almost two decades later Ewa Kłobukowska, a Polish sprinter, became another. She was stripped of her medals from the 1964 Olympics and struck from the record books. She too had a type of mosaicism, with some of her cells carrying an extra Y chromosome as well as two Xs. It is impossible to say to what extent her sporting ability was due to that Y chromosome. But there can be no doubt that her initial classification as female was correct. She later became a mother.

The press coverage of Kłobukowksa's case was so prurient that thereafter the results of sex tests were kept private. But the procedures remained grossly humiliating. Before the Track and Field Championships in 1966, female athletes had to walk naked in front of a panel of female doctors. At the Commonwealth Games that year, they underwent no-notice gynaecological examinations. Years later Mary Peters, a British pentathlete, wrote that it was 'the most crude and degrading experience I have ever known in my life. I was ordered to lie on the couch and pull my knees up. The doctors then proceeded to undertake an examination which, in modern parlance, amounted to a grope.'

Female athletes' anger and resistance meant that before the 1968 Olympics in Mexico City, these distasteful physicals were replaced by a test in which a mouth swab is examined for the presence of Barr bodies (deactivated X chromosomes present in the nuclei of XX cells). The test remained in use for many years. However, despite being more objective and less humiliating than a physical inspection, it also led to unfair exclusions. People with complete androgen-insensitivity syndrome (CAIS) are conceived with the XY chromosomes that would normally build a male body, but are immune to male hormones for genetic reasons. Such women fail the Barr body test, though their bodies develop along female lines (they have internal testes, not ovaries, however, and lack a womb and are infertile).

One woman who was unfairly excluded by the Barr body test was Spanish hurdler María José Martínez-Patiño. In 1985, before she was due to race in the World University Games in Kobe, Japan, she heard there had been a problem with her sex test. She was dropped and told to consult a specialist when she returned home. 'I sat in the stands that day watching my team mates, wondering how my body differed from theirs,' she wrote in *The Lancet* medical journal years later. Two months later, as she prepared for the Spanish hurdling championships, a letter arrived informing her that she had XY chromosomes and that she should feign an injury and withdraw 'quietly, graciously, and permanently'. When she refused, her story was leaked, and she was stripped of her sports scholarship and erased from Spain's athletic records.

Convinced she had been the victim of an injustice, Martínez-Patiño found doctors to support her. In 1988 the International Association of Athletic Federations (IAAF; now World Athletics) accepted that it had made a mistake. But after three years away from competition, she had lost form. She never fully regained it, and missed out on qualifying for the 1992 Olympics in Barcelona. That was the end of her career.

In the run-up to that competition, the IOC changed to yet another method of sex determination: the polymerase chain reaction (PCR) test. In this, the mouth swab is checked for a gene normally found on the Y chromosome that drives the growth of testes in the womb. In other words, PCR tests for genetic maleness rather than femaleness. But it was not used for long. The history of misfires had undermined confidence in sex-testing. In 1991 the IAAF stopped. The IOC soldiered on, and in the run-up to the 1996 games picked up eight women with XY chromosomes, all of whom it cleared to compete. In 1999 it too stopped routine testing. The new plan was to do a genetic work-up if suspicions were aroused by a virilised appearance or anomalous drug-test result.

Meanwhile, the question of what to do with males who transitioned to live as women was hotting up again. In the two decades since Renée Richards had sued the US Tennis Association, the issue had remained quiescent – when the Berlin Wall came down and the East German sports-doping programme was revealed, it became clear that an unscrupulous government could bulk female people up with male hormones, rather than surgically converting males into women *en masse*. But now governments were granting people who had undergone sex-reassignment surgery birth certificates with the sex changed. For sports officials, being unable to rely on government documents posed a challenge.

At a meeting in Stockholm in 2003, the IOC and IAAF decided that post-operative transwomen could compete as women, starting from two years after surgery. But the waiting period was never enforced – how could it be? Without testicles producing testosterone, transwomen did not show up as male in blood tests, and the authorities were no longer routinely doing sex tests. The IOC does not know if any transwomen ever competed under the Stockholm rules.

With the benefit of hindsight, the most significant aspect of the new rules was that they gave a new answer to the question behind decades of sex-testing: where does male sporting advantage reside? The authorities had looked for a masculine appearance and male body parts, then for XX chromosomes and finally for the gene that drives male development. Each time, athletes with rare disorders of sex development (DSDs) had shown that exceptions needed to be made. But the new transgender policy offered an appealingly simple framing: male sporting advantage consisted of testicles and a body capable of using testosterone.

The authorities had arrived at a definition of Woman similar to that of second-century Greeks: a woman is a human who lacks (functioning) male body parts. And that, in turn, shaped their response to the next row over DSDs.

In 2009 South African teenager Caster Semenya came from nowhere to win gold at 800 metres in the African Junior Championships, and then in the IAAF World Championships. Questions were asked about her sex straight away. Her deep voice, broad shoulders, narrow hips, defined muscles and explosive power all suggested to anyone knowledgeable about sports physiology that here was an athlete who had developed under the influence of male hormones.

The issue soon became poisonously political. Journalists in South Africa were warned by government ministers not to cast doubt on Semenya's right to compete in female events. Anyone who mentioned the link between a masculine physique and male hormones was accused of racism – of implying that Semenya's blackness made her unfeminine. One sports writer says a senior politician warned him to stop discussing the impact of testosterone on sporting performance, and said that if Semenya's medals were taken away, it would be 'World War Three'.

Semenya's story is so intimately entwined with the emerging understanding of male sporting advantage that I am going to cut to the chase and discuss her DSD, which can be inferred from a later decision in the Court of Arbitration for Sport (CAS). It is a genetic condition called 5α-reductase deficiency (5-ARD), named for an enzyme that converts testosterone into dihydro-testosterone (DHT), which in turns triggers the develop-ment of a male foetus's genitalia. Without the genetic instruc-tions to create that enzyme, a baby with male chromosomes will be born with ambiguous genitalia, somewhere between female-looking with an enlarged clitoris, and male-looking with a micropenis. The testes will be either internal or in the labial folds.

DHT plays no known role in puberty, and so people with 5-ARD, who have male levels of testosterone and the ability to use it, grow up along male lines. They do not grow breasts. Their voices break, their muscles strengthen, their shoulders broaden and their hips stay narrow. Sometimes, the genitalia become more clearly male. In a few regions of South America where a mutation that causes 5-ARD has become concentrated in the gene pool, the condition is called variations on *huevos a los doces*, or 'eggs [testicles] at twelve'. In these places, children with the condition who were thought to be female at birth are generally reclassified as male during puberty.

Elsewhere, whether a baby with 5-ARD is registered male or female depends on the degree of genital ambiguity and stand-ards of medical care. Until recently, babies in Europe or North America who were diagnosed young with 5-ARD, and whose genitalia were ambiguous or broadly female in appearance, often had their testes removed and were registered female – shades of John Money's theory that if you castrated a baby boy, what you got was a baby girl. Recent research has shown, however, that 5-ARD males are usually psychologically more comfortable if registered as their biological sex, no matter how under-virilised their genitalia. A study that looked at nearly 100 children with XY intersex conditions in India found that all those diagnosed with 5-ARD and registered male at birth kept that designation, whereas nearly all those with the condition who were registered female at birth chose to change their legal sex as they grew up.

But all this was by the by when Semenya was born in a poor South African village in 1991. She was registered as female, and although she has talked of playing sport with the boys and finding girls boring, she continued to regard herself and be recognised as a girl and then a woman.

Conditions such as 5-ARD that can lead to an XY person being registered female at birth are extremely rare, with a global frequency of less than 1 in 20,000. Some confer little or no sporting edge (CAIS, for example). But the advantage conferred by male-pattern puberty is so towering that the IAAF estimates that XY DSDs are over-represented in women's elite competitions by a factor of 140 – and by even more among medallists.

The trans-inclusion policy crafted in Stockholm set the pattern for how the sporting authorities thought about Semenya. She was told to withdraw temporarily from competition and suppress her testosterone, which can be done by taking oestrogen or spironolactone, a hormone blocker. Around the same time, other women with DSDs were undergoing more extreme measures.

The treatment of four, who have not been named, was written up in the *Journal of Clinical Endocrinology and Metabolism*.

Sometime in 2011 or 2012 the IAAF invited them for assessment, after which they were advised that the standard treatment was to have their internal testes removed, take oestrogen and undergo plastic surgery to make their genitalia appear more female. In effect, they were steered towards sex reassignment – even though they were already legally women, and none had sought treatment for gender dysphoria. All complied, though for unclear reasons none returned to elite competition.

The episode is not only distasteful; it is incomprehensible. For around the same time as these women were being suggest-sold surgery and dependence on artificial hormones, the IAAF and IOC were weakening their trans-inclusion rules. Now, rather than undergoing genital surgery, transwomen merely had to suppress their testosterone. The level in blood serum differs widely between males and females, so it was easy to set a cut-off between the two. In a female, any level above 1.7 nanomoles per litre (nmol/L) suggests the presence of testicular material or a tumour, whereas 7.7 nmol/L is right at the bottom of normal for an elderly man. The authorities settled on 10 nmol/L, much lower than healthy males in their prime, to be maintained for a year before a transwoman could compete as a woman.

Once again, the conception of womanhood had changed. No longer was a woman someone who lacked testicles; now all that had to be lacking was testosterone. Since this can be suppressed with drugs, anyone who wanted could become a woman in sports officials' eyes. Womanhood had become a provisional status.

In one way, dropping the requirement for sex-reassignment surgery makes sense. Both the old rule and the new one were predicated on the notion that male sporting advantage comes from testosterone in the blood – so why worry about the presence or absence of male body parts? As the transwoman cyclist Veronica Ivy (who argues that transwomen should be entitled to compete as women without any conditions) memorably said to Martina Navratilova (who disagrees): 'Genitals do not play sports. Which part of tennis do you play with your penis?'

The trouble is that regarding circulating testosterone as the pre-eminent marker of maleness was never justified. Male sporting advantage does not depend on hormone levels on a given day; it is mostly the result of having gone through male puberty. But at least the requirement for surgery had restricted the number of males eligible to compete as women and excluded nearly all males of prime sporting age, since until recently hardly anyone underwent sex-reassignment surgery in their twenties. The new rules were close to a free-for-all.

But sports administrators were under pressure from many directions. Some commentators used the Semenya case to accuse them of sexism – of thinking that a woman who was fast or strong must be a man. Some intersex advocates argued that anyone registered female at birth should be allowed to compete, whatever their hormone levels, chromosomes or physique. And transactivists sought to conflate gender identity and DSDs to demand the same for transwomen.

In the run-up to the 2016 Rio Olympics, research appeared that seemed to say what sport's highest authorities wanted to hear. After sex-reassignment surgery in 2004, Joanna Harper, a medical physicist and recreational runner, became convinced that her lack of testosterone was hammering her race times. She sought to find out whether this was a general phenomenon. In 2015 she published a paper fitting running performances from eight transwomen to age-standardised tables: male pre-transition and female post-transition. For anyone seeking to equate circulating testosterone with male sporting advantage, the pattern she found was fortuitous: a speed loss of 10–12 percent – pretty much the performance gap in running between males and females.

It is hard to imagine a shakier basis for a big policy shift. Harper's paper was a collection of anecdotes: self-reported times from a handful of transwomen, of varying ages and training regimes, gathered over many years and lacking any controls for the multitude of factors that can affect performance. One participant became a much keener runner after transition; another put on weight and gave up running soon after submitting times. The paper looked at recreational runners, not elite ones. (Harper is frank about all these flaws.) Moreover, it considered only running, one of the sports where the male advantage is slightest.

But the IOC suspected that transactivists in countries where sex-reassignment surgery was not required for changing legal sex were preparing challenges against the Stockholm rules. Meanwhile Semenya and other athletes with DSDs were seeking to overturn the rules requiring them to bring their testosterone levels down. At the CAS, which hears policy challenges from professional athletes, they argued that high testosterone levels and androgenised development were natural advantages, like any others an athlete might benefit from.

The authorities made a convincing case for keeping male advantage out of female sports. But their desire to be trans-inclusive meant they were unwilling to simply exclude anyone who benefited from it. Instead they argued that lowering testosterone would be enough to maintain fairness when it came to DSDs too.

In response to the CAS's demand for evidence about athletes with DSDs specifically, rather than males in general, they restricted the rules to events where they could point to specific elite athletes, and said that as others emerged, they would consider adding new events. The outcome was intellectually incoherent: testosterone benefits athletes in all events, not just those where athletes with high testosterone currently compete. And it gave the unfortunate impression of being targeted at Semenya. As I write, she is ineligible to run at any distance from 400 metres to a mile, which covers the events where she has excelled.

With hindsight, the seventy-year history of attempts to locate male sporting advantage looks like a shell game. Each time sports officials thought they had figured out where it was – in physiology; in the presence of the Barr body; in the absence of the 'make male' gene revealed by the PCR test; in the presence of testes – rare DSDs, and latterly gender-identity ideology, meant the search continued. By the time they arrived at absence of functional testosterone, they had turned womanhood into something provisional. But they had not quite made it vanish. The shell game had one more round to go.

*

The final step happened in community sports, when national bodies tried to follow the IOC's lead. It is one thing to demand of elite athletes, who are subject to no-notice anti-doping tests, that they maintain low testosterone levels, but quite another to do so of non-professionals. In most settings, therefore, admitting transwomen who are on hormone treatment amounts to admitting males on demand.

Which brings us back, finally, to deckchairs. And to World Rugby, which knew from bitter experience that if it exposed players to avoidable risks, it could expect to pay the price in court. The IOC, which had rushed into trans inclusion without confirming that it could be done fairly, had not even considered safety. World Rugby would have to do that itself.

'We had to go back to the drawing board and develop a proper evidence-based process,' says Ross Tucker, the eminent sports scientist who advises World Rugby on scientific matters, player welfare and performance. The body had learned a hard but valuable lesson as it struggled to reduce spinal injuries and concussions: that safety concerns cannot be resolved by anecdote or emotion. 'Whenever there is a tragedy, there are so many criticisms,' he says, 'and your best fall-back is evidence.'

So World Rugby arranged a two-day workshop in London in early 2020, at which experts argued for and against including transwomen in women's rugby. They considered science (sex differences in performance), medicine (how to lower testosterone, and the impact of doing so), law and risk (human-rights arguments for trans inclusion, and the consequences for injury and liability), and ethical and social issues (the losses to transwomen from exclusion and female players from trans inclusion). All this was weighed by a working group consisting almost entirely of women, some of them former players and all experts in their field. World Rugby thus avoided a crass error made by the IOC, where the decision to open up women's sports was made by its male-dominated medical and scientific commission.

Among those presenting were Emma Hilton, a developmental biologist at Manchester University, and Tommy Lundberg, a specialist in exercise physiology at the Karolinska Institute. Their review paper has appeared in *Sports Medicine*, one of the most prestigious journals in the field. It demonstrates that, contrary to Harper's anecdotal paper, testosterone suppression has barely any impact on the sporting performance of people who have been through male puberty. Longitudinal studies, which track people over time, find that transwomen's lean body mass, muscle area and strength typically fall by less than five percent after one year of suppression, and very little more thereafter.

This may be enough to put an elite athlete out of competition – taking five percent off Semenya's time in the women's 800-metre race in Rio would have knocked her down from gold to barely eligible to enter. But it is still far less than the male advantage, which varies by sport from around twelve percent to as much as fifty percent. 'With regard to transgender women athletes, we question whether current circulating testosterone level cut-off can be a meaningful decisive factor, when in fact not even suppression down to around 1 nmol/L removes the anthropometric and muscle mass/strength physical advantage in any significant way,' Hilton and Lundberg write.

In contact sports, safety, not merely fairness, is at issue. Here, mass, strength and speed are all important, and there is no evidence that these are meaningfully lowered by testosterone suppression. World Rugby commissioned a biomechanics expert to explore the impact of introducing male bodies to the women's game on head and neck mechanics during tackles. The model didn't even incorporate differences in strength and power caused by the application of force during tackles, but even so found that these risk factors for head injuries increased by at least twenty to thirty percent.

Over the past decade World Rugby has set player welfare as its top priority. Even if it was willing to countenance female play-ers being outmatched by male ones, it was quite another matter to raise their risk of injury as well. So the regulator decided to bar transwomen from the international women's game, over which it has authority, and advised national federations to do the same in domestic tournaments.

Several, including those in Australia, Canada, the UK and the US, have said they will ignore the guidance. They have, however, been put on notice that if women are injured in collisions with transwomen, World Rugby will not support them. If a woman took a personal-injury claim, federations would have to defend their choice to ignore evidence-based advice from their global regulator. 'If you remove a protection made for players' safety and someone is injured, then you will be sued,' says Tim O'Connor, a barrister who specialises in personal-injury claims and presented at World Rugby's workshop. 'And historically, the reason for women's segregation has been safety.'

In a country with *de facto* gender self-ID, like Canada, the national body could perhaps argue that it had no choice. In Australia and the UK, where national laws explicitly allow males to be excluded from female sports on safety grounds, any half-decent lawyer would have a field day. And win or lose, such a public airing of the evidence of elevated risk would surely nudge insurers to push federations' and clubs' premiums through the roof.

World Rugby knows the evidence it has so painstakingly gathered will not save it from human-rights challenges in countries with legal gender self-identification. Meanwhile, women's groups may also bring challenges to trans inclusion against national federations. Under British law, failing to exclude males from women's sports is arguably indirect discrimination. A case would be hard to win, since indirect discrimination is hard to prove. But even a failed challenge would provide campaigners with a chance to make their argument in the court of public opinion.

If you want to know how sporting bodies got into this pickle in the first place, you could do worse than consider the presentations made at World Rugby's workshop. The experts opposing trans inclusion drew on research and statistics, and explored the pros and cons for everyone on the pitch. Those in favour presented anecdotes, appealed to emotion and considered the consequences for transwomen only. They had no concrete or logical arguments. 'Perhaps the most striking aspect of the workshop was the gulf in methodological and scientific robustness between the arguments for and against inclusion,' says Tucker. 'The positions were obviously different, but the difference between the evidence bases underpinning those differences was enormous'.

To British swimmer Sharron Davies, one of the few big sporting names to have called publicly for women's sports to be reserved for females, it comes as no surprise that advocates for trans inclusion have never had to make a case. 'I can't tell you the number of parents, and the number of athletes, who've told me privately that they agree with me 100 percent,' she says. 'It's not that people disagree with me, it's that they're frightened of the activists.' She thinks sporting authorities should return to sex-testing: 'It's the simplest thing in the world, a mouth swab that takes three seconds. It's not at all intrusive.' She also wants to see them work with advocates for trans people and athletes with DSDs to create open categories so everyone can compete fairly.

Davies is painfully familiar with competing against virilised bodies and knowing that, no matter how hard you train or how talented you are, you will lose. The nearest she got to an Olympic gold was in 1980, in Moscow, when she came in behind East German Petra Schneider, who later admitted to doping. 'Twenty years swimming against East Germans who'd been pumped full of male hormones,' she exclaims. 'It's obvious in the same way now, that allowing people with male physiques and the benefits of male puberty into a female race is categorically unfair.'

Also familiar to her is the IOC's supine attitude. Despite persistent rumours about East Germany's muscular female athletes, it sought to keep the peace rather than catch the dopers.

Then, as now, female athletes were victims of its failures. And then, as now, women who complained were dismissed as 'sore losers'. What is new today is that female athletes are not merely shamed, but bullied, into silence. By and large only those retired from competition dare speak up – and even then, they face consequences.

Alongside Davies, the other high-profile sportswoman who has said most is tennis legend Martina Navratilova. She was one of the first lesbian athletes ever to come out, and is obviously not transphobic in any meaningful sense: she is close to Renée Richards, who coached her for years. But even Navratilova is called a bigot for recognising male sporting advantage. She stumbled into the controversy in 2018, when she discovered that sporting federations were switching to self-ID. 'You can't just proclaim yourself a female and be able to compete against women,' she tweeted. 'There must be some standards, and having a penis and competing as a woman would not fit that standard.'

Startled by the vitriolic response, Navratilova apologised, deleted the tweet and agreed to do some research. The effect was far from what her harassers had intended. 'If anything, my views have strengthened,' she wrote in the *Sunday Times* a couple of months later, describing self-ID in sport as 'insane' and 'cheating'. That made her *persona non grata* with LGBT groups that had regarded her as a heroine ever since she came out in 1981. Athlete Ally, an American group that campaigns against homophobia in sport – and latterly for gender self-ID – dropped her as an ambassador. Transactivists wrote to companies whose products she endorsed, and to the Tennis Channel and BBC, for whom she commentates, pressing them to cut ties too.

Navratilova draws a distinction between everyday life and sport: 'However you see yourself, this is how I will speak to you, and about you to other people. But when it comes to sport, that's about biology, not feelings.' And she no longer seems to think, as the tweet that started the row implied, that post-operative transwomen should be included in women's competitions. Asked whether it was fair for Richards to play as a woman, she responds: 'Renée was in her forties, not training particularly hard. I was number one in the world and I had my hands full to beat her. I think that says everything you need to know.'

Both Navratilova and Davies see speaking out as a moral imperative. 'My life has been all about fairness, and when something is not fair it drives me absolutely bonkers,' says Navratilova. 'If I were still playing I would be speaking out about this; for me it's like speaking out about being gay.' That also lost her endorsements, she points out. 'I couldn't have lived with my conscience otherwise,' says Davies. 'Nobody did it for me and my generation. The doping was allowed to go on for Olympics after Olympics. I've only ever wanted the science to come before the rule changes, not after.'

10

REGARDLESS OF SEX

The American Left's embrace of gender self-identification

'It passed, it passed! I'm ecstatic,' says a teenager in a Queen t-shirt, with asymmetrical pink hair. A burly, middle-aged man in a suit – a spokesman for the ACLU – hurries over for a hug. The camera cuts to another teenager, whose eyes are shiny with tears. 'I feel uncomfortable that my privacy is being invaded,' she says. 'As I am a swimmer, I do change multiple times, naked, in front of the other students in the locker room. I understand that the board has an obligation to all students, but I was hoping that they would go about this in a different way that would also accommodate students such as myself.'

The scene is a school in suburban Chicago in late 2019. The board of School District 211 has just voted to allow trans students unrestricted access to private facilities corresponding to their stated identities, rather than their sex. Transgirl Nova Maday – the teenager with the pink hair – recently graduated, having fought to be allowed to use the female toilets and changing rooms since starting to identify as a girl at age fifteen. The other teenager, Julia Burca, is on the swim team. She has just watched the board, which fought to maintain single-sex spaces for several years, give in.

The room is a sea of placards. 'Anatomy NOT identity. Protects all equally' jostles with 'Trans students belong in locker rooms'. Surveying the scene are police officers, reporters and camera crews. When the board splits 5–2 in favour of acceding to the federal government's demand that trans-identified students be granted unconstrained access to facilities for the sex they identify as, the room erupts in cheers and jeers. 'Just wait till election time,' shouts one woman as she leaves. 'Home school, that's the answer,' shouts another.

What the news cameras have captured is the culmination of District 211's six years on the frontlines of the 'bathroom wars' – a dismissive tag for a nationwide fight about the reality and salience of biological sex. It unfolded in schools, public places, Washington bureaucracies, state legislatures and – this is America, after all – courtrooms. The backdrop was increasing political polarisation, with the Democratic Party captured by an identitarian youth wing and the Republican Party poisoned by its own right-wing brand of ethno-nationalist identity politics under Donald Trump. As the Democrats and their fellow travellers in think-tanks, campaign groups and civil-rights organisations embraced gender self-identification, defenders of women's sex-based rights – even secular feminists – found themselves with few allies other than Christian conservatives.

District 211's fight started in 2013, not with Maday, but with an unnamed transgirl at another high school. 'Student A' was granted access to single-stall facilities, but, with the support of the ACLU, sued to be allowed to use the girls' toilets and changing rooms. In an attempt to square this demand with other students' privacy, the school curtained off a section of the girls' changing room for Student A. But in 2015, towards the end of

Obama's second term, the federal Department of Education laid down an ultimatum: either the school board allowed Student A unrestricted access to female single-sex spaces, or District 211 would lose funding of $6 million a year.

In December 2015 the school board held a public meeting to discuss its response. The overwhelming majority of comments from parents were against allowing male people into female spaces at all. Some cited religious objections; others, anger at federal overreach; and still others, their daughters' privacy. When the board voted to give in and comply with the department's demand on the basis that Student A voluntarily used the curtained area, opponents cried 'gutless cowards' and 'shame on you'. Afterwards, some parents told the *Chicago Tribune* that their daughters did not want a transgirl using their facilities, but had not dared say so (the handful of students who spoke at the meeting were in favour). One student, who would not give her name, told the reporter that personal modesty and religious beliefs made her 'uncomfortable changing in front of someone I believe is a guy'.

A group of parents of varied ethnicities, faiths and political affiliations started to organise against allowing male students access to female facilities under any condition. Among them was Vicki Wilson, whose son was at the school and daughter expected to go there in the future. 'Gender dysphoria is real, and we empathise with those kids,' she says. 'If it had been my child, I would have wanted the school to make it comfortable for him. I'd have said: "let's get you another place to change." But never would I have said: "change with your sister and her friends and violate their privacy." '

A friend put Wilson in touch with the Alliance Defending Freedom (ADF), a conservative Christian group that takes legal cases to protect religious liberty and opposes abortion and same-sex marriage. It offered to represent the families, by now about fifty of them. In May 2016 they filed a lawsuit against the education department and District 211. Their argument can be summarised easily: Title IX of the Education Amendments of 1972, which bars discrimination based on sex in federally funded educational institutions, also expressly permits single-sex toilets, changing rooms and other 'living accommodations' (as well as single-sex sports).

But a week later, the federal government upped the ante. Much of its power is exercised via administrative orders issued by departments and agencies, which ensure compliance by threatening to cut off funding. Often these are minor rule changes – an endless blizzard of paperwork flying out from Washington to the country at large. But sometimes they can be highly consequential – attempts to force through a new policy by decree, rather than going via Congress. On this occasion, the Departments of Education and Justice informed all schools, universities and colleges that the word 'sex' in Title IX – the law that bars educational institutions from committing sex discrimination – should be understood to refer to self-identification.

A 'transgender male is someone who identifies as male but was assigned the sex of female at birth', the departments declared, and vice versa for a transgender female. When a person transitions, they 'begin asserting the sex that corresponds to their gender identity instead of the sex they were assigned at birth'. This is so confusing that I will spell it out. The words 'sex', 'male' and 'female' are being used to mean two entirely different things: the immutable biology observed at birth and the identity later declared. The claim is that people born male who identify as girls or women thereby change *sex itself* (and vice versa for people born female who identify as boys or men). Transgirls are therefore *literally female*, and have the right under Title IX to use female single-sex spaces.

The departmental circular is worth reading as an example of gender-identity ideology's self-referential nature and incoherence (a source is supplied in the further reading section). The words 'male' and 'female' cannot mean both biology and identity. And setting aside the thorny question of what it might mean to *feel* male or female, why would such a feeling matter, if *being* male or female does not? It is impossible to frame arguments against gender self-identification using such language, since the necessary words are lacking – which is presumably part of the point. The accusation of Orwellianism is often made too lightly, but this time it is justified. 'Don't you see that the whole aim of Newspeak [the language of the totalitarian superstate Oceania] is to narrow the range of thought?' Orwell wrote in *Nineteen Eighty-Four*. 'In the end we shall make thoughtcrime literally impossible, because there will be no words to express it.'

The order to introduce gender self-identification never came into force. Two dozen states brought lawsuits; court orders stayed its implementation; and a few months later Donald Trump was elected president. It seems surpassingly unlikely that the new president, a man demonstrably unconcerned with women's rights or boundaries, cared about the threats gender self-identification posed to both. Nonetheless, the policy was a left-wing creation and had gained no traction with Republicans, and so, after he took office, his administration let the nation's schools and universities know that 'sex' no longer meant 'gender identity', but should be understood to refer to biology once more. Other departments, including those overseeing federal prisons and homeless shelters, had sent out similar edicts. One after another, they were countermanded.

Democrat-controlled states and cities, however, continued to write self-ID into laws and regulations, both in schools and elsewhere. To give a typical example, an anti-discrimination law passed in New York City in 2019 defines sex as 'a combination of chromosomes, hormones, internal and external reproductive organs, facial hair, vocal pitch, development of breasts, gender identity, and other characteristics'. When these do not align, it says, 'gender identity is the primary determinant of a person's sex.'

Legal cases continued as well. Between 2018 and 2019 three were heard in Illinois. Two related to District 211: one taken by the ACLU with Maday replacing Student A, who had graduated; and one opposing gender self-ID brought by Wilson and the other parents, supported by the ADF. The third was taken by a transboy at school in another Chicago suburb to Illinois's human-rights commission. The contradictory rulings show how impossible it is to form a coherent body of law when core terms have been destabilised.

First, a judge ruled that the curtained-off area in the girls' changing room provided a reasonable compromise between Maday's trans identification and other students' privacy (note that to even consider privacy in this context is to accept that a transgirl is not a girl exactly like any other, since entering a changing room constitutes consent to see and be seen by everyone who has right of entry). Then another judge ruled that transgirls' access to female areas should be unrestricted because Americans do not have a 'visual right to privacy' over their 'unclothed or partially clothed bodies' (note that the logical implication of denying that people have rights to visual privacy is not gender self-identification, but the abolition of single-sex spaces – or indeed changing rooms). Finally, the state human-rights commission decided that insisting that 'transgender males' use a curtained-off area constituted adverse treatment of them in comparison with 'similarly situated nontransgender males' (note that the people it calls 'transgender males'

– transboys – are actually female, and that as soon as you say so, the logic collapses).

Soon afterwards, District 211 folded, settling with Maday and the ACLU for $150,000. From January 2020 it has allowed unrestricted access to all facilities according to gender identity. Its six-year fight had cost it $500,000.

Gary McCaleb worked as an attorney for the ADF for eighteen years, retiring around the time that the parents and students of District 211 dropped their lawsuit. Politically, he and I do not agree on much. But we are able to talk about our differences, because neither of us redefines essential terms while denying that we are doing so. 'Judges would agree that separation by sex is perfectly legal, and then say: "but a transgirl is a girl",' he says. 'Our country was founded on a statement that "We hold these truths to be self-evident." But you cannot have a self-evident truth when everyone can declare their own reality.'

*

Even before the bathroom wars broke out, transactivists had started to promote gender-identity interpretations of existing civil-rights laws. Besides Title IX – the ban on sex discrimination in educational institutions – the main target was Title VII of the Civil Rights Act of 1964, which bans workplace discrimination based on five 'protected classes': race, colour, religion, sex and national origin. Their big moment came in mid-2020, when three test cases bundled together under the name of the only surviving plaintiff, Gerald Bostock, came before the Supreme Court. They concerned two gay men and a transwoman, all of whom had been fired for coming out at work.

Aimee Stephens, the transwoman, had been hired as a man by Harris Funeral Homes in Detroit, and six years later announced the intention to 'live and work full-time as a woman'. The business had a strict dress code – suits for men, dresses or skirts for women – and a largely conservative, religious clientele. The owner told Stephens that it 'would not work out' and let her go.

The Supreme Court's ruling in Bostock v. Clayton County, by a 6–3 majority, was identical in its reasoning for both sexual orientation and gender identity. It declared that workplace discrimination on grounds of either was prohibited by a strictly textual reading of Title VII, because such discrimination is logically impossible to commit if you do not take the employee's sex into account. You cannot even observe that someone is homosexual or transgender, let alone discriminate against them, if you are not aware of their sex – and considering sex in employment decisions is barred. An employer 'who fires an individual for being homosexual or transgender fires that person for traits or actions it would not have questioned in members of a different sex', the majority wrote. 'Sex plays a necessary and undisguisable role in the decision, exactly what Title VII forbids.'

The judges cautioned that their ruling concerned only employment law. 'The employers worry that our decision will sweep beyond Title VII to other federal or state laws that prohibit sex discrimination,' they wrote. 'And, under Title VII itself, they say sex-segregated bathrooms, locker rooms, and dress codes will prove unsustainable after our decision today. But none of these other laws are before us; we have not had the benefit of adversarial testing about the meaning of their terms, and we do not prejudge any such question today.'

You may notice that the Bostock judgment is incompatible with the notion that 'sex' means the same thing as 'gender identity', as the Obama administration had insisted four years earlier. Its entire point is that employers must be aware that there is a mismatch between sex and gender identity even to notice that someone is trans and then discriminate against them. But it leaves unanswered a thorny question: what, precisely, are the 'traits or actions' that it refers to, which an employer might deem unacceptable in a transwoman but not a female person (and *mutatis mutandis* for transmen and males)?

The answer is obvious in the case of sexual orientation, to which Bostock applies the same reasoning. An employer who is prejudiced against a gay man objects to him having or desiring male sexual partners, and would not have minded if the employee had been a woman with a male partner (similarly, an employer who objects to a lesbian having female partners would not have minded if she had been a man). But for trans people, there is nothing as clear-cut.

The sole clue in the judgment is that Aimee Stephens announced to her employer that she intended to 'live and work full-time as a woman'. What does that mean? I live and work full-time as a woman, and I can think of only a few things that might change if I were to live and work full-time as a man. Some are trivial, some would require me to actually become male, rather than merely declare myself so, and some raise genuine issues for employers that the Supreme Court did not acknowledge.

Among the superficial things that would change if I were a man are my name and title. Certain biological issues would too, such as no longer having to cope with menstruation, pregnancy or menopause in the workplace. I might be seen differently by my employer and colleagues, in ways that are hard to pin down. And finally, there are the situations where distinctions of sex are permitted in the workplace despite general prohibitions on discrimination, such as toilets and changing rooms, and the 'bona fide occupational qualifications' exemption that permits employers to hire a person of one sex or the other for certain jobs (for example, a health-care provider may lawfully seek to hire only females to carry out gynaecological examinations).

If the Supreme Court meant that employers should not be able to penalise trans workers over trivia such as names and titles, that seems reasonable. It cannot have been thinking of such matters as pregnancy and other biological functions of one sex or the other, since these cannot be changed by declaration. Nor can it have meant nebulous matters of perception and treatment, since any change to these for someone who decides to 'live and work' as a member of the opposite sex would definitely constitute sex discrimination. That leaves only situations where single-sex provision is legal, such as washrooms.

But by acknowledging that the true sex of trans people is not the same as their gender identity, the Supreme Court seems to undercut any argument that they should have right of access according to their declared identity. Would Harris Funeral Homes have been in the clear if it had accepted Stephens's announcement that henceforth she would 'live and work' as a woman, but had continued to expect her to follow the men's dress code and use the men's toilets? If not, why not, since the Supreme Court accepts that transwomen are not female? If so, then its protestations that its ruling did not reach to such matters ring hollow.

And indeed, lower courts have already started to cite Bostock in support of gender self-identification more generally. A notable example came in August 2020, when an appeals court found that a school in Virginia had discriminated against Gavin Grimm, a transboy, by barring him from the boys' toilets and changing rooms. 'After the Supreme Court's recent decision . . . we have little difficulty holding that a bathroom policy precluding Grimm from using the boys' restrooms discriminated against him "on the basis of sex"', the judges declared. They acknowledged that sex-separated toilets are legal, but went on to say that 'Grimm does not challenge sex-separated restrooms; he challenges the Board's discriminatory exclusion of himself from the sex-separated restroom matching his gender identity.'

This evokes another of Orwell's coinages in *Nineteen Eighty-Four*: doublethink, which means holding two contradictory ideas simultaneously. You can interpret what happens when a trans person is barred from a single-sex space that matches their declared identity in two, mutually exclusive, ways. The first is to claim that the word 'sex' means 'gender identity', as in the Obama-era departmental circular: the person's declaration has changed their sex and they are barred because they are trans, not 'cis'. The second is the logic of Bostock: their sex has not changed and they are barred because they are the wrong sex (and note that some single-sex spaces are legal). The appeals court claims, in effect, that the first happened – that Grimm was excluded from the 'sex-separated restroom matching his gender identity'. But it then cites Bostock, which distinguishes between sex and gender identity, to claim that this exclusion is illicit.

It is, of course, a good thing that the Supreme Court gave gay and transgender people employment protections, and a great shame that Congress did not act to do so much earlier – and indeed to legislate against harassment, violence, and discrimination in housing, health care and so on. Such protections have long been standard in Europe (I will have more to say about anti-discrimination law in the UK in chapter 13). But they are merited because employers should be able to mandate employees' beliefs or behaviour only when these affect job performance, and because everyone deserves freedom, safety and equal access to public goods. As the UK shows, none of this requires removing sex-based rights. And yet I fear that the Bostock ruling, by skating over what it might mean for a male person to 'live and work as a woman', paves the way to do exactly that.

The Supreme Court is likely to be called on to make a decisive ruling in the coming years. It will probably concern the other major carve-out for sex-separation in federal civil-rights law: sports. Several duelling legal challenges are in progress: some by transwomen and campaigners against state laws that reserve female sports for females; others by female athletes against state laws mandating gender self-ID.

Among the former is a lawsuit being taken by Lindsay Hecox, a twenty-year-old transwoman at Boise State University in Idaho who wants to be eligible for the women's track team. With the support of the ACLU, Hecox is suing the state government, which passed a law in 2020 reserving girls' and women's sports for females. Two other states have also passed similar measures, and bills are in front of legislatures in around twenty more. But for now Idaho's law has been suspended by a federal judge until Hecox's suit is heard.

Meanwhile in Connecticut, which is one of at least eighteen states that allow males to enter female sporting competitions, three teenagers, Selina Soule, Chelsea Mitchell and Alanna Smith, challenged this inclusion. In 2017 two transgirls, Terry Miller and Andraya Yearwood, started to compete as girls in high-school athletic events. Neither had impressive form when competing as a boy, but in the following three years they set seventeen women's state meet records and won fifteen girls' track championship titles – titles held by nine different girls in 2016. Nearly a hundred girls lost the chance to progress to the next level of competition because they finished behind one or both of them. In April 2021 a judge dismissed their suit because Miller and Yearwood had graduated; as this book went to press the girls' lawyers were seeking to continue the challenge, since the underlying issue was not limited to specific trans athletes.

Mitchell, who is the fastest biological girl in Connecticut at 55 metres, has lost four girls' state championships and two all-New England awards to Miller and Yearwood. 'It was very overwhelming and intimidating to go up against them, knowing that you are going to lose,' she says. 'We deserve to win, just as men get to win.' The girls are often misrepresented as seeking to get transgender athletes banned, whereas in fact all they want is that everyone competes in their own sex class. 'In sports it's your body that's competing, not your mind,' says Soule.

Perhaps the most bizarre consequence of the adoption of gender self-identification by the Left is that the loudest voices speaking up for women's rights are conservative Christians. The three girls are supported by the ADF, though they are not all from conservative Christian families. The simple fact was that nobody else was willing to help them. They approached many attorneys, some of whom were sympathetic but concerned about the inevitable backlash, and big women's rights organisations, including the Women's Sports Foundation and the National Women's Law Center – either of which would seem a perfect fit for girls facing unfair competition. But no luck. 'They were trying to pretend nothing was happening, or that it wasn't a big deal,' says Christy Mitchell, Chelsea's mother. 'I saw it as a women's rights issue and still do. The media try to make it an LGBT issue, and it really isn't.'

'For anyone to watch this real-time and see it as fair is mind-boggling to me,' says Smith's mother, Cheryl Radachowsky. 'Until I got to see it myself, I never realised there would be people who'd think this was okay. It's just a race for second place.'

*

It is impossible to make sense of the push for gender self-identification on the American Left without understanding the historical and political context. Three peculiarities have shaped the

213

national discourse on the subject: the scars left by the country's dire racial history; the way the fight for gay marriage played out; and, lastly, its partisan and polarised politics.

Chattel slavery and racial segregation have marked America in many more obvious ways, but for the purposes of this book, the most significant are that they have invited false analogies between race and sex, and poisoned words and phrases such as 'exclusion', 'segregation' and 'separate but equal'. It has become close to impossible for left-leaning Americans to articulate arguments based on material differences between the sexes. For them, all 'discrimination' is patterned on white privilege and black oppression. The word's original meaning of acknowledging difference is almost completely inaccessible.

And so the bathroom wars were mentally slotted into a narrative in which bigots attempted to exclude a marginalised group and were beaten back. This is not me reaching for effect; analogies with the civil-rights era are routinely deployed in support of gender self-identification. To cite just one striking example, when North Carolina passed a state 'bathroom law' in 2016 that barred people of one sex from facilities intended for the other, the Department of Justice sued the state, alleging discrimination (the law was repealed a year later in the face of a boycott organised by the ACLU). 'This is not the first time that we have seen discriminatory responses to historic moments of progress for our nation,' declared then-justice secretary Loretta Lynch – as it happens, a black woman from North Carolina. 'We saw it in the Jim Crow laws that followed the Emancipation Proclamation. We saw it in fierce and widespread resistance to Brown v. Board of Education [the Supreme Court ruling that ordered school desegregation] . . . It was not so very long ago that states, including North Carolina, had signs above restrooms, water fountains and on public accommodations keeping people out based on a distinction without a difference.'

I am not American; I don't know what it is like to have a psyche shaped by the legacy of slavery, lynching and the Jim Crow laws. All I can do is fall back on logic and science, and say once again why single-sex spaces are not analogous to racial segregation.

The differences between the sexes are material and significant, with consequences that go beyond matters of law or custom; those between people of different skin colours or ethnicities are not. Feelings of modesty and privacy related to the presence of the opposite sex appear to be common to all cultures, and have an obvious origin in the facts of reproduction. Women have an extra reason for wanting single-sex spaces when they are vulnerable or naked: as protection against male sexual violence and harassment. Their spaces do not constitute privilege, but revolt against the age-old oppression of females by males. And if you really must analogise race and sex, you should line up the two oppressed groups: women and black people. Feminist philosopher Marilyn Frye does so very tellingly in *The Politics of Reality*, her collection of essays published in 1983: 'it is always the privilege of the master to enter the slave's hut. The slave who decides to exclude her master from her hut is declaring herself not a slave.'

Moreover, even if the analogy between racial segregation and sex-separation held, it would not support gender self-ID. The solution to racial segregation was not to allow some whites to identify as black, and vice versa, but to integrate. Someone who truly believed that the physical differences between male and female people who declared the same gender identity were so trivial that only a bigot would notice them would logically have to support a unisex world. They would not argue that sex-separation should stand while sex became a matter of self-declaration.

The impact of the fight for gay marriage was two-fold. It yoked the 'T' to the 'LGB' more tightly and earlier than happened elsewhere; and it dealt the Right a loss that made it reluctant to accept what looked like a rematch.

American campaigners had long sought to add sexual orientation to the list of protected classes in the Civil Rights Act, either in an amendment or in a new, freestanding Employment Non-Discrimination Act (ENDA). Latterly, transactivists sought to tag on gender identity. In 2007 two proposals for such a new law arrived in Congress, one with just sexual orientation, and, for the first time, one with gender identity too. Their Democrat sponsors canvassed colleagues and determined that the broader proposal had no chance of passing. With the support of the Human Rights Campaign (HRC), a campaign group for gay rights established in the 1980s, they dropped it, reasoning that a chance to improve life for millions of gay Americans should not be missed.

Furious transactivists not only withdrew support for the slimmed-down bill, but campaigned against it. It failed to pass. Hundreds of civil-rights groups joined a 'United ENDA' front, promising never again to seek a benefit for gay people without also helping transgender ones.

From the viewpoint of transactivists, the strategy made sense. Americans were well on their way towards accepting gay rights, but gender self-identification would be a much harder sell. Few ordinary people had any idea that transactivists seriously regarded man and woman as opt-in categories, and hardly any would have agreed with the implications for settings such as changing rooms. If gay people were allowed to win their rights alone, trans people would end up without allies.

It is less obvious why gay people did not rebel against their cause being hitched to a less popular one that had already cost them a likely legislative victory. One reason was no doubt natural sympathy for another minority. At least as salient, however, was that the main demands of transactivists – namely, that transwomen should gain access to women's spaces and, if sexually interested in women, be regarded as lesbians – did not discommode gay men, whose interests had always taken precedence in LGB activism.

And finally, the HRC's punishment for accepting the sexual-orientation-only version of the proposed new law put the entire Left on notice. Transactivists picketed its fundraisers, including its gala dinner in Washington. Then came the legalisation of gay marriage. Some veteran campaigners stepped down, making way for graduates stuffed to the gills with queer theory. Campaign groups needed a new marquee cause – and the transactivists had one ready and waiting. With barely a pause for breath, civil-rights organisations big and small changed their focus to gender self-identification.

The extent of the makeover is remarkable. In 2019, Michael Biggs of Oxford University analysed words relating to identities – 'lesbian', 'bisexual', 'gay' and 'trans', including plurals and variants – in the annual reports of the HRC and GLAAD. In 1999, 'trans' and 'bisexual' hardly appeared in the HRC's reports; 'gay' accounted for nearly two-thirds and 'lesbian' for a third. But by 2018 'lesbian' had been almost entirely squeezed out, 'gay' was down to a tenth – and 'trans' was over three-quarters. Biggs analysed GLAAD's reports from 2007, at which point 'trans' accounted for fifteen percent. By 2018 the pattern was very much the same as for the HRC.

The HRC, in particular, has the zeal of the converted. In an interview in 2017 Sarah McBride, a transwoman who is now a Democratic senator for Delaware and was the HRC's press secretary at the time, explained that it had blocked any LGB activism that did nothing for the T 'forcefully and aggressively'. The very history of gay liberation has been rewritten to position transwomen at the forefront – for example, in claims that they led the Stonewall uprising in 1969. This is rebutted by Fred Sargeant, a veteran gay-rights campaigner who was present. Marsha P. Johnson and Sylvia Rivera, two names often cited, were gay drag queens. Johnson never called himself a transwoman, and Rivera did not identify as trans until thirty years later. And anyway, says Sargeant, neither played any significant role.

In the fight for same-sex marriage, the American Left had become particularly closely associated with the winning side. (Compare, for example, the UK, where gay marriage was introduced by a Conservative government, which presented it as part of a pro-family agenda that emphasised autonomy and personal responsibility.) The Defense of Marriage Act passed by Congress in 1996, which restricted marriage to opposite-sex couples, was proposed by Republicans. Some Republican-dominated states refused to recognise same-sex marriages solemnised elsewhere until forced to by the Supreme Court ruling. The connection between Republicans and opposition to gay marriage was reinforced by the 'God made Adam and Eve, not Adam and Steve' style of rhetoric favoured by evangelical preachers.

In fact, the split between the two parties on this issue was not as sharp as it looks now. Many Democrats voted for the Defense of Marriage Act. A sizeable minority on the Left opposed same-sex marriage, which they disliked for tying gay people into heterosexual norms – and not a few people on the Right supported it for precisely the same reason. But in the simplistic version of events that has become canon, on gay marriage the Left was right, and the Right was wrong. So when the same campaign groups moved on to gender self-identification, Republican politicians did not embrace the new demand, but they let its proponents take the floor unchallenged. This silence allowed an extreme demand from the far left of the Democratic

Party not only to become party policy, but to escape wider scrutiny in the mainstream media and other public forums.

And lastly, America's highly polarised political landscape meant that the form of transactivism adopted by the Left was particularly radical. Polarisation feeds on itself, as extremes on one side provide the cautionary tales used by extremes on the other to whip up fear and hatred. Moderates within each party stay silent, since the opposition seems a greater threat than their own hardliners.

On the Right, the extremists are white ethno-nationalist majoritarians; on the Left, they are identitarians who see progress as a process of bringing one marginalised group after another in from the cold. Spokespeople for each marginalised group are regarded as 'owning' its policies, meaning transactivists get to promote gender self-identification without hard questions about how it impacts on everyone else. And as the Left has adopted their creed, it has descended to depths of science-denialism formerly associated with the climate-change and evolution deniers of the Right. Indeed, denying the materiality and immutability of human sex is not merely akin to denying evolution – it *is* denying evolution, since the two sexes are evolved categories, and immutable in all mammals.

Another malign consequence of polarisation is legislative gridlock. Several major issues of public policy remain outstanding in America long after having been settled elsewhere in the rich world, such as universal access to health care, maternity leave and gun control. This is partly because richly funded interest groups oppose laws that would command broad electoral support. But it is also because the legislature is finely balanced and lawmakers refuse to work across the aisle.

When a legislature is functioning well, lawmakers seek compromise, balance competing interests, consider the broader implications of a proposed policy and carve out necessary exceptions. Draft abortion laws in many countries, for example, have brought some social conservatives on board by restricting access to the early months of pregnancy. Severely ill women and rape victims are usually treated as special cases. Whatever the issue, the eventual law should be something that most politicians and voters think is at least bearable, and that is regarded as legitimate by even those who don't like it – an important aspect of democracy known as 'losers' consent'.

When gridlock is the usual state of affairs, the issues a legislature fails to resolve often end up in courts. These, by contrast, can answer only the questions before them, and will generally argue from principle and precedent, rather than consequences. If the issue is tidy, the impact on others is minimal and public opinion has already strongly shifted, as with gay marriage in the US, little is lost. But with messier subjects, and when the only principles and precedents are a poor fit, the ruling may be seen to lack legitimacy.

An example is the Supreme Court's 1973 ruling in Roe v. Wade. It concluded that abortion was a privacy right, as conferred by the Fourteenth Amendment. Privacy was not something that seemed at all relevant to legislatures elsewhere as they considered abortion, and the ruling failed to manufacture losers' consent since it sidestepped the central question, namely whether the foetus has any rights. That does much to explain why abortion is still such a live question in American politics. Trump's overwhelming support from evangelicals owed in large part to his promise to fill Supreme Court vacancies with judges who would see things their way – on abortion above all.

Every now and then, the logjam in Washington shifts. On the rare occasions that one party holds both houses and the presidency, it tends to be maximalist, since another chance may not come for ages. And that is the approach Joe Biden is taking to gender self-identification, even though the issue is highly polarising and he has only a bare majority in the Senate.

On his first day in office in January 2021 he issued an executive order to all federal agencies, instructing them to examine their rules and regulations in light of the Bostock judgment. They have been given a pretty firm steer as to what they should conclude. On the campaign trail, Biden pledged to allow male prisoners to serve their sentences in women's prisons on the basis of self-ID, and to pass a so-called Equality Act that would interpret the word 'sex' to mean 'gender identity' right across federal law.

Either the passage of the Equality Act or a flurry of new edicts from Washington bureaucrats mandating gender self-ID in schools, prisons, homeless shelters and so on would surely provoke a further flurry of legal challenges. If not the question of whether males can self-declare into women's sports, one of these could provide the case in which the Supreme Court finally rules on gender self-identification. And even the best-case scenario – that it reaffirms the reality of sexual dimorphism and the lawfulness of sex-separation in situations where sex matters – has a big downside. Large swathes of the American Left have become convinced that such a reaffirmation could be motivated only by hate. Many of the country's culture wars have become 'frozen conflicts', where the combatants have dug in and a peace deal seems out of reach. The issue of gender self-identification could easily become another.

11

BEHIND THE SCENES

Transactivism's long march through the institutions

For a movement that is supposedly about the latest oppressed minority gaining full human rights, transactivism has progressed remarkably far and fast. Usually, civil-rights movements start by winning hearts and minds, and that takes time. You might think it a good thing that such delay seems a thing of the past. In fact, this is a major indication that transactivism is not a civil-rights movement at all.

Consider the movements commonly claimed as its forerunners. Three decades passed between the AIDS crisis that re-galvanised the gay-liberation movement and the Supreme Court's ruling that legalised same-sex marriage across the US. In 1996 the share of Americans supporting gay marriage was barely a quarter. It did not become a majority until 2011. Similarly, the movements to enfranchise women and to end segregation in the American South had to be built from the ground up. Campaigners gave speeches and held rallies to raise awareness and win supporters. Solid majorities had to favour the social and legal shifts these groups demanded before politicians and judges implemented them.

What same-sex marriage, women's franchise and the end of segregation all have in common is that they extend the rights of a privileged group to everyone. And when people hear the phrase 'trans rights', they assume something similar is being demanded – that trans people be enabled to live without discrimination, harassment and violence, and to express themselves as they wish. Such goals are worthy ones, but they are not what mainstream transactivism is about. What campaigners mean by 'trans rights' is gender self-identification: that trans people be treated in every circumstance as members of the sex they identify with, rather than the sex they actually are.

This is not a human right at all. It is a demand that everyone else lose their rights to single-sex spaces, services and activities. And in its requirement that everyone else accept trans people's subjective beliefs as objective reality, it is akin to a new state religion, complete with blasphemy laws. All this explains the speed. When you want new laws, you can focus on lobbying, rather than the painstaking business of building broad-based coalitions. And when those laws will take away other people's rights, it is not only unnecessary to build public awareness – it is imperative to keep the public in the dark.

This stealthy approach has been central to transactivism for quite some time. In a speech in 2013, Masen Davis, then the executive director of the American Transgender Law Center, told supporters that 'we have largely achieved our successes by flying under the radar . . . We do a lot really quietly. We have made some of our biggest gains that nobody has noticed. We are very quiet and thoughtful about what we do, because we want to make sure we have the win more than we want to have the publicity.'

The result is predictable. Even as one country after another introduces gender self-ID, very few voters know this is happening, let alone support it.

In 2018 research by Populus, an independent pollster, crowd-funded by British feminists, found that only fifteen percent of British adults agreed that legal sex change should be possible without a doctor's sign-off. A majority classified a 'person who was born male and has male genitalia but who identifies as a woman' as a man, and only tiny minorities said that such people should be allowed into women's sports or changing rooms, or be incarcerated in a women's prison if they committed a crime.

Two years later, YouGov found that half of British voters thought people should be 'able to self-identify as a different gender to the one they were born in'. But two-thirds said legal sex change should only be possible with a doctor's sign-off, with just fifteen percent saying no sign-off should be needed. In other words, there is widespread support for people describing themselves as they wish, but not much for granting such self-descriptions legal status. The same poll also asked whether transwomen should be allowed in women's sports and changing rooms, sometimes with a reminder that transwomen may have had no genital surgery, and sometimes without. The share saying yes was twenty percentage points lower with the reminder than without – again demonstrating widespread confusion about what being trans means, and that support for trans people does not imply support for self-declaration overriding reality.

A poll in Scotland in 2020 suggests that even young women, the demographic keenest on gender self-ID, become cooler when reminded of the practical implications. A slight majority of women aged sixteen to thirty-four selected 'anyone who says they're a woman, regardless of their biology' as closer than 'an adult human female, with XX chromosomes and female genitalia' to their conception of what the word 'woman' means. (Young men were much less keen on the self-ID definition, though keener than older men. Overall, 72 percent of respondents chose the biological definition.) But that slight majority of young women fell to 38 percent answering 'yes' to: 'Do you think someone who identifies as a woman, but was born male, and still has male genitalia, should be allowed to use female changing rooms where women and girls are undressing/showering, even if those women object?'

This pattern of broad sympathy for trans-identified people combined with opposition to the practical consequences of gender self-ID also holds in the US. In 2020, public-opinion polling in ten swing states found that at least three-quarters of likely voters – including a majority of registered Democrats – opposed allowing male people to compete in female sports. Proposals to ban puberty blockers and cross-sex hormones for minors also polled extremely well. Two more polls the same year, one in California shortly before state laws changed to grant male convicts who identified as women the right to be held in women's prisons, and one in Idaho to gauge support for the state legislature's efforts to keep males out of women's sports, found large majorities supporting separation by sex rather than gender identity.

Gender self-ID does not even play well with left-leaning voters. In early 2020, Eric Kaufmann, a politics professor, gave a random sample of likely British voters some text about a 'trans rights' pledge signed by all but one of the candidates for the Labour Party leadership. It described women's groups campaigning to maintain sex-based rights as 'trans exclusionist hate groups', and said Labour members supporting them should be expelled. The share who said they were likely to vote Labour at the next election was ten percentage points lower than in a control group who read nothing. Progressive campaigners have used 'taboos around minority sensitivity to amplify their influence', Kaufmann concluded, enabling them to 'advance unpopular platforms that both weaken the Left and contribute to cultural polarisation.'

A movement that focuses on the levers of power rather than building grassroots support is one in which a few wealthy people can have considerable sway. They have shaped the global agenda by funding briefing documents, campaign groups, research and legal actions; endowing university chairs; and influencing health-care protocols.

One is an American transwoman billionaire, Jennifer (James) Pritzker, a retired soldier and one of the heirs to a vast family fortune. Pritzker's personal foundation, Tawani, makes grants to universities, the ACLU, GLAAD, HRC and smaller activist groups. To cite a couple of examples, in 2016 it gave the University of Victoria $2 million to endow a chair of trans-gender studies, and throughout the 'bathroom wars' it supported Equality Illinois Education Project, which is linked to a group campaigning for gender self-ID in the state.

Two other billionaires, neither transgender, also spend lavishly on transactivism. One is Jon Stryker, another heir to a fortune. His foundation, Arcus, supports LGBT campaign group ILGA, and Transgender Europe, which channels funding to national self-ID campaigns. Arcus funds the LGBT Movement Advancement Project, which tracks gender-identity advocacy in dozens of countries (and partners with President Biden's personal foundation on the Advancing Acceptance Initiative, which promotes early childhood transition). In 2015 Arcus announced that it would give $15 million in the next five years to American trans-rights groups. Among the recipients were the ACLU, the Transgender Law Center, the Trans Justice Funding Project and the Freedom Center for Social Justice, which campaigned against North Carolina's bathroom law. In 2019, it gave $2 million to found a queer-studies programme at Spelman

College in Atlanta, Georgia, and it funds Athlete Ally, the group that dropped Martina Navratilova as an ambassador when she opposed trans inclusion in female sports. In March 2021 he gave a further $15m to the ACLU, to be spent in part on pressing for legal change.

A third billionaire funder of transactivism is George Soros, via his Open Society Foundations (OSF), a network of independently managed philanthropic institutions. OSF has made large donations to the ACLU, Planned Parenthood, Human Rights Watch (including $100 million in 2010, its biggest donation ever) and the HRC, all of which campaign for gender self-identification. OSF pays for the production of model laws and 'best-practice' documents on trans-related issues. To highlight just one example, in 2014 it supported 'License to be Yourself', a guide to campaigning for national gender self-ID laws. This argued, among other things, that children of any age should be able to change their legal sex at will.

This pattern of funding helps explain the gap between trans campaign groups' rhetoric and the policies they pursue. The talk is about the world's downtrodden: poor, homeless trans people forced into survival sex work, lacking health care and harassed by the police. But the money comes in large part from the world's most powerful people: rich, white American males. The two groups' needs and desires barely overlap at all.

There certainly are trans people in harrowing circumstances. Many of the murders cited by transactivist groups to support the claim that trans people are uniquely at risk are of South American *travestis* – transwomen who retain male genitalia and often work in street prostitution. But the risks they face have little to do with being trans. Street prostitution is dangerous for anyone, as is being a gender non-conforming male in South America. Mostly, these people need the same as their fellow citizens: better health care and policing, economic development and an end to America's drug war. They also need exit strategies from prostitution. Amended birth certificates stating *travestis'* sex as female will do nothing to disguise their maleness, or protect them from violent pimps and johns.

Fortunately, the limited statistics available suggest that trans people in safer places are not at greatly elevated risk of violence. Their life expectancy depends mostly on the same things as everyone else's – sex, occupation, state of health and so on – and not on their identity. But they do have specific needs that would be worth addressing. They are on average poorer than their fellow citizens, and more likely to have mental-health problems. Above all, they would benefit from high-quality research into the origins of cross-sex identities, and how to care for a body altered by cross-sex hormones and surgeries as it ages.

But mainstream transactivism does none of this. It works largely towards two ends: ensuring that male people can access female spaces; and removing barriers to cross-sex hormones and surgeries, even in childhood. These are not the needs of people on low incomes at risk of poor health. They are the desires of rich, powerful males who want to be classed as women. Everything I have written about – the harm to children's bodies; the loss of women's privacy; the destruction of women's sports; and the perversion of language – is collateral damage.

*

The way these desires become laws is via 'policy capture': the distortion of policymaking to benefit a minority at the expense of the general public. It has three elements: lobbying and funding; shaping knowledge production and dissemination; and threats of trouble. Much of it is done by groups that were founded to fight against government overreach and for gay rights, and which adopted gender self-ID to keep donations coming in after gay marriage was won.

In the US, the two most influential are the ACLU and the HRC. The ACLU takes lawsuits in favour of gender self-ID in 'bathrooms' and sports. Both groups lobby lawmakers directly, and fund electoral materials praising candidates who favour gender self-ID and attacking those that don't. They influence young people via educational programmes that describe innate gender identity as scientific fact, and sexual orientation as about which genders you are attracted to. And they present trans-identified pupils gaining access to spaces intended for the opposite sex as a civil-rights cause.

Trans campaign groups influence media organisations, courts and the public discourse in a variety of ways. One is by writing guidance for journalists. This is accepted gratefully – and uncritically – by editors fearful of tripping up on a sensitive topic, and in an increasingly censorious climate. Guides by GLAAD and the UK's journalism watchdog, the Independent Press Standards Organisation (produced with input from nine trans campaign groups and no one else), give the distinct impression that mentioning a trans person's biological sex or pre-transition name is both bigoted and unnecessary.

Journalists following these guides will struggle to report clearly on such subjects as the rise in paediatric transition and the scientific basis for keeping transwomen out of women's sports. And their articles on crime will mislead their readers: an axe-wielding woman laying waste to customers in a supermarket; police warning about a homicidal, sex-offending teenage girl; a woman punching and squeezing a one-year-old to death out of frustration; a female paedophile prosecuted for grooming children online and then meeting up with and raping them. (These are all real examples, and in every case the fact that the 'female' person was in fact male was left out of many reports.) Women almost never commit these sorts of crimes – and yet reports of women committing them are becoming commonplace.

The same sorts of issues have started to come up in court cases, perhaps because many judges have attended so-called educational sessions run by transactivists. Take, for example, the lawsuit in Connecticut opposing transwomen's inclusion in women's sports. In a pre-hearing discussion, the judge told lawyers representing the girls that using the word 'male' for transgirls was 'not accurate' and was 'needlessly provocative'. I suspect he had been told by some activist group that mentioning trans people's sex is transphobic. So, without any thought for freedom of speech or women's rights, he ordered the plaintiffs to avoid mentioning the very fact upon which their argument hinged.

Similar distortions are visible in the *Equal Treatment Bench Book*, a quasi-official guide for British judges. It uses jargon that appears nowhere in law, such as 'gender assigned at birth'. It presents preferred pronouns as compulsory and deadnaming as 'highly disrespectful'. Never mind that a defendant's sex and former name may be salient to a case – or that other people in a courtroom may be under oath to tell what they regard as the truth.

The main route whereby campaign groups influence public discourse and policy is via businesses keen to virtue-signal at little cost. Take the HRC's Corporate Equality Index, which companies join to demonstrate commitment to diversity and inclusion. The scoring rewards those that implement programmes such as the HRC's 'Transgender Inclusion in the Workplace'. This recommends that companies advocate publicly for gender self-ID, and presents self-ID as the proper criterion for access to single-sex spaces and schemes intended to help women advance at work.

The British equivalent of the HRC is Stonewall. More than 850 organisations, employing around a quarter of the national workforce, are signed up to its 'diversity champions' scheme. The training and materials they receive claim falsely that UK law gives employees and customers the right to use single-sex spaces that match their self-declared identities. Companies rise in the rankings if they put up signage encouraging the use of toilets and changing rooms on the basis of gender self-identification, or make all facilities gender-neutral. That such policies dispropor-tionately harm female people, and thus arguably constitute ille-gal indirect discrimination, is never mentioned.

Such schemes are generally thought to encourage corporate good-citizenship. But they lead companies to focus on the wishes of some employees and ignore the rest. Moreover, they can be used for the third element of policy capture – threats of trouble. Companies that resist the recommended policies risk a social-media storm, and perhaps a boycott.

In fact, most businesses are happy to play along. In an age of corporate social responsibility, it is convenient to have a tiny oppressed minority to focus on. Rainbow lanyards, pronoun badges and 'all-gender' toilets cost little or nothing. Opening a crèche, offering paid internships for working-class youngsters or adapting the workplace for disabled employees would do more for genuine diversity and inclusion. But these policies would be expensive and, without powerful lobbies promoting them, do less to burnish a company's reputation.

One business sector, in particular, has benefited from trans-activism: health care. Helping gender-dysphoric people feel comfortable in their bodies makes no one much money; turning them into lifelong patients is highly profitable. In the US, puberty blockers cost around $20,000 a year. Cross-sex hormones are cheaper, but taken for decades. 'Top surgery' – breast implants for transwomen and double mastectomy for transmen – costs at least $10,000. Vaginoplasty costs $10,000–30,000; more for someone whose missed out on puberty and hence has child-sized genitals, since skin will have to be harvested from elsewhere. 'Bottom surgery' for transmen starts at around $20,000 for metoidioplasty, which takes advantage of the clitoral growth caused by testosterone to create a small pseudo-phallus. Phalloplasty costs as much as $150,000.

For reshaping facial features to look more typical of the opposite sex – shaving bone from the jaw, nose and brow for transwomen and building them up for transmen; plumping up or slimming down lips; altering the eye sockets – the sky is the limit. And the rise of novel gender identities is creating new, lucrative possibilities. The US has a few doctors willing to satisfy the fantasies of men who want vaginas but not to sacrifice their penises. In 'penile preservation vaginoplasty', skin is taken from the scrotum, and perhaps also the abdominal lining, to create a neovagina. Other non-binary surgeries include 'gender nullification': the removal of all sex organs, and perhaps the nipples and navel too.

Until recently, gender clinicians tried to treat only patients whom they were sure would benefit, and to go slowly to minimise regret. Now that caution has been thrown to the winds, groups that promote gender-affirmative treatment have some of the world's most powerful lobbyists in their corner. American hospitals and nursing homes spend $100 million a year on lobbying the federal government. Big Pharma spends more. A paper published in *JAMA Internal Medicine* in May 2020 estimated that between 1999 and 2018 the pharmaceutical and health-product industry spent $4.7 billion on lobbying the federal government; another $414 million on contributions to presidential and congressional candidates, national party committees and outside spending groups; and $877 million on contributions to state candidates and committees.

This money is intended to influence a broad range of policies. But it would be naive to think that manufacturers of puberty blockers and cross-sex hormones, or hospitals offering gender surgeries, do not seek to shape policies on gender medicine. And indeed, in the past few years the number of Americans whose health insurance covers gender procedures has increased hugely. That includes everyone with plans bought on Obamacare exchanges, Medicaid in many states, and most universities' and big employers' schemes.

Lobbyists also seek to influence the 'standards of care' produced by expert groups. As medicine becomes more special-ised, these have growing influence on which procedures are done, what insurance will pay for – and what will get you sued. America's National Academy of Medicine has drawn up guid-ance on ensuring independence and high standards when setting standards of care. Those for gender dysphoria drawn up in 2011 by WPATH – the renamed Harry Benjamin Foundation – fall woefully short.

They were not based on any systematic review process, since the necessary research base did not exist. And by the National Academy's criteria, the working group that drew them up was far from independent. Those criteria place great weight on avoiding conflicts of interest, which may be financial or intellectual, such as having published in the field. Not everyone involved needs to be independent, in this sense – it is reasonable to include some subject specialists. But most members should be experts in weigh-ing evidence, such as statisticians and epidemiologists, who are not associated with any particular treatment approach.

Every single member of the committee that produced the WPATH standards had potential conflicts of interest, in this sense. Some were simply experts (Ken Zucker was one). But others had received grants from trans-advocacy groups, and several members, including the chair, came from a single department at the University of Minnesota that receives funding from Jennifer Pritzker's Tawani Foundation.

The membership of WPATH has long included trans people and advocates, as well as gender clinicians. In recent years it has tilted ever further from evidence-based medicine and towards activism. In 2017, between Zucker's sacking and his vindication, he was invited to speak at WPATH's annual conference. Activists protested, his presentation was cancelled and the organisation apologised for inviting him. New standards of care are being drawn up as I write. But I see no reason to expect any turn back from ideology and towards evidence.

*

One effective technique for capturing government policy is to persuade bureaucrats and courts to take baby steps. None individually raises concerns, but you can still end up very far from where you started. And since it is rare to reverse legal changes, the movement is mostly one way.

In country after country, campaign groups have first argued that if governments allow doctors to offer sex-change operations at all, they are recognising a lived sex role that may differ from natal sex, and should therefore grant it legal status. Anything else, they say, would be cruel to post-operative transsexuals who live in stealth and should not have to 'out' themselves when asked to show official documents. Once the principle of legal sex change has been established, campaigners seek to weaken the conditions. Even though they started by talking about post-operative transsexuals, they now describe making surgery a condition of legal sex change as a human-rights violation, since that surgery causes sterilisation. In 2017, that argument persuaded the European Court of Human Rights, and it ordered all European countries to allow legal sex change without surgery.

Campaigners also engage in another reframing: from gender dysphoria, which requires diagnosis, to gender variance, a supposed natural human characteristic. They then argue to remove medical gatekeeping. Over time, a legal exception for a few suffering individuals becomes a right to receive cross-sex hormones and body-modifying surgeries, and to be treated on demand as a member of the opposite sex.

The steps can be accelerated by taking advantage of governments' tendency to look abroad for policy models. An official-sounding group in one place writes a document laying out ambitious demands. One elsewhere then cites that document as a 'benchmark' or 'model law' or 'international best practice'. Any success it has sets a new baseline for lobbying efforts around the world.

This international, multi-step journey towards legal gender self-identification started in 1992, when Phyllis Frye, an American transwoman and lawyer, founded the International Conference on Transgender Law and Employment Policy. It met annually until 1996, and produced an impressive-sounding 'International Bill of Transgender Rights'. (One of the founding members was Martine Rothblatt, the author of *From Transgender to Transhuman*, whom I introduced in chapter 7.) Some of its demands would probably have garnered widespread support at the time: to be able to wear what you want, and to be gender non-conforming without losing your job. But others would have seemed crazy: to be able to enter 'gendered space' and participate in 'gendered activity', even if your gender identity is not 'in accord with chromosomal sex, genitalia, assigned birth sex, or initial gender role'.

Around the same time two British transmen, Stephen Whittle and Mark Rees, set up Press for Change. In 1997 it published 'Five principles for the evaluation of legislative proposals covering transgendered people in the United Kingdom', a similar document to that produced by the American group, with which it had made contact shortly after both were founded.

When the UK government set up an Interdepartmental Group on Transsexual Rights in 1999, Whittle was an adviser. Three years later, the British government lost a case in the European Court of Human Rights brought by Christine Goodwin, a transwoman who wanted to count as a woman for the purposes of marriage and government bureaucracy. The groundwork had been laid, and Whittle was one of those who ensured that the Gender Recognition Act of 2004 did not restrict legal sex change to post-operative transsexuals – even though that was all the European judgment had required. The first national law to take this position, it was immediately cited as a new baseline by campaigners elsewhere.

The next step in the journey was the biggest: the publication of the 'Yogyakarta Principles' in 2007. They are the parallel in human-rights law to the addition of the 'T' to the 'LGB' in American activism around the same time. They established a new acronym, SOGI (sexual orientation and gender identity), thus yoking the two disparate concepts together in legal discussions, public policy and education. And though they have no official standing and have never been adopted by any international body, they are constantly cited by lobbyists as 'best practice' and a model for governments to follow.

The principles were drawn up at a meeting in 2006 in Yogyakarta, a tourist destination in Indonesia, organised by NGOs seeking to support national and international gay-rights campaigns. The focus was supposed to be on decriminalisation of homosexuality. Whittle was one of the few attendees who was a proponent of the idea, still marginal in the coalescing LGBT community, that gender identity, rather than sex, should be centred in law. The principles took the most extreme position encoded in national law at the time – the UK's Gender Recognition Act – and claimed that international human-rights law required all governments to copy it.

Ten years later, at another meeting, the principles were updated. By then Argentina, Malta and Ireland had introduced gender self-identification, and 'YP+10' again proclaimed that the outlier should become the baseline. Indeed, they went further, claiming that all gender identities should gain official recognition, and governments should allow citizens to change their sex on any document whenever they want. Gender self-identification should hold in every conceivable circumstance. Everyone should be allowed to play sports without regard to 'sex characteristics' and to receive 'gender-affirming' health care – that is, hormones and surgeries – on demand, covered by insurance or the public purse.

Even these extreme policies – beyond anything any government had ever implemented – were presented as temporary measures on the way to an ultimate goal. Principle 31 of YP+10 declared that governments should 'end the registration of the sex and gender of the person in identity documents such as birth certificates, identification cards, passports and driver licences, and as part of their legal personality'. This is the logical endpoint of gender-identity ideology: the abolition of sex as a concept in law.

Robert Wintemute, a professor of human-rights law at King's College London, attended the first Yogyakarta meeting. His focus at the time was gay rights, though he had been sufficiently influenced by trans ideology to have written a book chapter entitled 'Sexual orientation and gender identity', which had appeared the previous year. His thinking has changed considerably since then. He now questions whether governments should ever have enabled legal sex to be changed in the first place, rather than protecting trans people by passing laws against violence, harassment and discrimination triggered by a difference between appearance and sex. And he thinks the coalition of the LGB and T should be disbanded.

What has changed his mind is the 'escalation of demands', from post-surgery sex change to self-ID to the abolition of legal sex. 'The nerve of them, to say that all states must abolish sex on birth certificates!' he exclaims. 'To say that international human-rights law requires something of all states that not a single state had ever done.'

*

In 2015 it was the turn of my home country, Ireland, to take the baton in the international self-ID relay race. The story started almost two decades earlier, in 1997, when a post-operative transsexual, Lydia Foy, took legal action against the government for refusing to grant her a new birth certificate with the sex changed. In 2002 she lost her case in the Irish High Court. But the Goodwin judgment came two days later, and the following year Ireland adopted European human-rights law. The country's lack of provision for legal sex change was now unsustainable – though the government did not act until 2011, when an advisory group recommended a gate-kept process modelled on British law.

But policy capture ensured that Ireland ended up with something quite different. Only transactivist groups gave evidence to the parliamentary committee scrutinising the proposals. Among those lobbying for self-ID was Michael O'Flaherty, who had been rapporteur at the first Yogyakarta meeting. He recommended copying Argentina instead – at the time the only country with self-ID. No mention was made of women's safety or privacy at any point.

The lobbying succeeded. First, medical gatekeeping was reduced to requiring a doctor to sign off on applications. Shortly before the bill was passed, in mid-2015, even that safeguard was removed. With one leap, Ireland went from having no provision for changing legal sex to allowing anyone to do so 'for all purposes' by printing out a form, writing their name, address, email and government ID number, signing a declaration of serious intent in front of a solicitor or notary, and posting the form with their original birth certificate. There is not even a fee.

Gender self-identification was one of three big societal shifts in Ireland in just four years. The way it became law is in stark contrast with the other two. It provides a further demonstration, if any were needed, that this is no broad-based civil-rights movement, but the work of well-funded lobbyists carried out behind the scenes.

Earlier in 2015, a referendum on same-sex marriage passed with a high turnout and sixty-two percent in favour. In 2018, another referendum legalised abortion with an even larger majority. Both made me proud to be Irish, though as a non-resident I could not vote. The public discourse was exemplary. The government published model laws, and the independent Referendum Commission set out the issues in clear language. Many journalists, celebrities and ordinary people were moved to come out – about their sexuality, or about having travelled to England for an abortion. Both campaigns united the country, and taught us more about ourselves and our fellow citizens.

But there was no public consultation or information campaign about gender self-ID. Even now, hardly anyone I talk to in Ireland knows they could change their legal sex more cheaply and easily than they could get a passport. And that, it turns out, was deliberate.

In 2019 Dentons, the world's largest law firm, published a report it had prepared pro bono for IGLYO, a European network of youth LGBT organisations. Entitled 'Only Adults? Good Practices in Legal Gender Recognition for Youth', it argued for the right to change one's legal sex at any age without parental consent. It acknowledged that this would be unpopular with the public. But other unpopular trans-rights policies had already become law, it explained – citing gender self-identification in Ireland. It recommended linking such proposals with unrelated ones that commanded broad support; in Ireland, it said, self-ID had been brought in under cover of same-sex marriage. And it advised staying out of the news. Irish transactivists had 'directly lobbied individual politicians and tried to keep press coverage to a minimum'.

Neither Argentina nor Malta, which introduced gender self-identification just before Ireland, has Ireland's friendly, wholesome image. Now transactivists had their poster child. Mention gender self-ID anywhere else, and you will probably hear that Ireland introduced it 'with no problems'.

It never seemed likely that legally recognising males as female 'for all purposes' would cause no problems. But it took time before any came to light. At first limited public awareness helped, since only people engaged with transactivist groups availed themselves of the new law. But if you create a loophole, soon enough someone undesirable will use it – and it will be the most vulnerable who suffer.

Ireland is a small country with relatively little crime. Around a thousand women receive prison sentences each year, almost all short ones for petty offences. At any moment, around 170 are behind bars, of whom between zero and three have committed sex crimes. Until 2019, not a single woman had ever been imprisoned for a sex crime against an adult. Since then, Irish prisons have experienced a sudden influx of 'female' sex offenders – according to official records. As you will have guessed, the perpetrators are in fact male.

The first, whose name is not public, was convicted in July 2019 on ten counts of sexual assault, and one of cruelty to a child. This person has changed legal sex but undergone no surgical or hormonal transition – in other words, is a physiologically normal male. The sentence is being served in a women's prison, where the prisoner is accompanied by two guards whenever in communal areas.

'The law that was enacted in 2015 did not envisage this situation,' said Robert Purcell of the Irish Law Society when the case came to light. 'And it puts the prison service and the courts in a difficult position.' With all due respect to Purcell, it certainly does – but the law did envisage it. This is what treating a male person as female 'for all purposes' means, even if Irish politicians did not think it through.

The next case was more disturbing still. Reporting restrictions in Ireland mean I cannot name the transwoman concerned – absurdly, since the case was widely reported before the restrictions, and the information is from official sources. So I will call this person Kandi, which captures some of the obsession with plastic femininity that clearly inspired the female name this transwoman chose.

In 2020, Kandi was charged on two counts of sexual assault and four counts of threatening to murder women. Kandi's history merits a good deal of compassion. But I am sorrier for the women who are Kandi's targets, and I think that the fiction that this horrifyingly damaged male is a woman only causes further harm to everyone.

Here, in brief, is Kandi's life story. At the end of 2001 a male child was born to a woman with a sadistic and abusive partner.

Straight away, the father started to abuse the child, too. As he grew older, the child was recruited to join in the abuse of his mother. Later psychiatric reports found that he identified with his father and had learned to be violent to order. His mother fled home with him when he was eight. Aged ten, he carried out a serious attack against her. In the years following, his behaviour became more violent and sexualised.

Aged thirteen, he committed another serious assault on a woman. He was twice sentenced to young offenders' institutions for violent crimes. At fifteen he said he was a girl. He was assessed at the Tavistock (Ireland has no paediatric gender clinic), where clinicians could not tell whether he truly had gender dysphoria, or whether his cross-sex identification was sincere. They suspected that he had researched gender-identity issues and was responding by rote.

Aged seventeen, he attacked another woman, trying to gouge out her eyes, ripping her eyelids and pulling out clumps of her hair. Fortunately, a witness called the police. He told the police that the victim's screams were music to his ears and he was sorry he had not killed her. A psychiatric assessment predicted further assaults. He expressed a desire to rape and murder women, and to kill his mother – and to move to Los Angeles after sex-reassignment surgery to work in the porn industry and prostitution.

When he turned eighteen, the police advised his mother to go into hiding. He changed his name to a female one by deed poll and used the provisions of self-ID to become legally female. The arrests came shortly afterwards. As I write, Kandi is held in a women's prison and Ireland continues to enable violent males to identify as women 'for all purposes'.

12

THROUGH THE
LOOKING GLASS

How transactivism is chipping
away at civil society

As human-rights organisations have embraced gender-identity ideology, they have adopted policies that harm the most disadvantaged, all the while spouting the language of intersectionality. And they have abandoned the constituencies they were founded to fight for. In the US, this trend is so pronounced that anyone on the Left who opposes gender self-identification has to seek allies on the Right – and be dismissed as a sell-out – or accept not being heard at all.

Established women's groups are the most obvious culprits. If they had stood up for women's right to single-sex spaces and services, gender self-ID could never have made such inroads. Instead, as they adopted a postmodern, 'woke' style of feminism, they abandoned the women who needed them most.

It is remarkable that in the US – the only developed country lacking paid maternity leave and universal health care, and where women's reproductive rights are under constant attack – so-called feminists have prioritised the demands of transwomen, that is, of males. Poor women and girls of colour, who are more likely to attend state schools, to need homeless and rape-crisis shelters, or to fall victim to the war on drugs and end up in prison, depended on feminists to stand up for single-sex spaces. It is a perfect example of when intersectional thinking is needed – and a travesty that gender self-identification is so often described as intersectional.

The Gavin Grimm 'bathrooms' case had been due at the Supreme Court before Donald Trump became president. No established American women's organisation filed an amicus brief defending single-sex spaces before the federal government's gender self-ID policies were withdrawn, and it was sent back down. That was left to Safe Spaces for Women, a tiny, ad-hoc grouping of rape and assault survivors – a constituency you would have thought any women's organisation would keep front of mind. Its brief expressed 'a strong interest in ensuring that the voices of women who have suffered sexual abuse are heeded when policies are made that may directly affect their physical, emotional, and psychological well-being . . . survivors of sexual assault are likely to suffer psychological trauma as a result of encountering biological males – even those with entirely innocent intentions – in the traditional safe spaces of women's showers, locker rooms, and bathrooms.'

No established women's organisation opposed the idea that, by identifying as a woman, Aimee Stephens thereby became covered by an employer's female dress code. It was left to the Women's Liberation Front (WoLF), a small radical-feminist network, to argue that Stephens's demand to be allowed to dress as a woman made sense in the context of sex-separated dress codes only if you define manhood and womanhood as the performance of masculinity and femininity.

WoLF's positions are those of feminism's second wave, and had Stephens argued instead that neither men nor women should be required to follow sex-stereotyped dress codes, it would have agreed wholeheartedly. But filing an amicus brief to the Supreme Court in support of a conservative employer represented by the Alliance Defending Freedom meant that both it and its arguments were dismissed by pretty much every other left-wing group. It is a catch-22 that Natasha Chart, chair of its board until mid-2021, is very familiar with: speak up against gender self-ID and get called a shill for the Right; or stay silent and see other left-wingers claim that only the Right is opposed.

In 2015, Chart had been sacked from her job with a reproductive-rights campaign group for writing about her opposition to legalised prostitution and gender self-ID. None of the allies from her long history of feminist and environmental activism supported her; instead they 'unfriended me, denounced me, described me as a physical threat to trans people, said I was genocidal'. Then, as one left-wing group after another adopted the self-ID cause, she watched those former allies campaign for male rapists and murderers to be allowed to transfer to women's prisons on demand.

'I did not come to politics to work with people who gave this little of a fuck about women prisoners, who everybody knows have overwhelmingly been victims of child-abuse, domestic violence and commercial sex exploitation,' she says. 'These women have no political representation, cannot vote, cannot talk to the press. And the people who should be speaking up for them have abandoned them. If my two options are talk to the ADF, or talk to somebody on the Left who calls me a fascist KKK bleep bleep bleep and hopes I die in a fire, is it even a choice?'

The taboo on aligning with the Right to oppose gender self-ID goes far beyond what is standard for America's polarised politics. The Women's Human Rights Campaign, a global group of volunteer women aligned with second-wave feminism, has written a Women's Declaration on Sex-Based Rights, which women everywhere are invited to sign. Its American arm is non-partisan, and willing to work with like-minded individuals and organisations across the political spectrum. 'We get pushback,' says Kara Dansky, who now works for the organisation's American arm (and is a former ACLU attorney and former member of WoLF's board). 'It's astounding to me, because men's groups work across the aisle all the time. Everyone who understands American politics knows that you have to work across party lines. The ACLU is very open and proud about its associations with conservative organisations on topics such as criminal-justice reform and the First Amendment.'

That support for self-ID has led self-proclaimed feminists to abandon the most vulnerable women is remarkable enough. Even more remarkably, it has led organisations right across civil society not only to abandon their core principles, but to actively work against them. This is further evidence – if any were needed – that the campaign for self-ID is the opposite of a civil-rights movement.

The idea that what makes someone a man or woman is perfor-mance of, or identification with, gender is incompatible with the foundational feminist belief that women, like men, are fully human and should not be restricted by stereotypes. Same-sex orientation cannot be defended if people are self-defined identi-ties, rather than fleshly mortals whose sex can easily be perceived by others. Free speech is incompatible with privileging discourse over material reality. Feminist and gay-rights groups that adopt gender-identity ideology therefore end up promoting policies that harm women and gay people. Children's charities tear up safeguarding procedures. Scientific societies repeat cultish mantras. Anti-censorship campaigners whip up witch-hunts.

The American National Women's Law Center, which was instrumental in using civil-rights law to strengthen women's sports, endorses the Democrats' proposed Equality Act, which would destroy them. Its director, who also sits on the board of the Transgender Law Center, claims that no females will be harmed by the inclusion of transwomen in sport. The girls forced to compete with males in Connecticut who lost out on medals and opportunities to be seen by university talent scouts would beg to disagree.

Established gay-rights groups have stood by as people who assert same-sex orientation are told that they have a 'genital fetish' and lesbians are told to accept penises as female sex organs. Indeed, those groups have joined in the bullying. Stonewall was founded to fight homophobia. Yet, at a Pride March in 2019, when lesbians waving banners that read 'Lesbians don't have penises' and 'Pro women not anti-trans' were threatened, the chair of Stonewall's board praised the bullies, tweeting: 'Thank you! The right instinct'.

Magazines for lesbians used to rail against 'compulsory hetero-sexuality' – the homophobic notion that a lesbian was simply a woman who hadn't yet met the right man. Now they denounce women who describe themselves as same-sex-attracted, rather than same-gender-attracted. They call their core readership 'vagina-havers' and the like, and run articles on subjects such as how to pleasure bepenised transwomen (top tip from *Autostraddle*: avoid saying 'blow job' so as not to trigger dysphoria).

Planned Parenthood, which used to provide contraception and evidence-based sex education to teenagers, now prescribes puberty blockers and cross-sex hormones practically on demand, and presents gender-identity ideology as scientific fact. ActionAid UK, which campaigns against female genital mutilation and period poverty, says there is 'no such thing as a biologically female/male body'. The NSPCC, Britain's largest children's charity, provides training in child-safeguarding principles, which include separating children's sleeping quarters by sex and ensuring that concerns about child safety are not ignored. But it cancelled an 'ask me anything' session on Mumsnet because most of the pre-submitted questions concerned the impact of gender self-identification on child safeguarding.

The British Humanist Association says it aims to 'make sense of the world through logic, reason, and evidence'. But its president, Alice Roberts, has blocked Twitter users who asked her to define sex and cited clownfish as evidence that no such definition exists. Its American counterpart says it opposes all pseudoscience, whether religious or secular. But in 2021 it withdrew an award it had bestowed a quarter-century earlier on eminent scientist and freethinker Richard Dawkins. His heresy was to express an interest in the differing treatments of transracialism and transgenderism.

The ACLU's support for free speech was once so absolute that in 1978 it defended neo-Nazis' right to march through a Chicago suburb where Holocaust survivors lived. But an internal document leaked in 2018 revealed that its support is now conditional, because 'speech that denigrates [marginalised] groups can inflict serious harms and is intended to and often will impede progress towards equality'. Members of the global anti-censorship group PEN must pledge to 'oppose any form of suppression of freedom of expression'. But in 2020, when Scottish writers were no-platformed for supporting sex-based rights, PEN's Scottish branch refused to support them, saying that free expression was 'complex', and 'any policy that ignores such complexity can stifle the free expression of a range of stakeholders, most notably members of marginalised communities'.

*

Another plank of liberal democracy is also buckling under the strain of gender-identity ideology: journalism. Parts of the British press are still willing to sin against modern pieties. The tabloids – and a couple of quality dailies and magazines – judged correctly that their readers would want to know that women were losing their jobs for arguing against gender self-ID, and that gender-dysphoric children were being medicalised. But much worse happens in the US and Canada, and their mainstream media remain silent. In 2017 CBC, Canada's public broadcaster, abandoned plans to air a BBC documentary about paediatric transitioning – filmed largely in Canada – within hours of transactivists complaining.

As journalism became a graduate profession, new entrants brought the censoriousness of campus activism with them. Beat specialists, detailed reportage and fact-checking became casualties as advertising revenue dried up. Activist groups learned that biased, or even false, press releases had a good chance of being quoted verbatim. I could find no mainstream, liberal American outlet that quoted the Obama-era departmental circular ordering gender self-identification in schools. Instead, they cited transactivists and described it as 'preventing transphobia' or 'advancing trans rights' – suggesting a benign crackdown on bigotry that affected no one but trans people. It was left to conservative and religious publications such as *The Federalist*, *National Review* and *Daily Signal* to report what the document actually said.

No mainstream or liberal outlet published anything about Natasha Chart's sacking. The only newspaper that ran a story about a feminist fired for defending sex-based rights and opposing legalised prostitution was the *Christian Post*. As WoLF became active in opposition to gender self-identification, Chart and the other members received rape and death threats. This too

went unremarked by mainstream outlets. 'We could be threatened and attacked, and they wouldn't care,' says Chart. 'If we
didn't try to get the message out in the conservative media,
anything could happen to us and it would be like it never
happened.'

The first duty of journalists is reporting: describing the world
as it is. This should ensure that public opinion is never a mystery,
and the outcomes of votes are never a shock. A referendum or
election may be too close to call, but the result should never
have seemed inconceivable beforehand. Mainstream outlets are
often criticised for their political and intellectual monoculture,
which makes for one-sided reporting on issues where the elec-
torate is split down the middle, such as Brexit and the rise of
Donald Trump. But more of an indictment is how long it took
them to notice how many voters did not share their views.

Journalists' secondary role is to offer commentary: to describe
the world as it might be. But increasingly, they are doing something deceptively similar with a quite different purpose: describing the wished-for world as if it already existed. This is not journalism, or even advocacy. It aims at bringing about change by
decree rather than argument and evidence.

Take an article in the *New York Times* in October 2020:
'World rugby bars transgender women, baffling players'. A well-
reported story would have explained two things this piece failed
to: why World Rugby acted as it did, and that most people
agreed with the move. An op-ed could have argued for gender
self-ID in sport, either by picking holes in World Rugby's
evidence or by contending that other considerations mattered
more than fairness and safety. But this article consisted only of
assertions. It read as if it had emerged from a parallel universe in
which humans were not sexually dimorphic, and to think they
were was 'baffling'. This sort of faux journalism, which presents

an extreme agenda as a fait accompli, has undermined trust in the media and left governments and electorates flying blind.

The problem of biased reporting is amplified by biased moderation on social media. Twitter rarely censures sexualised insults and threats directed at women, but comes down heavy on the use of incorrect pronouns and the like. A Twitter user who calls himself Sam Barber tracks accounts sanctioned for crimes against gender. Among the hundreds on his list are women suspended or banned for saying that 'only women get cervical cancer'; for saying that 'we need to talk about male violence'; for quoting verbatim from the parliamentary debate in 2004 on the UK's Gender Recognition Act; for stating the definition of rape in British law; and for saying, correctly, that the limited statistics available suggest that transwomen in the UK are more likely to commit murder than to be murdered.

This bias chills opposition to transactivism and silences valuable voices. Lara, the detransitioner I quoted in chapter 5, got into an argument on Twitter with a transwoman who insisted she was every bit as female as an 'AFAB' (someone 'assigned female at birth') who had undergone hysterectomy. When Lara, who is still traumatised by the hysterectomy she underwent at age twenty-one, responded 'delusional male', she lost her account. Miranda Yardley, a British transwoman whose scepticism about gender-identity ideology is shared by many other older post-operative transsexuals, though few are as willing to say so, was barred from Twitter for saying that trans people remain of their natal sex.

Meghan Murphy, the founder of the Canadian radfem site 'Feminist Current', was among the first people to write about Jessica Yaniv's repeated litigation against female beauticians. She lost her Twitter account for using male pronouns to refer to Yaniv. The Irish comedian Graham Linehan became an opponent of gender-identity ideology after criticism of an episode of his hit show *The IT Crowd*, in which a man discovers his girlfriend is trans. Linehan's large and heterogeneous following meant he brought gender-identity ideology to the attention of many who would otherwise not have noticed it – and made him a target for mass reporting (assisted, it must be said, by the ease with which he could be goaded). He was suspended from Twitter several times, and finally banned in 2020.

This is part of a general pattern that has been evident throughout this book: the enforcement of gender-identity ideology by threats and silencing. Among the examples I have already discussed are gender clinicians, like Blanchard and Zucker; and researchers and writers, like Bailey and Lawrence. In autumn 2019 Selina Todd, the Oxford historian of women whom I cited in chapter 5, had to be escorted by security guards during lectures because of death threats. Meghan Murphy needs a police guard when she speaks publicly, and venues hosting her routinely receive bomb threats. And there are many others. To cite just a couple, an Australian senator, Claire Chandler, faced a human-rights inquiry after a transactivist complained about a speech in which she argued for female-only spaces and sports. Lidia Falcón, the president of Spain's Feminist Party, was investigated on hate-crime charges because she said that gender self-identification endangers women.

Intimidation and harassment are carried out openly and proudly. Like all social-justice activists, gender-identity ideologues reject the concepts of viewpoint diversity and open debate. In their worldview, speech either opposes or upholds oppression, according to who is speaking and whether their words align with narratives promoted by historically dominant groups. They think that a person speaking from a privileged position – defined in 'intersectional' terms, meaning white, male, 'cis', straight, able-bodied and so on – must be either actively seeking to counter that privilege or else shoring it up. Opposing gender self-identification, then, is by definition bigotry.

If this is how you think the world works, listening to your opponents is not merely pointless, it is harmful. Liberal arguments in favour of free speech, for example that robust debate exposes you to arguments you hadn't thought of and helps you hone your reasoning, are dismissed as irrelevant. Your opponents' speech reinforces injustice, and silencing them is moral, even if that takes violence or the threat of it. Control the discourse, and you control reality.

*

Universities are supposed to perform many roles essential to civil society: submitting received wisdom to re-examination; producing fresh research; and turning out graduates who are familiar with a broad range of ideas and able to reason clearly. But as they have adopted gender-identity ideology, they too have taken the side of the censors. The attacks on Rebecca Tuvel for comparing transracialism with transgenderism, or Lisa Littman for researching teenage gender dysphoria, should have been met with a ringing defence of academic freedom. Instead, academics joined the witch-hunts – or led them.

In 2019 Kathleen Stock, a British philosopher who is one of very few in her field to argue publicly against self-ID, solicited testimonies about the chilling effect of gender-identity ideology in universities. She heard about HR investigations, disciplinary hearings, threats of violence and demands from students that academics be fired. One respondent was removed from the editorship of a journal and another lost a book contract. None had ever harassed a trans student or expressed any bigotry. Their crimes included liking a tweet by a known opponent of self-ID, arguing to include material about sex as well as gender identity in a course, objecting to the word 'cis' and signing an open letter in support of academic freedom.

Even as academics who oppose gender-identity ideology are silenced, others are playing a leading role in the 'knowledge production and dissemination' part of policy capture. As gender studies replaced women's studies, and queer theory leaked into other disciplines, the number of academics who make their living from gender-identity ideology grew. You do not have to be particularly cynical to think that the holder of a chair of transgender studies funded by a trans billionaire or campaign group is unlikely to produce research showing that gender self-identification is harmful for women. A sociology professor with a large grant to study pregnant men is unlikely to suggest that female people taking male hormones should be studied by medics, not sociologists. A law professor with government funding to look at 'gender decertification' – the removal of the male/female marker from birth certificates – is unlikely to conclude that birth certificates record sex, not gender, and should remain unchanged.

These academics' work ripples out into wider society. Some of their ex-students become teachers or HR professionals, and pass on what they have learned to children or write it into company policies. Together with campaigners and lobbyists in human rights and health care, they form an interest group that far outnumbers transgender people themselves. Their interests are in spreading their ideology and keeping their jobs, rather than in making trans people's lives better. And they bring to mind the famous remark of the American writer Upton Sinclair, that 'it is difficult to get a man to understand something when his salary depends upon his not understanding it.'

Women's sports provide a case study in how this new interest group imposes its will via institutions. Every poll finds that allowing males into women's sports is one of the most unpopular aspects of self-ID. If you publicly oppose it, as I have, you will hear privately from athletes of both sexes that they do too. And yet sports regulators are scrambling to introduce self-ID. World Rugby is the only one to have reversed course, and many national federations have rejected its advice.

The idea of self-ID in sport obviously originates with lobby groups. But it would never have become policy without the 'Upton Sinclair crowd', in particular the graduates hired by sports authorities to promote diversity and inclusion. They were brought on board to root out racism and homophobia, and attract new participants and audiences. But when people who claimed to speak for the next minority came knocking, they were ready listeners. They had been hired explicitly to increase 'diversity and inclusion', after all, and the wider the net is cast, the more important their jobs are. They were neither paid nor qualified to consider safety and fairness.

Why didn't female athletes kick up a fuss? The answer has three parts: the difficulty of co-ordinating; the fact that young women are gender-identity ideology's foot-soldiers; and, finally, the third element of policy capture – threats.

Trans inclusion presents female athletes with what economists call a collective-action problem. The classic example is the 'tragedy of the commons', whereby jointly owned land becomes infertile because everyone entitled to graze their animals on it has an incentive to take more than their fair share. All female athletes will lose from admitting males into women's sports, but each individually has incentives to stay quiet. Trans athletes are, after all, not numerous, so each woman can cross her fingers and hope to get through her career without coming up against one. Athletes' professional lives are short, so even a year or two distracted by a fight that may not be of personal benefit is a huge sacrifice. And sponsors do not like controversy, even in a noble cause.

Female athletes are also prone to the same psychological biases and societal pressures as other women. Compared with men, women score higher in tests of agreeableness and anxiety, and are keener to get along with others and easier to guilt-trip. They face harsher social sanctions for asserting themselves and prioritising their own needs. And gender-identity ideology is the main shibboleth of progressive circles – I know young women who lost their entire friendship group because they refused to say that transwomen should be regarded as women in all circumstances.

One of the draws of gender-identity ideology is that it allows women to deny that they are physically weaker and more vulnerable than men. Of course, physical differences are precisely why men's and women's sports are segregated – but that segregation also means women are not faced with the performance gap as a daily reality. Pretending it does not exist may appeal to female athletes because they will have spent their lives insisting they are as good as men. Rather than adding the rider, 'within my own sex class', it may be tempting instead to say, 'I'll take any man on' – knowing in a corner of their mind that no one is likely to call their bluff.

Another societal pressure comes from what social scientists call 'intra-group status jockeying'. The idea is that people seek not only to elevate groups they are part of, but also to elevate themselves within those groups. You see this when successful women oppose extending maternity rights because they didn't need 'handouts' to get where they are; or when women blame rape victims for being 'careless'. These women are positioning themselves as superior to others who are too feeble to make it in a man's world, or too silly to stay safe. Of course, this makes them sound like bitches. A female athlete who supports trans inclusion, by contrast, gets to appear generous and inclusive, even as she positions herself as superior to women who acknowledge that they require a separate sex class to be competitive.

I will give an example, while emphasising that it is in no way exceptional. In an article for *The Advocate*, an LGBT magazine, American rugby player Naima Reddick says she supports trans inclusion because she has competed against males during training 'without hesitation because I'm confident in my skill set'. She compares playing against transwomen to playing against tall women (she is shorter than the average female rugby player). 'When I play, I look across the field to judge my opponent, go into my toolbox, and pick what I can use to win the one-on-one battle,' she says. If any of this was an argument for allowing males to play against women, then Reddick would be able to qualify for the men's national team, and sports would never have been sex-separated.

Opponents of trans inclusion in sports are not only belittled, but dismissed as whiners. *Slate* described Selina Soule as a 'sore loser' for objecting to males entering her races. Sharron Davies still recalls with resentment hearing the same phrase when she complained about her virilised East German competitors. In 1976 Shirley Babashoff, the star of the US Olympic swimming team, responded snappishly to a reporter who asked her opinion of those East Germans: 'Well, except for their deep voices and moustaches, I think they'll probably do fine.' She was mocked in the press, described as 'shrill' and 'angry', and nicknamed 'Surly Shirley'. *Sports Illustrated* captioned a picture of her: 'Loser'. The message to women comes through loud and clear: complain about unfair competition, and it will be open season.

If all that weren't enough, any female athlete who speaks out risks being dropped from her squad or team. The diversity, inclusion and anti-bullying policies now universal in sport were written in partnership with LGBT groups, and impose fines and suspensions for racist and homophobic behaviour, and latterly for 'transphobia' – defined to include any questioning of someone's gender identity. I doubt many senior administrators or female athletes understood the full import when those policies were written. But by the time sports administrators decided to allow males to self-ID as females, the people most affected had already been silenced.

13

THEY CAN'T FIRE US ALL

How British women are starting to fight back

In 1925, John Scopes, a teacher in Tennessee, was charged with the misdemeanour of teaching the theory of evolution. William Jennings Bryan, a three-time presidential candidate, made the case for the prosecution. Scopes lost, and teaching evolution remained banned in Tennessee for another forty years. The 'Scopes monkey trial' became a byword for science denialism and the battle between faith and reason.

Fast-forward almost a century to see the modern-day equivalent play out in an employment tribunal in London, in late 2019. Like the Scopes trial, it was a depressing reminder of the power of a state-backed belief system to compel citizens' actions and speech, and to punish those who dissent. It was also the start of a fightback against gender-identity ideology that is gathering pace in the UK, and inspiring similar movements around the world.

The protagonist is Maya Forstater, who has lost her job in the London office of the Center for Global Development, a think-tank headquartered in Washington. It objected to her stating a scientific fact as incontrovertible as evolution – that in humans, male and female are distinct, immutable categories – and adding that she regarded acknowledging this fact as essential to protecting women's rights. The previous year, Forstater had tweeted that sex was a matter of biology, not identity, and that making it easier to change legal sex would harm women. The think-tank claimed she was transphobic and let her go.

Forstater argued before the tribunal that her views constituted a 'protected belief' under the UK's Equality Act of 2010, and that her employer had unlawfully discriminated against her. Some of the questions she was asked were as ridiculous as those posed to Scopes. How had she formed her 'novel' belief that sex in humans was immutable, the barrister for her former employer asked? On what basis did she think male people couldn't become female? Could she name philosophers who agreed with her? How could she know someone's sex if she hadn't been present at their birth? Doctors 'assigned' sex by looking at newborns and using 'guesswork', did they not? (At which the room, packed with women supporting Forstater, erupted in laughter.)

Forstater did her best to present her awareness of the objective reality and significance of mammalian bodies as a distinctive creed, like Judaism or ethical veganism. But the judge ruled against her. Her belief that human sex is binary and immutable was 'absolutist', he said. Quoting the case of Grainger v. Nicholson, which laid down guidance on when beliefs are legally protected, he ruled that Forstater's satisfied several of the conditions, by being sincere, cogent, serious and important – but failed the final one, by being 'not worthy of respect in a democratic society'.

First-instance employment tribunals in the UK do not set precedent. Forstater's appeal was heard in April 2021, and at the time of writing, the judgment had not been issued. But whether she wins or loses, it seems possible that there will be a further appeal. The case may end up in the UK's Supreme Court. And her initial defeat, like that of Scopes, was a triumph in the court of public opinion. News of how entrenched gender-identity ideology had become went worldwide when J. K. Rowling tweeted to her fourteen million followers: 'Dress however you please. Call yourself whatever you like. Sleep with any consenting adult who'll have you. Live your best life in peace and security. But force women out of their jobs for stating that sex is real? #IStandWithMaya #ThisIsNotADrill'.

'All hell broke loose,' says Forstater. 'It was in the papers in Australia; it was in *Variety*; I had the *Daily Mail* on the doorstep.' Gaining the support of one of the world's most beloved authors was surreal, but also a much-needed boost. The ruling had been 'completely devastating', she says. Some reports had claimed that she had harassed a trans colleague – though she had no trans colleagues and had not harassed anyone. 'The judge concluded that by using the definition of "woman" in the Equality Act I had said something that was not worthy of respect in a democratic society,' she says. 'It's Kafkaesque to say that when you quote the law that protects your rights you are being offensive, and should therefore have no rights.'

Forstater had become interested in issues of sex and gender a decade earlier, when her children were small, and she had spent time on the Mumsnet feminism chat board. In 2012 she co-founded the Let Toys Be Toys campaign, which called out retailers for sexist stereotyping – such as science kits marketed to boys, with a pink-and-sparkles version for girls. When she first heard of gender self-identification, she assumed it was 'the next gay marriage'. Then she started to see women who seemed to be neither religious nor conservative expressing doubts online. When she searched for information, she found nothing from women's or civil-rights groups, or the liberal media.

She returned to Mumsnet, where she found 'a think-tank of smart women considering safeguarding and legal issues;

collecting and analysing evidence in ways that civil-society organisations were not doing'. She became convinced that self-ID would harm women, angry that those whose responsibility it was to do this work had abdicated – and determined to say something. 'I didn't think I was vulnerable', she says, 'because I worked for a think-tank that welcomes evidence and debate.'

So she started to tweet about her concerns. Her employer asked her to remove its name from her Twitter profile and to avoid 'exclusionary statements'. Then a few American colleagues complained to HR. Step by step the offer of a contract for the next few years was walked back. Because she had stated publicly why she thought laws banning sex discrimination and protect-ing single-sex spaces should remain anchored in material reality, she found herself out of a job.

She decided to sue her ex-employer, and launched a campaign on CrowdJustice to cover the costs. It hit her initial target of £30,000 in five hours, and £60,000 stretch target in less than a day. Thousands of people donated, on average £27. Many added messages to the effect of 'thank you for standing up to this'.

Forstater had waded into a pitched battle. British transactiv-ists, like those elsewhere, were seeking to redefine sex to mean gender identity – but British law presented obstacles. They had proceeded along several tracks: promoting novel legal interpre-tations in academic writing and public advocacy; convincing businesses to go beyond the law; and finally, for complete certainty, pressing to get the law changed.

Six years after the Gender Recognition Act was passed, the Equality Act consolidated dozens of anti-discrimination laws into a single, over-arching framework. It illustrates how much better it is to create such protections by writing laws, which can consider exceptions and trade-offs, rather than via court cases, as in the US. It protects nine characteristics, both at work and in the provision of services. 'Religion or belief' covers formal religions and any serious personal philosophy – for example environmentalism. But it excludes beliefs that trample on other people's rights – Holocaust denial, for example. It was in this category that the Forstater judgment placed feminist belief in the significance of biological sex.

Two of the other characteristics are 'sex' and 'gender reassignment'. The first is defined as 'male' and 'female'; the second covers anyone who is 'proposing to undergo, is undergoing or has undergone a process (or part of a process) for the purpose of reassigning the person's sex by changing physiological or other attributes of sex'. This category probably includes around a hundred times more people than the 6,000 or so who have used the Gender Recognition Act to change their legal sex.

Crucially, having the protected characteristic of gender reassignment does not give someone the right to use facilities intended for the opposite sex: rather, it covers discrimination in work and everyday life, such as being sacked or refused service in a pub. The act expressly cites many single-sex settings for women where even transwomen who have changed legal sex can be excluded, including group counselling for victims of sexual assault, hospital wards and communal accommodation. Women's sport can also be reserved for natal females, if that is necessary for safety or fairness.

All this shows that it is possible to grant trans people legal protections without destroying women's rights or denying the reality of bodily sex. And it leaves British transactivists who are determined to press for gender self-ID far less room for manoeuvre than their counterparts in the US. So they promote novel interpretations of both laws. For the Gender Recognition Act, they have made much of seemingly inconsequential switches between 'sex' and 'gender' in its wording, and the fact that it does not mandate genital surgery. For the Equality Act, they take a leaf out of the American playbook and argue that the terms 'male' and 'female' actually refer to gender identity.

At the time of the Gender Recognition Act, transactivists argued successfully against making genital surgery a precondition for legal sex change. They pointed out that not everyone is healthy enough for such surgery – and that for females, especially, it is brutal and dangerous. With hindsight, these concerns appear secondary to the long-term strategy of transactivists, in the UK and elsewhere, to detach legal sex from material reality. A paper in 2007 co-authored by Stephen Whittle argued that the act had achieved that goal, partly by removing the pre-condition for surgery and partly because of some wording that switches oddly between 'sex' and 'gender'. In it, the authors write, 'gender identity becomes and *defines* legal sex', and sex becomes 'disembodied'.

In another co-authored paper, published in 2020, Whittle claims that his campaign group, Press for Change, 'heavily influenced' the wording of the Gender Recognition Act. I have no reason to doubt this, but very much doubt that civil servants and politicians regarded that wording as significant. At the time, Westminster insiders say, the bill was seen as a harmless concession to a few thousand people with difficult lives. And other aspects of the act undermine the 'disembodied' interpretation. Legal sex change requires a diagnosis of gender dysphoria, two years presenting as the opposite sex and two doctors' sign-off. And although the law says that it changes a person's 'gender . . . for all purposes', it immediately states exceptions.

In these, it is easy to spy material reality behind the legal fiction. The act permits barring people from competing in sport as if their acquired sex is their natal one. A legal sex change does not change whether you are legally your child's father or mother.

It does not enable an elder daughter to disinherit a younger brother. (It says a lot about the UK that it occurred to lawmakers to worry about women using the new law to 'cheat' the rules of primogeniture.) If someone who has changed legal sex perpetrates or is victim of a sexual crime, the crime remains the same. (The point here is that British law defines rape as the non-consensual penetration of vagina, anus or mouth with a penis. Now, for the first time, a penis could belong to a woman and a vagina to a man.)

As for the Equality Act, the argument that 'male' and 'female' refer to gender identities not only seems weak, given common usage, but contradicts the most relevant precedent-setting court case since the law passed. That concerned Craig Hudson, who was sentenced in 2004 for murder. Over the two years of his marriage, he and several relatives tortured his wife, Rachel, to death. The autopsy found eleven fractured ribs, a detached lower lip and dozens of bruises, burns and scalds. She died of a blood clot on her brain. 'I see a lot of people who have been beaten,' the Home Office pathologist said. 'I have to say, I have never seen anything like this before.'

By 2013 Hudson was identifying as Kimberley Green, and demanded outsize women's clothes, a wig, tights, prosthetic breasts and a prosthetic vulva. They were refused on security grounds – the clothes were available only from specialist websites, and prisoners were banned from going online; make-up and a wig could aid in disguise and escape; tights could be used as a ligature, and the prosthetics, to conceal drugs. Green claimed discrimination on the basis of gender reassignment.

In such cases, British anti-discrimination law mandates a kind of thought experiment, considering whether the treatment would have been different if everything apart from the protected characteristic had been the same. Green argued that the comparison should be with a (non-trans) woman; the prison governor, that it should be with a (non-trans) man. This gets to the heart of the matter. If gender identity defines whether a person is a man/male or woman/female, when you take away a transwoman's 'transness' you get a (cis) woman. But if biological sex does, what you get is a (cis) man.

Unlike the judges in the Gavin Grimm appeal in the US, who mixed and matched the two interpretations, the British judge in the Green case picked one. It was not gender self-identification. He ruled that Green, who had not changed legal sex, was both biologically and legally male. This did much to establish that, for the purposes of British anti-discrimination law, transwomen who had not used the provisions of the Gender Recognition Act are unambiguously both males and men.

All in all, the law in the UK has proved far more resistant than in the US to activists' attempts to introduce gender self-identification by the back door. Nonetheless, it is routinely ignored. The Equality Act is permissive, not prescriptive: you are not explicitly obliged to offer female-only swimming sessions, domestic-violence shelters and so on. And when single-sex spaces are likely to get service-providers threatened and smeared as bigots, many will simply give up.

It is a testament to the trans lobby's influence that most companies' 'equality and diversity' policies now refer to 'gender' or 'gender identity', rather than sex, and declare themselves 'trans-inclusive'. To the extent that they are doing more than the law requires, that is fine. But by trans-inclusive, they often mean policies that arguably discriminate indirectly against women, and against believers in some religions too.

Alan Henness, a retired electronics engineer, has made it his mission to highlight employers' infractions of equality law. He became interested in the issue after his wife, Maria MacLachlan, was assaulted by a transactivist in 2017. Under the influence of the *Equal Treatment Bench Book*, the judge ordered her to refer to her transwoman assailant as 'she' while giving evidence. Though the defendant was found guilty, the judge reprimanded MacLachlan and denied her financial compensation because she kept forgetting to use female pronouns for the obviously male person who had punched her in the face.

Henness's method is quirky but revealing. He starts the application process for jobs in order to receive the equality-monitoring form – and then writes to the employer and tweets about what he finds. Few, it has to be said, bother to reply, so he has created a website to publicise his findings and, with luck, increase the pressure. He has semi-applied for more than 200 jobs and been asked to select his 'gender' and 'gender identity' from some weird and wonderful menus. The silliest was probably from Kent and Essex police: female; gender fluid; intersex; male; non-binary; prefer not to say; prefer to self-describe; transexual; transgender. If the police forces were to be sued for sex discrimination in hiring, they would not have the data to defend themselves, since this form muddles up sexes, identities and medical conditions.

Some organisations go beyond ignoring the law; they express contempt for it. Amazingly, this includes the Law Society, which represents solicitors. In a guide for members, it says that the Gender Recognition Act and Equality Act 'fall short in protecting and assisting the trans and non-binary community'. It recommends that members get rid of single-sex toilets and changing rooms (potentially exposing them to liability under health and safety legislation), and subject any employee who complains to disciplinary proceedings.

None of this could have happened if the Equality and Human Rights Commission (EHRC) and Government Equalities

Office – official bodies with a remit to tackle discrimination – had not also lost sight of the law. A parliamentary committee in 2019 concluded that official guidance on single-sex provision was vague and contradictory, and needed a total rewrite. In some documents, the two bodies say that everyone should be allowed to use whichever facilities they want – clearly not the Equality Act's intention. Elsewhere, they say that trans people should be allowed to use the facilities they want if they pass well enough – even while also saying that such gatekeeping would constitute unlawful direct discrimination.

Both bodies talk a lot about trans inclusion, and rarely about the rights of women. In late 2020, when World Rugby advised national federations to exclude transwomen from women's rugby, it cited safety and fairness. But when England Rugby said it would ignore the advice, neither body said anything, even though transwomen can legally be excluded from women's sports on precisely those grounds.

It all adds up to gender self-identification in practice. But transactivists wanted it in law, too. And it was here that British feminists dealt gender-identity ideology its first serious reversal.

*

The push for gender self-identification began in earnest in 2015. Politically, it was a momentous year. The Conservative Party's surprise election victory committed it to a referendum on membership of the European Union – and the rest is history. Everything else in politics became a side issue.

One of those side issues was a parliamentary inquiry into transgender equality. It was yet another object lesson in policy capture. No women's representatives were invited to give evidence; no transactivists were too fringe to be included. The committee heard from Action for Trans Health, a tiny group with eccentric demands, including puberty blockers and hormones to be available at any age without prescription, the release of all trans prisoners, and 'the total abolition of the clinic, of psychiatry and of the medical-industrial complex'. It was as if a parliamentary transport inquiry had heard from yogic fliers, or a health inquiry from crystal healers.

Unsurprisingly, given the lack of balance, the inquiry recommended legal gender self-identification. It also recommended removing the exceptions in the Equality Act that allow service-providers to separate facilities by biological sex despite the provisions for legal sex change. For a while the report gathered dust. First the Brexit referendum was announced. Then voters unexpectedly voted to leave the EU. The prime minister resigned. His successor lost her majority in a disastrous snap election. But through it all, a few MPs continued to press for self-ID. In late summer 2017, a public consultation was announced for the autumn.

Some women's groups now admit that they fell for the spin that self-ID would affect no one except trans people, and had no idea single-sex spaces were under threat. Others feared that objecting publicly would jeopardise their funding. Still others had followed American feminism down the gender-identity path. And by this point, almost all competent politicians and civil servants were fully occupied by Brexit. Women who cared about single-sex spaces would, it seemed, have to speak up for themselves.

One was Venice Allan, a Labour Party activist. In September 2017 she planned a debate on gender self-ID. When the venue cancelled under pressure from transactivists, Allan told attendees to meet in Hyde Park at Speakers' Corner, a place that has long been associated with free speech, from where they would proceed to a substitute. It was while they were assembling that Maria MacLachlan was assaulted. Earlier, her assailant had posted on Facebook: 'I wanna fuck up some terfs. They're no better than fash [fascists].' Afterwards, members of Action for Trans Health praised the assault, likening punching TERFs to 'punching Nazis'.

Another event a couple of months later landed Allan in court. Alluding to the assault at Speakers' Corner, one of the speakers, veteran gay-rights and anti-racism campaigner Linda Bellos, said that if 'one of those bastards comes near me, I will take off my glasses and thump them'. A transwoman who watched the event streamed on Allan's Facebook page claimed to have felt threatened and brought a private prosecution against Bellos and Allan. The pair had to attend two hearings before the case was thrown out.

No doubt the fear of assault and prosecution intimidated some women. But others shouted louder. Among them was Woman's Place UK. 'Our first demand was that women's voices should be heard on this issue,' says co-founder Judith Green. 'The legal definition of sex is something that affects everybody, and in particular women, because we suffer from sexism. The second demand was that women-only spaces must be upheld and if necessary extended.'

WPUK started to hold its own events. Every one provided more evidence of the threat to women's speech. Almost every venue came under extreme pressure to cancel. Leeds Civic Hall did so, with just a few hours' notice. Its capitulation was thrown into sharp relief by an exhibition celebrating the centenary of women's suffrage that it was holding at the same time. Attendees reconvened in a pub. A meeting eight days earlier in another pub, the Harlequin in nearby Sheffield, had gone ahead as planned. But two years later, transactivists were still trying to get its licence removed, sending threatening messages to the owner and complaining about her to the police.

A second was a recently founded women's charity, FiLiA. As gender self-ID looked like becoming law, the trustees decided that they had to take a position. After intense internal discussions, they endorsed WPUK's principles, which are agnostic on whether governments should recognise gender identities, but firm on the need for female-only spaces. 'We have to deal with this issue, but it's a huge distraction,' says Lisa-Marie Taylor, the charity's chief executive. 'While we're forced to defend the legal definition of woman, women are still being raped and battered. Female genital mutilation continues.'

A third group, Fair Play for Women, grew out of conversations on Mumsnet and Facebook. In mid-2018, when the public consultation on gender self-ID finally started after several delays, it printed up t-shirts reading 'Hands Off My Rights', and organised women to hand out leaflets in town centres each weekend. 'We were all really scared, because we'd heard that everyone hated "TERFs",' says Nicola Williams, its spokeswoman. 'But every time you told somebody what was happening, they would say: "I don't believe it." Ordinary people had no idea that gender self-identification was even on the cards.'

Kellie-Jay Keen, a women's rights campaigner and YouTuber who goes by the name Posie Parker, took a different approach to raising awareness. (For non-Brits, a nosey-parker is someone who asks prying questions.) In 2015, she had discovered that no questioning of gender-identity doctrine was allowed. A transwoman in a Facebook group she belonged to made a misogynistic joke with a punchline about a feminist tied to a radiator in a basement, and Keen responded: 'Are you sure you identify as a woman?' The resulting pile-on astonished her, so she started to probe further, in person and online.

'I asked, does my eleven-year-old daughter have the right to go into a women's space and not see a penis?' she says. 'I heard I was a bigot, a pervert, disgusting, transphobic, obsessed with genitals.' In February 2018 she was interviewed by the police on suspicion of hate crime. On Twitter, she had referred to Susie Green of Mermaids taking her child to Thailand to get 'castrated'. Green made a police report. (Needless to say, the sex-reassignment surgery Jackie Green underwent at age sixteen does involve castration.)

No charges were brought, and the attempt to silence her made Keen more determined to be heard. She decided that the main thing she wanted to say was that women were losing the ability to define themselves. So she started selling t-shirts with the dictionary definition: 'Woman (noun): adult human female'. She saved the profits to put the same slogan on a billboard in Liverpool during the Labour Party conference in September 2018. 'It was a damp squib, nobody noticed,' she says. Then Adrian Harrop, a doctor and transactivist who lives in the city, complained that it was 'transphobic hate speech'. The billboard company took the poster down and tweeted an apology – thereby neatly illustrating Keen's point. The story got picked up widely. When the pair were invited onto Sky News, Harrop described the dictionary definition of woman as a 'symbol that makes transgender people feel unsafe'. 'It was perfect,' says Keen. 'To win this fight, all we have to do is get transactivists to speak.'

Parents worried about the impact of gender self-ID in schools started organising too. Transgender Trend, which was founded in 2015 by Stephanie Davies-Arai, a communication specialist, produced a legally accurate and evidence-based guide on supporting gender-variant and trans-identified children in schools, and an early-years picture book that counters the wrong-body narrative so often pushed in children's books, entitled *My Body is Me!* Just how far gender-identity ideology takes adherents away from that gentle message of self-acceptance and body positivity can be judged by the vitriolic reaction to the book. Transactivists likened it to 'Nazi propaganda'. Clara Vulliamy, a children's author, said it presented an 'extreme ideology that explicitly targets children'. The author, Rachel Rooney, was subjected to such sustained harassment that she considered leaving the publishing industry.

Safe Schools Alliance, a newer group focused on child safeguarding, succeeded in getting many councils to withdraw guidance which incorrectly stated that children who identified as members of the opposite sex had the legal right to use that sex's toilets and changing rooms, and which normalised harmful practices for trans-identified children such as 'breast-binding' – strapping breasts down under clothing to give a male silhouette, which causes pain and faintness, and can permanently deform the lungs, spine and ribcage.

Throughout all this, a group of gay people, including founders and long-time supporters of Stonewall, were trying to get the lobby group to row back on its support for gender self-ID. Private requests for meetings and an open letter asking for dialogue were rebuffed. In October 2019 the group called a meeting in London. Running the show were two lesbians, Kate Harris and Beverley Jackson. Until a few years previously, Harris had been a major fundraiser for Stonewall. Jackson is a former firebrand, one of the founders of the Gay Liberation Front in 1970 – 'the token lesbian, along with nineteen gay men'.

Out of that meeting the LGB Alliance was born. It aims to elevate the voices of lesbians, since they are side-lined within LGBT groups, and to defend free speech, fight the elision in law of sex and gender identity, and get gender-identity ideology out of schools. But most of all it intends to ensure that the voices of gay people, whose interests have been abandoned in the push for gender self-identification, are once more heard.

*

The government consultation had closed in October 2018, but the results failed to materialise. Rumour in Westminster suggested that senior Conservatives had finally realised that gender self-ID was not the cost-free political win the activists had promised. In yet another election, at the end of 2019, the party won a stunning victory. Working-class voters in Labour heartlands elected Conservatives for the first time in living memory. No doubt the main reason was that the Labour Party was hopelessly divided on Brexit – but the Conservatives were becoming convinced that their opponents' growing 'wokeness' also played a part.

During the campaign, Labour MPs had gained unflattering attention for saying things that would naturally astonish anyone unfamiliar with gender-identity ideology. The third-largest party, the Liberal Democrats, went further, running on a pledge to implement full gender self-ID, including for non-binary identities. In an interview their leader, Jo Swinson, couldn't give a straight answer when asked if male and female people even existed. She lost her seat.

By this point, the Conservatives had decided to ditch self-ID. Some spied the chance for an American-style culture war that they thought they could win. But all the trends they would have to decry had started or accelerated while they were in power. Moreover, the party leadership's private polling suggested that, although self-ID was stunningly unpopular with the public once it was explained, awareness was still too low for it to be electorally salient. Instead, the party decided to let the opposition continue shooting itself in the foot.

In September 2020 the minister for women and equalities, Liz Truss, made a low-key announcement. Self-ID had been shelved, she said, but more would be spent on treating gender dysphoria, and the medically gate-kept process for changing legal sex would become cheaper. Simultaneously, the education department warned schools not to tell children that they might be a different gender from their sex 'based on their personality and interests or the clothes they prefer to wear', and not to work with external groups that suggested any such thing.

As I write, the fightback continues in the courts. Keira Bell's challenge to the use of puberty blockers, discussed in chapter 4, was merely the first of several crowdfunded legal challenges to gender self-identification, of which I will highlight a few.

In March 2021 Fair Play For Women won a stunning victory in a lightning judicial review of the decision by the Office for National Statistics to blur the meaning of 'sex' in the decennial census. The ONS had added guidance suggesting that respondents should tick 'male' or 'female' according to what it said on any of their official documents – which amounted to gender self-identification in practice, since almost all such documents can be changed on demand. Campaigners crowdfunded £100,000 in just ten days, and the judge ordered the ONS to edit the guidance to make it clear that 'sex' means 'sex'. He ruled that, in changing the definition of a fundamental demographic group by stealth, it had overstepped its legal powers.

Meanwhile campaigners are seeking a test case to establish that female-only services, which the Equality Act permits in certain circumstances, may exclude transwomen as a matter of course. This seems straightforward, since transwomen are not female, and yet the EHRC has said service-providers must assess each individual case. Separately, a grassroots group, For Women Scotland, is challenging a law about representation on company boards that defines a woman as anyone who 'describes themselves and is described by others' as a woman – a group that does not fit the criteria for permissible discrimination. After its initial challenge was rejected, it is seeking to appeal.

Another case is being taken by Harry Miller, a former policeman, against the College of Policing. Miller is challenging its guidance on handling 'hate incidents', which seemingly include anything at all a trans person complains about. In 2019 Miller was investigated for a handful of tweets, which ranged from saying that Sheffield women knew the difference between boys and girls to an off-colour piece of doggerel on transgender women's anatomy. The High Court has already ruled that the police acted unlawfully in investigating Miller, denouncing their overreach with references to the Cheka, Gestapo and Stasi. Now he is seeking to have the guidance itself overturned.

And lastly, important cases are under way concerning employers' rights to silence their employees' concerns about gender self-ID. Alongside Forstater's, another employment tribunal has started, taken by barrister Allison Bailey against her chambers and Stonewall. Bailey, the daughter of Jamaican immigrants, is one of a handful of British barristers who is black and from a working-class background. She accuses the charity of working behind the scenes to encourage her chambers to victimise her in retaliation for her connection with the LGB Alliance. Emails presented as evidence in a preliminary hearing showed that a Stonewall employee contacted her chambers to say that its ongoing association with her 'threatens [its] positive relationship' with Stonewall, and put the charity 'in a difficult position' going forward. The words were interpreted by the judge as plainly intended to put pressure on the chambers to take action against Bailey, accompanied by a threat to sever ties if it did not. A full hearing is due in 2022.

The flourishing grassroots groups and flurry of legal challenges are likely to embolden further opposition to gender self-ID, as each person who speaks out gives others the courage to do likewise. As Forstater said in her talk at a conference in London in January 2020 organised by WPUK to mark fifty years of the Women's Liberation movement, there is safety in numbers: 'They can't fire us all.' It all raises an interesting question: why did the secular, feminist resistance appear in the UK, rather than elsewhere?

Size mattered, for a start. The UK is small enough that a single group can arrange events nationwide, but not so small that policy could be captured in a single move, as in Ireland. It was also lucky with timing. Stonewall added the T to its remit only in 2015, almost a decade after American LGB groups. From 2016 Brexit side-lined other government business. British women could look across the Atlantic to see what was coming, and had time to organise.

Culture mattered, too. The idea that life's central purpose is to search for your true self is American, not British. The UK never had chattel slavery on its own soil, the legacy of which has so warped American thinking about material differences between the sexes. It is less religious than the US, and less polarised. Abortion is not politicised, which makes it easier for left-wing feminists to work with Christian conservatives on a single-issue campaign. Many of the women leading the UK's feminist resurgence were teenagers in the 1980s, the era of New Romantics and glam rockers. They are comfortable with men who gender-bend and still see themselves as men. Some of those women came up through unions, where they learned to build a movement.

A centralised political system allowed them to focus on just two legislatures: Westminster and Holyrood, in Scotland. In the federal systems of the US, Australia and Canada, the enemy was Hydra-headed. And the achievements of British feminism, from reproductive rights to paid maternity leave, gave them confidence and authority. American feminism has no comparable record of success.

The UK also had a useful legal framework. The Equality Act's protections for trans people meant that British women could fight for single-sex spaces without feeling guilty. Moreover, despite some motivated reasoning by transactivists in the legal profession and academia, UK law is pretty clear about the importance of biological sex. The law on child safeguarding is world-class, too, giving parents a tool to fight back against gender self-identification in schools.

The National Health Service played an important role, in several ways. Since British workers' health care is not tied to their jobs, they are less easily silenced by their employers than Americans are. It is the world's most centralised health system, the most insulated from lobbying by suppliers and users – and among the stingiest in any rich country. These are hardly unalloyed virtues, but they were useful when lobbyists started to press for gender-affirmative care. The NHS is also unusually committed to cost-benefit analysis. The excesses of paediatric gender medicine are being opposed in the UK first, not because the Tavistock is worse than clinics elsewhere, but because it is more easily held to account.

British political culture is deeply suspicious of extremists, including liberal ones (in the American sense). The Left is more communal and less individualistic than in the US, and performative social-justice activism is not a condition of university entrance, meaning 'wokeness' has been relatively slow to spread from the liberal arts, humanities and social sciences to other fields. The UK lacks the human-rights tribunals that act as a parallel justice system in Canada and some American states. Those in Canada have a mandate to push anti-discrimination laws into new areas, and have adopted gender-identity ideology with enthusiasm. Canada is also hobbled by its self-image as more progressive, kinder and all-round nicer than the US, which predisposes its politics to virtue-signalling and institutional capture.

In any list of the UK's advantages, though, Mumsnet takes pride of place. Its importance is partly because of Silicon Valley bias and censorship, but also because it is highly unusual in being a female-dominated online space. More than ninety-five percent of its users are women. A survey in 2018 found that discussions about women's rights were a draw for nearly two-thirds of users. It is committed to free speech, and in 2018, when it came under pressure to ban 'transphobia', it bent but did not break. It now deletes posts that call transwomen men or trans-identified males, or that deadname or misgender them. But it also deletes posts that call women cis or TERF. And discussions about male violence and human biology are still possible without circumlocution.

In her 2020 book, *The Politicization of Mumsnet*, Sarah Pedersen of Robert Gordon University in Aberdeen describes the site's feminism chat board as a 'subaltern counterpublic'. The term was introduced by political theorist and philosopher Nancy Fraser for places where members of subordinated social groups – in this case women – create and circulate narratives, and formulate interpretations of their identities, interests and needs, that run counter to narratives and interpretations in the dominant culture.

The feminism chat board and the new women's organisations are symbiotically linked, says Pedersen. Women flocked to Mumsnet to discuss the parliamentary inquiry into transgender equality. Some campaigns were cooked up on the site, like 'Man Friday' in 2018, which saw women highlight the absurdity of gender self-identification by identifying as men on Fridays and performing 'random acts of manliness', such as going to the men-only bathing pond on Hampstead Heath in London. Whenever WPUK holds an event, or a gender-related case is heard in an employment tribunal or court, Mumsnetters provide a running commentary.

British activists are inspiring counterparts elsewhere. By the time the LGB Alliance was a year old, a dozen similar groups had formed as far afield as the US, Canada and Brazil. WPUK is in contact with sister groups in other countries, including Canadian Women's Sex-Based Rights (CaWsbar), which is campaigning to add safeguards to federal gender-identity laws. And detransitioners are organising in several countries, seeking better medical care for themselves and better transition information and protocols for everyone. All hope campaigners in the UK will succeed in demolishing the aura of inevitability around gender self-identification. But they are miles behind, and battling on tougher terrain.

CONCLUSION

TRANS RIGHTS ARE
HUMAN RIGHTS

Where do we go from here?

One of the jobs of social scientists and political analysts is to predict how public opinion on a controversial issue might evolve. To do this, they sometimes build a model grouping people with similar attitudes, and consider the forces or trends that lead to movement between those groups. To think about how attitudes towards gender self-identification might develop, let's start with five groups. Four already have some opinion on the issue: enthusiasts; 'lukewarms' who know little about it but are positively disposed; those who are equally ignorant but suspicious; and committed opponents. And finally, probably the largest group comprises those who are oblivious to the issue.

Here's how an enthusiast might interpret the current situation and expect things to unfold. The committed opponents are simply bigots. Silencing them will make it less likely that others join them and more likely that trans people will come out, thereby increasing societal acceptance. The people who started in the suspicious or oblivious groups will gradually become lukewarms; the lukewarms will become enthusiasts. Opposition will become ever more stigmatised, and eventually gender self-ID will gain widespread support.

There is a precedent for precisely such a societal shift: that in attitudes towards homosexuality over the past half-century. And many transactivists, analogising transphobia with homophobia, confidently expect history to repeat itself with gender self-ID. But for several reasons, I do not think it will.

The first is that genuine transphobia – disgust or animus towards trans people – is far rarer than homophobia was fifty years ago. What is usually meant by the word – objection to gender identity overriding sex – is nothing like homophobia, and hence not likely to shift for the same sorts of reasons. The public polling discussed in chapter 11 suggests that people who oppose gender self-ID do not usually do so because they object to trans people as such, but because of their assessment of what is at stake for themselves and everyone else.

The second is that increased trans visibility will not have the same effect as increased gay visibility. As more gay people came out, starting in the 1960s and continuing through the AIDS crisis into the 2000s, straight people gradually realised two things: that gay people were just like everyone else apart from their sexual orientation, and that their orientation was no skin off anyone else's nose. Seeing and meeting more trans people may indeed encourage understanding and empathy. But when it comes to the ideology, rather than the people, it will only encourage hostility. The more males compete in women's sports, the more obvious the unfairness. It only takes one male person feeling entitled to use women's changing rooms to radicalise a lot of women. Silencing objectors will not change their minds; it will make them angrier, because something they genuinely value is being taken away.

The final reason relates to why beliefs are held. A half-century ago, people who regarded gays as perverts mainly did so because most other people did. Such baseless communal beliefs have a great deal of inertia, shifting only slowly at first in the face of new ideas or evidence. But over time, change gains momentum and at some point the incentives flip. Nowadays, a big reason for many people not to hold homophobic beliefs is that few others in their social circle do.

And once more, the analogy with 'transphobia' breaks down. People who oppose gender-identity ideology do so in spite of, not because of, cultural signals. Governments, academia, the media, publishing, HR departments: all are firmly behind gender self-identification. The social rewards go to proponents; vocal opponents risk harassment and sacking. Journalists who write human-interest stories about happy transkids or non-binary celebrities will easily find outlets; those who pitch articles about the risks of paediatric transitioning or the science behind keeping women's sport for females will struggle to get commissioned.

We humans are social animals, and 'because everyone else does' is not the only social reason we hold beliefs, or at least profess to hold them. Another is because we subconsciously think they will make us look good. And sometimes, in what social scientists call preference falsification, we claim to hold views that we are well aware we do not because we think others will despise us if we admit the truth. All this misrepresentation and second-guessing can create 'pluralistic ignorance' – a situation where people do not understand their fellow citizens' true views, but think they do.

Pluralistic ignorance can lead politicians to enact unpopular policies, thinking they are doing what voters want. Or it can keep undemocratic regimes in power. The end days of the Soviet

Union offer an illustration. The communist regimes were more widely hated than was generally realised, because the fear of persecution meant few people voiced their opposition, and hence that opposition was slow to organise. In the case of gender-identity ideology, ignorance is more common than outright opposition. But biased media coverage and the silencing of contrary opinions mean that anyone who seeks further information will get a highly inaccurate impression of what their fellow citizens think.

Pluralistic ignorance is fragile. People's beliefs, and their willingness to voice them, can shift remarkably quickly if they gain greater insight into other people's true views. One way this can happen is if anonymised polling alerts them to the existence of a silent majority that disagrees with the dominant narrative. Another is if a few truth-tellers inspire others to speak out in increasing numbers, as the child does in the fable of the emperor's new clothes.

Something like this is already happening, with the role of truth-teller taken by J. K. Rowling. At the end of 2019, her expression of support for Maya Forstater made worldwide news; six months later she ramped things up by sharing an article entitled 'Creating a more equal post-Covid-19 world for people who menstruate'. The avoidance of the word 'woman' clearly pushed her to her limits, and she tweeted: ' "People who menstruate." I'm sure there used to be a word for these people. Someone help me out. Wumben? Wimpund? Woomud?'

A few days later, she posted an article on her blog. It expressed compassion for and solidarity with trans people, but also her concerns regarding gender self-identification and the silencing of women. 'I refuse to bow down to a movement that I believe is doing demonstrable harm in seeking to erode "woman" as a political and biological class and offering cover to predators like few before it,' she wrote. She wondered whether, had transgender ideology been around during her teens, she would have identified as a boy and ended up regretful and sterile. And she revealed a history of domestic abuse and sexual violence that had given her a deep appreciation of the importance of single-sex spaces.

Then came a concocted row over *Troubled Blood*, the latest of the crime novels Rowling has written under the pen name Robert Galbraith. An early review mentioned a transgender killer; in fact, the killer merely disguises himself briefly in a woman's wig and coat. Journalists around the world who hadn't read the book credulously recycled the story. *Pink News*, which hadn't received a review copy, ran forty-two stories about Rowling's 'transphobia' in a week. Twitter allowed #RIPJKRowling to trend, and the threats and insults became ever more vile. It was the digital equivalent of a mob waving pitchforks – and, as the lies proliferated, a reminder of Jonathan Swift's epigram: 'Falsehood flies, and the Truth comes limping after it.'

If Rowling had been more vulnerable, all this might have worked to silence her. Instead, it served to alert more people to the illiberalism of gender-identity ideology, and activists' intolerance of even the slightest dissent. The idea that a children's author known for her liberal politics and donating most of her vast fortune to charity had somehow morphed into a bigot was wildly implausible. And anyone who actually read what she said would have found only compassion and good sense.

In Rowling, cancel culture had come up against someone too big to cancel – someone who could say that the emperor had no clothes. In her sole commentary on the row over *Troubled Blood*, she made the point nicely, tweeting a picture of herself in a t-shirt with the slogan 'this witch doesn't burn'. In democracies, policy capture can take campaigners only so far. Once voters openly disapprove of a measure, politicians start to take notice.

*

How might the beliefs of those who espouse gender-identity ideology change, if contrary views are no longer silenced and it becomes clear that the enthusiasts are in the minority? That depends on why enthusiasts hold their beliefs. Kevin Simler, an author and scientist, distinguishes between 'merit beliefs' and 'crony beliefs', which are held and abandoned for different reasons. It is my contention that many people's adherence to gender-identity ideology is cronyistic, in this sense, and will be abandoned when it is no longer in the ascendant.

The idea is that beliefs can be thought of as 'employees' of our minds, some of which are 'hired' because they are competent, and others because of whom they know. The two sorts earn their keep in different ways, says Simler: 'merit beliefs by helping us navigate the world, crony beliefs by helping us look good'. Merit beliefs are based on evidence, and if our understanding of the evidence changes, the beliefs do too. Crony beliefs, by contrast, are about fitting in, winning allies and making the right impression. Among Simler's examples of crony beliefs are conspiracy theories, which play well in certain circles, and fanatical devotion to a sports team, a belief some people's entire social circle is built around.

A merit belief may be false, just as an employee hired in open competition may turn out to be incompetent. And a crony belief may be true, just as one hired to curry favour with a powerful politician may turn out to be excellent. But the odds are against it. Generally, merit beliefs match reality better, because that is their purpose and when they do not work, they are adjusted or abandoned. The reasons for adopting or abandoning crony beliefs have little to do with evidence, and much more to do with perceptions about what other people believe.

People are often not conscious that a belief they hold could fall into this category. But they must be aware, at some level – just as *someone* in a company must understand why the mayor's idiot nephew is on staff, or else he would be fired. Similarly, we know at some level that our crony beliefs are fragile, and do not subject them to vigorous testing. Instead we become defensive when they are challenged, and seize on even the flimsiest arguments in their favour. We do not allow anything that really matters to depend on their truth. And we boast about them, since being known to hold them is the point. The main sign that a belief is cronyistic, says Simler, is exhibiting strong emotions about it, 'as when we feel proud of a belief, anguish over changing our minds, or anger at being challenged or criticized'.

The applicability to gender-identity ideology is obvious. Proclaiming that transwomen are women is a way of showing that you are a member of an elite intellectual tribe – university-educated, left-leaning and too sophisticated to categorise people by their physiology. Adherence is signalled with pronouns in email signatures and social-media bios. The frequent use of the word 'dangerous' for Rowling's blogpost was revealing, since it contained neither insults nor threats. If critics felt capable of rebutting it point by point, they would not have felt endangered by it. The true danger was that readers might find it convincing.

Further signs that gender-identity beliefs are cronyistic include the repetition of mantras and the insistence that there is 'no debate'. These quiet inner doubts and reduce the chance of seeing something challenging. Many believers in gender-identity ideology use blocklisting tools on social media, such as Terfblocker. All it takes to get on one of these is to retweet a few articles about, say, detransitioners – or even to follow a few accounts that tweet such articles. Their stated purpose is to protect trans people from harassment or doxxing. But by casting the net so wide they raise the suspicion that the true purpose is to protect believers from seeing anything that might shake their faith.

The final indication of a crony belief is that nothing important is allowed to ride on it. To show that this is true of gender-identity ideology, I offer the following thought experiment. Picture a person who insists that transwomen are women in every circumstance. If transwomen commit crimes, they belong in women's prisons; if they play sport, they belong on women's teams. If they are attracted to women, lesbians must regard them as potential sexual partners. Such a person will accept no distinction between sex and gender. Transwomen differ from 'cis women' only in having been mistakenly 'assigned male at birth'. Now, what will our true believer do if they need a gestational surrogate?

I am familiar with some men in this situation. They spend a good deal of time harassing the women they call TERFs, and trying to get them fired. But when it comes to something central to their own lives, their beliefs fly out the window. The distinction between male and female that they refuse to admit even exists is tacitly accepted once it is crucial to something they really want.

My point is not that the capacity to become pregnant is a necessary condition of being a woman. Some women are too young or too old, or have undergone hysterectomy, or have health conditions that make pregnancy unachievable or unsustainable. The point is that if a 'cis' woman cannot become pregnant, there must be some such reason, and if she is of child-bearing age you would need to ask about her medical history to be aware of it. But our imagined gender-identity ideologue – who insists that women prisoners accept males in their cells, female athletes accept males in their competitions and lesbians accept males in their beds – would not even ask a transwoman to be a surrogate, because at some unacknowledged level they know it would be futile.

Whether someone espouses a crony belief, and how long they hold onto it, depends largely on how rewarding it is. If it is very rewarding – if their job depends on convincing declarations of faith, for example – most people will quell any doubts that arise. But if the rewards change, the energy that people put into shoring up these beliefs will too.

The threshold for listening to doubts depends on personal situation and character. Most of the women I spoke to for this book started out regarding themselves as trans allies, out of empathy or because it seemed like the progressive position. Then a chance remark or troubling discovery made them see things differently. Some were parents of teenagers whose trans identification seemed to come from nowhere; others were inspired to look more closely by disproportionate reactions to factual statements about biological sex.

Many of those willing to express their doubts publicly were self-employed or retired, and did not need to worry about losing their jobs. But others spoke out despite having every reason to stay silent. People vary greatly in how much they care about being liked versus being right. Some loathe conflict, and will therefore stay silent even about big problems or worries. Others find cognitive dissonance so unbearable that they cannot stop themselves from probing weak points in socially convenient beliefs, and speaking out about what they find.

These gender apostates differed in many ways: sex, sexual orientation, religion, politics and profession. But almost all had either a compelling personal reason to speak out, or a character trait that could be described as courage – or pig-headedness. Each such person makes it more likely that people who fit into neither of these categories are convinced by their arguments and willing to say so, and harder to misrepresent those arguments as bigotry.

*

As famed negotiator William Ury wrote in the 1981 classic, *Getting to Yes*, we all negotiate every day, whether or not we realise it. Whenever we want to do something that requires other people's consent, we will have to try to strike a deal: in weighty matters such as agreeing the price of a house or the salary for a job; and in minor ones such as what's for dinner and when the children must go to bed. But when it comes to whether sex or gender identity should take precedence in law and everyday life, the conflict has been treated as if only trans people are affected, and there has been no negotiation at all.

That is no longer tenable. Too many other groups who regard gender self-identification as harmful are insisting on expressing their worries and stating their needs. Less obviously, negotiation is in trans people's interests. The 'with us or against us' approach taken by activist groups that claim to speak for them is very harmful to their long-term interests. This is already obvious when it comes to inclusion of transwomen in women's sports, which strikes most people as grossly unfair, and in the ideological approach to paediatric transitioning, which risks positioning trans people as careless of children's long-term health. Describing opposition to these policies as transphobia will simply denude that word of all meaning – to trans people's detriment. In this conclusion, I offer some pointers to a better approach.

Ury's most important negotiating principle is to focus on interests, not positions. Interests are the outcomes that matter to you; positions are the ways you think you can get there. If everyone's positions are compatible, no negotiation is needed. All other situations require creative thinking so that everyone gets enough of what they want. People who cling to positions risk the 'zero-sum fallacy' – the idea that any gain for one party is a loss for another. Emphasising interests, rather than positions, also allows third parties to decide which demands deserve precedence. In the conflict between sex and gender identity, many decisions will fall to governments and thus, in turn, depend on what politicians think voters will wear. The winners will be those who convince the general public that their interests are reasonable and just.

Among the parties to this long-overdue negotiation are, of course, trans people. Their interests differ according to whether they are male or female; pre-, post- or non-operative; or same-sex or opposite-sex attracted. And like any group of people who share a single personal characteristic, they come from across the political spectrum. The full range must be heard – not just the activists who present gender self-identification as the sole solution to every problem.

People with disorders of sex development also need a seat at the table. They have been badly injured by the conflation of their complex and varied medical conditions with cross-sex identities. Gay people have suffered as gender-identity ideology has denied the basis for same-sex orientation. Detransitioners require special consideration: many are traumatised by what they have been through. Women and children are particularly affected by the loss of single-sex spaces and weakening of safeguarding principles.

Among the relevant interests is self-determination for gender-dysphoric adults, who may decide that their best option is medical or surgical transition. They need comprehensive information about long-term health outcomes, and a clear idea of what it is realistic to expect from others post-transition. For gender-dysphoric children other considerations, such as avoiding long-term health problems and sterility, should weigh more heavily. It is in their interests that the facts about desistance, and the links between childhood gender non-conformity and adult homo-sexuality, are widely known.

Everyone has an interest in feeling assured that governments are taking them into account in policymaking. Inclusion matters to historically excluded groups, such as gender non-conforming people and women, as do such bedrock issues as physical safety and dignity, freedom from harassment and access to the full range of public services. People of both sexes have an interest in setting their own sexual boundaries, and in bodily privacy. For women, safety is another important consideration.

Casting the mind beyond gender self-identification in this way will ensure that everyone affected gets a say. It will also help governments write a new agenda for improving trans people's lives. For example, they could commission rigorous research into the causes and treatment of gender dysphoria, and into why transition is becoming more common and skewing younger and female.

Broadening the focus will also make it easier to predict where conflicts are likely to erupt. It is extraordinary how little thought has been given to the tensions between gender-identity ideol-ogy and religions that forbid the sexes to mingle. Liberal, secular democracies should not privilege one belief system over others, and yet governments have required everyone to ignore some people's sex, without considering the consequences for those whose conscience does not permit them to.

And it will force governments to ask themselves a fundamen-tal question: what are they trying to achieve by allowing legal sex change? The early gender-recognition laws were motivated in large part by difficulties that no longer exist, including the inability to marry someone of the same sex, and discriminatory rules regarding matters such as pensionable ages. Another concern was protecting the privacy of passing, post-operative trans people, who did not want to be outed by having to show documents that stated their sex.

But now same-sex marriage is legal across the rich world, and the few remaining bureaucratic distinctions between men and women concern biological facts, for example which sex gives birth. In everyday life, sex matters less than it used to – but when it does matter, it is sex that matters, not gender identity. As for intruding on the privacy of passing trans people, that worry seems quaint now that the trans umbrella covers a vast range of people for whom passing is neither a possibility nor even a goal, for example part-time cross-dressers.

And if legal sex can be changed, everyone who uses official statistics has an interest in play, since sex is one of the most predictive variables in the medical and social sciences, and one of the most important for planning public services. This may seem a minor issue, since trans people are rare – but they are hugely over-represented in certain subgroups. Some paediatric gender clinics say that half the children they assess have autistic-spectrum traits, and that most have mental-health disorders. Since these conditions manifest differently in males and females, it is essential that doctors continue to record and treat trans-identified children as members of their sex, not their stated gender identity. Another relevant subgroup is people who have committed crimes. The gulf between male and female patterns of criminality means that male people already make up a large share of all 'woman-identified' perpetrators of violent and sexual offences. If self-declared gender identity is recorded, and sex is not, soon what is 'known' about female offenders will be shaped by male-pattern offending. That would have serious consequences for crime-prevention and rehabilitation.

Trans people have an interest in being able to conceal their birth sex when it is irrelevant – for example, when applying for a loan or visa. Conversely, everyone has an interest in knowing the sex of others in certain sensitive situations – when undressing, undergoing an intimate medical examination or hiring someone for a sex-specific role, for example to provide intimate care, or counselling to victims of sexual crimes. UK law recognises this interest by allowing people of the 'wrong' sex to be excluded from sensitive settings, even if they have been issued with an amended birth certificate. But the amended birth certificate makes this exclusion impossible to enforce.

Putting this all together, people have legitimate interests in both concealing their sex when it is irrelevant to others, and knowing the sex of others when it matters. These interests could be reconciled without permitting legal sex change by continuing to record sex on 'long form' birth certificates, and removing it from the 'short form' version. Trans people would then automatically have an identifying document that did not clash with their social identity, but there would still be a way to confirm people's sex when necessary.

Requiring paperwork would obviously be overkill for everyday single-sex facilities, such as public toilets and changing rooms. Access to these has never been regulated by statute (except briefly in North Carolina's 'bathroom law'), but by everyone understanding and obeying the rules. On the rare occasions that someone of the wrong sex entered, other users would quickly alert them; a man who loitered in women's facilities would be dealt with by security staff and, in the last resort, police. The tiny number of people who underwent full medical transition either passed well enough to fit in, or – especially early in the process – explained the situation and asked for forbearance.

Under gender self-ID, however, if you challenge someone who looks out of place, you put yourself in the wrong. This is what motivated 'bathroom laws' like North Carolina's. But such laws are overly punitive – and, moreover, fail to consider people who cannot, or do not want to, use their own sex's facilities. I am thinking here not just of trans people, but of detransitioners, who sometimes talk of the burden of fitting in nowhere. And people who identify as non-binary or gender-fluid may look at home in facilities for their sex, but still not want to be there.

Accommodating these groups will require more unisex facilities. But these should add to, not replace, single-sex ones. It will often not be possible to build enough single-occupancy facilities to meet all demand, and multi-user unisex provision cannot satisfy women's interests in safety and privacy. No doubt some trans people will pass well enough to continue using facilities they are not, strictly speaking, entitled to. But stopping them would take a degree of intrusion into everyone's privacy that would not be in anyone's interests.

I will consider just two further situations of the many that will require attention. One is prisons. Inmates of both sexes and all identities share the same core interests: safety and dignity, decent living conditions, suitable training and rehabilitation. Trans people may also have an interest in receiving clothing and toiletries not normally available to prisoners of their sex, and, depending on local rules, being able to satisfy any requirement to 'live as the opposite sex' to qualify for medical treatment.

I see no way to protect female prisoners' safety and dignity if males are held alongside them. Prisons are not private enough for mixed-sex living, and the under-reporting of violent and sexual offending by males makes case-by-case risk assessment impossible. Moreover, accommodating males, who are physically stronger and far more likely to be dangerous offenders, would require women's prisons to increase security and operate along stricter, more punitive lines, causing female prisoners further harm.

The safety and dignity of transwomen matter every bit as much. But they need not be held with women in order for those interests to be met. They are by no means the only vulnerable group of male prisoners: young men and gay men are also at heightened risk of sexual assault and violence. Men's prisons already have to take such issues into consideration, and should be run well enough to protect the safety and dignity of all inmates. If transwomen are judged to be even more vulnerable than other groups, they may need to be held in separate wings – which could also be useful in enabling them to express their gender more freely.

My final example is sport. Other sports should follow World Rugby's lead: it is the only regulator that has sincerely tried to consider the interests of everyone concerned.

The core interest for all athletes is fair competition. In contact sports, safety is a consideration, too. World Rugby has shown convincingly that satisfying these interests for female athletes requires excluding all males. Safety and fairness can be achieved for transwomen by including them in men's events, where they can compete against other males. And this is where all those 'diversity and inclusion' officers can earn their keep: by ensuring that transwomen are welcomed and supported by male team-mates and competitors, and that clubs accommodate their showering and changing needs.

If you think this sounds odd, you may not realise that, in most sports, so-called 'men's competitions' are actually open to everyone. So I am not misgendering or insulting transwomen by saying that they can compete with men. Indeed, in some sports it is quite common for elite women to compete against men at a lower level in order to find sufficiently tough opposition – a top-flight female cricketer may turn out for an amateur men's side, or an elite female runner may race against the best men in her local club.

For transmen, the solution depends on whether they have ever taken testosterone. If not, they can compete fairly with other females. Otherwise, they will have gained an unfair advantage – no matter that the intention was not to cheat. The 'therapeutic use exemptions' governing athletes' use of medication need to be strengthened so that taking testosterone for transition-related purposes disqualifies an athlete from women's events. Transmen who have taken male hormones will need to compete against each other – if there are enough of them – or against men, though they will be at a disadvantage. If skilled negotiators can suggest a better solution for this group, I would be delighted to hear it.

I am well aware that none of this bears much resemblance to the demands of mainstream transactivist groups. But those demands are incompatible with the interests of several other groups, including women, children, same-sex-attracted people and members of certain religions.

Think what would have to happen if gender identity were truly to supplant sex, right across society. Everyone would have to stop caring whether other people were male or female, and instead concern themselves only with identities. Women would undress in front of males as comfortably as in front of females, provided those males identified as women. No other consideration would count – not religion, modesty, trauma or anything else. An Orthodox Jewish woman would willingly receive an internal examination from a male doctor, and a rape victim would pour her heart out to a male crisis counsellor – again, provided those males identified as women. Everyone would be open to sexual partners with any combination of primary and secondary sexual characteristics, provided they had the 'right' identity. Anyone who said they could desire only certain combinations would be regarded as a bigot, or perhaps a pervert.

I doubt any mammalian species could live like this: other people's sex is too evolutionarily salient. If you disagree, that's fine – but you will have to argue for your unisex utopia, and wait for the rest of us to buy in. You cannot simply declare that it already exists, and that the rest of us must live in it.

The gender-identity debate has become so heated, and the political climate so poisonous, that engaging in good faith looks difficult. It will take a renewed commitment to two interests shared by everyone in a secular, liberal democracy: freedom of belief and freedom of speech. As an atheist, I do not have to pay even lip service to any religion – in return for which I gladly accept the right of religious people to discuss their faith, wear its symbols, worship freely and proclaim positions I oppose, such as the immorality of same-sex marriage or the importance of wifely obedience. I demand the same freedom to reject and oppose gender-identity ideology, and in return gladly accept that others have the right to preach it and live by it.

All the harms I have described – the destruction of women's rights, the sterilisation of gender non-conforming children, the spread of postmodernist homophobia, and the corruption of medical and scientific research – would crumble before a renewed societal commitment to the Enlightenment values of open inquiry and robust debate. This book is my contribution.

AFTERWORD

February 2022

Like any journalist, I love a fast-moving story. But book dead-lines are very different from those in my day job on a weekly paper, and at times I found it challenging to write about events that I knew would have moved on before the hardback edition had hit the shelves. A year on, those stories are still developing, especially – as I predicted in my introduction – in sports and paediatric gender medicine.

In June 2021, in Tokyo, New Zealander Laurel Hubbard became the first openly transgender Olympian, competing under rules dating from 2015 that allow males to switch sex category provided they lower their testosterone. Hubbard, a 43-year-old weightlifter who had suffered a serious arm injury three years earlier, did not make the podium. And so the (consid-erable) criticism died down quickly – quite unreasonably, since it is unfair to include anyone with male sporting advantage in the female category, even if that person is out of condition and well past prime sporting age. (If you can't see this, ask yourself whether an injured 43-year-old female weightlifter could have qualified to represent her country at the Olympics. All the female athletes competing in Tokyo were in superb shape, and almost all were in their teens and twenties.)

In November 2021 the IOC published revised guidance on transgender inclusion and achieved the seemingly impossible: a new policy even worse than the old. Now male athletes who want to compete as women will no longer even need to lower their testosterone levels, a change made on the grounds that there was no evidence that suppression had any impact on fairness. The proper response to recognising that male sporting advantage cannot be removed by suppression would, of course, be to exclude males altogether. Instead the IOC said it would leave each regulatory body worldwide to set its own rules, based on 'robust and peer-reviewed science' and excluding males only if a 'consistent, unfair and disproportionate competitive advantage and/or an unpreventable risk to the safety of the athletes' was proven.

The consequence is twofold. First, regulators who care about the integrity of women's sports will have to commission studies to demonstrate that the general phenomenon of male advantage does indeed hold in their individual sport. Second, regulators who do not care have been given the perfect excuse to embrace full self-ID.

But even as the IOC abandons the last safeguards for women's sports, its stance is becoming untenable. At the end of 2021 a trans-identified athlete emerged who embodies the contradictions of self-ID in a way that the ageing, injured Hubbard did not. Lia (Will) Thomas, a 22-year-old student at the University of Pennsylvania, had been a strong enough swimmer to make the men's team between 2017 and 2020, though not fast enough to win gold, even in intra-university events. In 2021 Thomas started to compete as a woman and, as I write, is smashing women's college records and on course to do the same with national and perhaps global ones. The world's fastest female swimmers are at risk of being erased from the record books by an athlete whose times are decent but not outstanding for a male.

For now, proponents of self-ID in sport are doubling down. When parents of Thomas's teammates complained about the unfairness of self-ID, university officials brushed them off, saying that UPenn's 'counselling and psychological services' were available to help their daughters 'navigate Lia's success in the pool'. The Ivy League expressed 'unwavering commitment to providing an inclusive environment for all student-athletes while condemning transphobia and discrimination in any form'. The Human Rights Campaign, a US LGBT rights organisation, declared itself 'in solidarity with Lia and all athletes who compete in the sports they love and on teams consistent with their gender identity.'

Such statements may be understandable when they come from ideologically committed activists. After all, acknowledging that males should not be allowed to enter female sporting events means recognising that 'transwomen are women' is not literally true. Adherence to the mantra leaves these activists no choice but to defend the indefensible.

More puzzling has been the lack of pushback from people without fixed positions on the issue. But an internal 'messaging guide' produced for the Transgender Law Center and other American transactivist groups that was leaked in early 2022 sheds some light on the matter. Few of the ordinary people who are positively disposed towards gender self-ID are aware that it increasingly applies in sports, it explains – and maintaining that lack of awareness is essential, because such low-information supporters are 'extremely susceptible to our opposition's argument that excluding trans youth is necessary to protect the fairness of women's sports'. Many of those who insist that 'transwomen are women' have not followed the consequences of that claim all the way to the logical conclusion, it seems.

To keep things that way, the guide recommends redirecting the attention of these supporters if ever it should happen to stray in an inconvenient direction. If the topic of trans inclusion in sports arises, transactivists should seek to shift the discourse away from fairness (which it calls an 'individualist lens of competition') towards a 'collective frame' by highlighting 'teamwork and other values young people learn through sports'. Above all, they should seek to stop people from making 'transphobic connections of transgender girls and women as actually male'. Girls and women, in other words, should be told not to care about winning and to satisfy themselves instead with taking part.

Away from the ideological capture of the IOC and the political polarisation of the US, some developments were more encouraging. A joint report by the UK Sports Councils stated categorically that fairness for female athletes was irreconcilable with trans inclusion, and that sporting regulators would have to choose between the two. Amazingly, the first regulator to say that it would prioritise inclusion for males over fairness for females was the British Kickboxing Council, which oversees a sport where not just fairness, but safety, is a major issue. New guidelines from the national sports council of Denmark also pointed out this irreconcilable clash between inclusion and fairness – and went somewhat further, recommending that regulators choose fairness. Men's competitions, it said, should be open to everyone, and women's reserved solely for female people, except in the handful of sports where strength, speed and endurance play no role.

The other fast-developing area in which I predicted a backlash was paediatric gender medicine. Here, too, there has been a mixture of disappointing reversals and promising news. But overall, the trend has been towards growing awareness and increased scrutiny.

Several more jurisdictions have passed laws banning 'conversion therapy', that is, any attempt to change either sexual orientation or gender identity. Among them are some American states, and Canada at the federal level. As I write, a public consultation on such a law is under way in the UK.

These bans tend to garner support because of revulsion at the outrages therapists used to inflict on homosexual people in an attempt to 'straighten them out'. But nowadays medical and psychiatric regulators across the developed world understand sexual orientation to be an innate and harmless trait, and bar any attempt to change it. To the extent that 'gay conversion therapy' still occurs, it is exclusively in informal, usually religious, settings, where a ban would make little difference. A pastor in a fringe evangelical church, for example, may call a prayer meeting in which members who confess to same-sex attraction are exhorted to give up their sinful ways. (Coercion or violence in such settings would count as assault, which is therefore already illegal.)

The main impact will be felt in paediatric gender clinics, where therapists who follow anything but the gender-affirmative approach will risk criminal sanctions. As I explain in chapter 4, most gender-dysphoric children will outgrow their misery unless their therapists and parents reinforce their cross-sex identity. But therapists constrained by laws based on the notion that gender identity is innate and unchangeable will be unable to do the careful, exploratory work required to uncover the reasons behind their young clients' gender dysphoria, or even tell their parents that it is likely to be transient.

And so these bans will mean more gender non-conforming children are socially transitioned and put on puberty blockers and then cross-sex hormones. Such children are much more likely than the average to grow up gay, as long as they are left in peace to work that out themselves. That well-meaning people's revulsion at gay conversion therapy has been co-opted to support a treatment pathway that turns proto-gay children into 'straight' trans people is the most upsetting of all the harms done by gender-identity ideology, and the one I most fervently wish to see ended.

In another unwelcome development, in September 2021 an appeal by the Tavistock paediatric gender clinic against the Keira Bell ruling succeeded. The appeal court regarded the sorts of arguments made in the initial hearing, which centred on whether a minor could give informed consent to puberty blockers, as largely irrelevant. Judicial review was not appropriate to resolve such issues of capacity, it ruled. Instead clinicians should decide case by case, and if they got it wrong with an individual child, they could expect to be sued. Bell has applied for leave to appeal to the Supreme Court.

More hopefully, in recent months some Swedish paediatric gender clinics have stopped prescribing puberty blockers after a hard-hitting three-part documentary by *Mission Investigate*, the country's premier investigative news TV programme. 'The Trans Train' revealed that gender clinicians neither informed children and their families of the harmful side-effects of puberty blockers and cross-sex hormones, nor monitored patients for such effects. One girl, who spent four years on puberty blockers, experienced such catastrophic loss of bone density that she now suffers constant, debilitating pain from spinal fractures and malformed vertebrae. Under the *Mission Investigate* team's questioning, doctors, therapists and endocrinologists obfuscated, denied and blamed each other. None was willing to take responsibility – and that offers hope for the future, though no justice for those already damaged. Clinicians who are happy to proceed as long as they are receiving plaudits are likely to reverse course when they realise that they may be held liable for the harms they have done.

Increasing recognition of these harms is already changing clinical practice. Sweden's main paediatric gender clinic, at the famous Karolinska Institute, in Stockholm, has now ended the prescription of puberty blockers except as part of randomised controlled trials – in other words, as part of research designed to compare outcomes for children who are put on the gender-affirming pathway and those who are not. Meanwhile clinics in Finland have announced that the first line of treatment for gender-dysphoric children will be psychotherapy, rather than transition. And further afield, the professional regulator for psychiatrists in Australia and New Zealand has advised paediatric gender clinicians to prioritise support for broader mental health needs and move only slowly towards medicalisation.

Just as significantly, some of the best-known proponents of gender affirmation have started to express doubts publicly. One is Laura Edwards-Leeper, a child psychologist who was instrumental in introducing puberty blockers to the US in 2007, and who is now chair of WPATH's child and adolescent committee. Another is Erica Anderson, a clinical psychologist (and trans-woman) who was until recently on the board of USPATH, WPATH's American arm. In a joint op-ed published by the *Washington Post* in November 2021, entitled 'The mental health establishment is failing trans kids', the pair criticise their professional peers for paying too little heed to trauma and mental illness in gender-dysphoric children and teenagers. Although both still support gender affirmation for carefully screened children, they warn that many clinicians are eschewing 'comprehensive assessment and gender-exploratory therapy' and providing 'sloppy, dangerous care'. And they express concern about the rising number of regretters, acknowledging that 'many trans activists want to silence detransitioners or deny their existence' for fear that their testimony will raise concerns about gender medicine more broadly.

A couple of months later American journalist Lisa Selin Davis published an interview with Anderson in *Quillette*, in which Anderson attests to the accuracy of Abigail Shrier's book, *Irreversible Damage*. 'I keep hearing these stories, and I believe them…I hear from people who say, "We took our child to a therapist who said, 'Your child is trans. I recommend hormones.'" And this is happening all over.'

Marci Bowers, another transwoman working in gender medicine, this time as a surgeon, has also expressed concern about the way gender medicine is evolving. In an article published in October 2021, Bowers is quoted by Shrier as saying that puberty blockers cause such huge difficulties for genital surgery that their use should be abandoned. (Jazz Jennings is among the 2,000 transwomen who has undergone vaginoplasty at Bowers's hands.) Bowers also spoke frankly about paediatric gender medicine's dirty little secret: that it produces adults with severe sexual dysfunction. 'If you've never had an orgasm pre-surgery, and then your puberty's blocked, it's very difficult to achieve that afterwards… I worry about their reproductive rights later… These young children who never experience orgasm prior to undergoing surgery are going to reach adulthood and try to find intimacy and realize they don't know how to respond sexually.'

Unlike these three clinicians, I think children can *never* provide valid consent to the destruction of their sexual response and reproductive capacity, no matter how gender-dysphoric they are. But I do not underestimate the bravery it has taken them to speak out. I regard them as whistle-blowers, albeit ones who continue to work within an immoral, exploitative industry. They have received vicious criticism and pushback from their peers – as they must have expected. Very few of those implicated in previous medical scandals have ever accepted that they and their colleagues have caused their patients needless harm. Instead they conceal their doubts, even from themselves, until that is no longer tenable. And then they quietly move on.

*

On another major theme of this book, the erosion of women's rights to self-definition and boundaries, the news was also fast-moving – and mixed. Depressingly often in the year since it was published, authorities of various kinds have demonstrated their lack of concern for women, forcing through gender self-ID despite clear warnings about the impact on vulnerable women.

One example came in mid-2021, when Edinburgh Rape Crisis Centre announced that its new CEO would be Mridhul Wadhwa, a self-identified transwoman who lacks a gender-recognition certificate (and who is therefore legally, as well as biologically, male). The job ad had availed of provisions in UK employment law that permit sensitive roles to be restricted to female people only. Wadhwa was therefore ineligible, but none-theless applied and was selected for the job. The appointment was a remarkable demonstration of why such positions should be reserved for female people. In an interview for a popular feminist podcast, Wadhwa boasted about the Edinburgh centre's commitment to self-ID, describing rape victims who sought female-only spaces in which to recover as 'bigoted people' with 'unacceptable beliefs' who should 'expect to be challenged on [their] prejudices' and told to 'reframe their trauma'.

The same lack of concern for women's needs and

vulnerabilities was visible in attitudes towards female prisoners. In mid-2021, a judicial review brought by an inmate of an English prison to the High Court in London failed to overturn the government's policy of placing transwomen in women's jails as long as they had either changed legal sex or passed a risk assessment. Among the male prisoners transferred were some who had undergone no physical transition; a female prisoner told the court of the fear and trauma that she and her fellow inmates, many of whom had suffered violence and sexual assault before being imprisoned, experienced as a consequence.

In its ruling, the court agreed that female prisoners were being put at heightened risk by the policy, that their human rights were potentially being violated, and that they were likely to suffer 'fear and acute anxiety' and 'significant' psychological impact. And it acknowledged that many British people found it 'incongruous and inappropriate that a prisoner of masculine physique and with male genitalia should be accommodated in a female prison in any circumstances'. But male prisoners' wishes had to be taken into consideration, it ruled, and the policy was 'capable of being operated lawfully'. In other words, the government was legally entitled to prioritise male prisoners' desires over female ones' dignity, safety and mental well-being if that was what it wanted to do.

Empathy for female prisoners was even more conspicuous by its absence in the US, as the number of states prioritising gender identity over sex continued to rise. Under a new law giving 'transgender, intersex and gender non-binary' prisoners the right to request transfer, California saw 288 male convicts requesting transfers to women's prisons in 2021, with 41 approved and 25 moved. (Eight women applied to move the other way; in a rare moment of sanity, none were granted permission.) The law specifies that transferred prisoners have the right

310

to mingle with the general prison population, and that 'genital status' must play no part in decisions about cell allocation. The Women's Liberation Front has taken a lawsuit against the policy, arguing that it cannot be applied 'in any manner that avoids violating the federal and state constitutional rights of incarcerated women'.

Even by the standards of America's partisan media on this subject, the coverage was abysmal. Newspapers and radio programmes in California, and other states with similar policies, ran soft-focus profiles of transwomen awaiting transfer, with no mention of the crimes they had been locked up for. In some cases, these included rape and murder. Rayne Bennett (Jacob Lawrence Pina), who was tried and sentenced (as a man) in Kansas for abducting and raping a fourteen-year-old girl and who later adopted a transgender persona in prison, was portrayed sympathetically by the Kansas branch of NPR and several local papers, without any mention of his crime. Female inmates' concerns were described as inspired by transphobic prison staff: the *San Francisco Chronicle* claimed that women had been perfectly happy with transfers from men's prisons until 'guards began to stir up the female prison population by warning that men would be housed with them'.

Similar biases and naivety about unintended consequences were on display in coverage of the 'Wi Spa affair', the story that came closest to breaking through the American media's code of omertà on gender self-ID. It started in June 2021, when a mobile-phone recording made in a spa in Los Angeles was posted on Reddit and promptly went viral. It shows a woman complaining to reception staff about a naked man entering the women-only section and exposing his semi-erect penis to the (also naked) women and girls. Staff tell her – accurately – that under Californian law anyone who says they're a woman has right of access to women-only spaces, even ones where the users are naked.

The following days saw protests and counter-protests outside the spa, some degenerating into violence. Again, the way the story was covered was as revealing as the facts. An editorial in the *LA Times* is worth quoting at length. 'There is no doubt that Wi Spa did the right thing in defending the right of a transgender customer to be nude in the women's area, even though the sight of male-appearing genitalia discomfited at least one female customer,' it says. After acknowledging, albeit grudgingly, that not everyone who 'feels uncomfortable in such scenarios' is 'a bigot', it comes down firmly on the right of male people who identify as woman to expose their genitalia in women's spaces. 'Everyone – transgender customers, members of every faith and women who are upset by the sight of penises – has the right to use the spa and other public accommodations…People have a right to use the spa, but that doesn't include with it a guarantee that they all will feel at ease with everything they see.'

Soon after this editorial was published, it emerged that the individual at the centre of the Wi Spa incident had been charged with five offences in relation to it, including indecent exposure, and had been on California's sex offenders' register since 2006. Under Californian law, indecent exposure does not mean merely exposing your genitals non-consensually – how could it, when people of one sex are entitled to go naked into spaces intended for members of the other? Rather, the exposure must be done in pursuit of sexual arousal or with the aim of committing a (further) sexual offence. As I write, it is not even clear whether the individual does in fact identify as a woman.

It has become no easier for women to speak up about such issues; however, the attempts to silence them are finally coming to wider notice. In October 2021 philosopher Kathleen Stock, whose gender-critical book *Material Girls: Why Reality Matters for Feminism* was published some months earlier, resigned from the University of Sussex because of intensifying harassment by some students and staff. As pandemic restrictions eased and in-person lectures restarted, police warned her to stay away from campus for her own safety and to install security measures in her house. The university's vice-chancellor issued a statement of support – somewhat belatedly, given that the harassment had been happening for years. But when the local branch of the national union of academic staff refused to support her, called for an investigation into 'institutional transphobia' and warned that employment rights should not be 'instrumentalised' to harm trans people, she had had enough and handed in her notice.

The story gained wide coverage, almost all of it sympathetic to Stock and outraged at the cruelty of her attackers. Just as importantly, many commentators noted that her positions are shared by most people, both in the UK and worldwide, and cannot be described as 'transphobic' by any fair reading. It was just one of several encouraging indications in the year since this book was published that those attempting to silence critics of extreme transactivism have overreached.

Another was the judgment in December 2021 in Harry Miller's case against the College of Policing, which ruled that police guidance originally intended to stop racist abuse escalating into physical violence, but now largely used to silence gender-critical women, was unlawful. For the past decade, police have been supposed to record any allegations that someone has said something hateful as a 'non-crime hate incident', which can show up in a pre-employment check. This has been the case even for allegations that are clearly malicious or even nonsensical. In several high-profile cases, reports were used to harass and intimidate opponents of gender self-ID by giving them a police record.

A month later, a long-running attempt to force a bakery in Northern Ireland owned by evangelical Christians to ice a cake with the slogan 'Support gay marriage' was thrown out by the European Court of Human Rights. That ended seven years of successive rulings and appeals in which activists had sought to present the bakers' refusal to express a slogan they profoundly disagreed with as a violation of other people's dignity – in other words, to create a 'human right' to compel others to affirm your beliefs at the expense of their own conscience.

As I make clear several times in this book, I wholeheartedly support same-sex marriage. But I also support freedom of belief and freedom of speech, including for opinions I disagree with. I am puzzled that the campaigners, who spent all that time trying to force evangelical Christians to endorse a political position they regard as sinful, never thought about their own free-speech rights – how would they like to be forced to bake a cake that said 'Sodomites will burn'? Personally, I'm grateful for the right to refuse to make a cake that says something I disagree with: 'Transwomen are women', say, or 'Wives, obey your husbands'.

My hope is that, together, these the two rulings will make it harder for authorities to compel either speech or silence, and safer for employees to stand up against self-ID. For example, someone who refuses to put 'preferred pronouns' in her email signature can now tell HR that she is exercising her legally protected right not to express a belief she does not hold. Doing so will still not be easy – taking a stand against orthodoxy, no matter how recently established, never is. But the risk is now lower, and consequently the number of people doing so can be expected to rise.

Which brings me, finally, to Maya Forstater's victory in her employment tribunal appeal. It is perhaps the most heartening development in the UK since this book was published and the one that will make the biggest difference to women's rights in the coming years.

As readers will recall, in December 2019 a judge ruled that Forstater's beliefs – namely that biological sex is binary and immutable, and that acknowledging this matters for women's rights – were so extreme and hateful that the think-tank she worked for was justified in letting her go. In June 2021 that judgment was overturned. Since her former employer declined to appeal to the Supreme Court, 'gender-critical' beliefs are now explicitly covered by British equality and employment law, meaning that anyone holding them is protected against discrimination in work and the provision of services. In March 2022 Forstater will have attended a hearing to establish whether she did indeed lose her job because of her beliefs, in which case she is due compensation, or for some other reason. A judgment is expected later in the year.

When the hardback edition of this book was published, Sex Matters, the human-rights organisation co-founded by Forstater to fight against the erosion of sex-based rights, was just getting off the ground. Like the other grassroots groups springing up in the UK to defend causes I care about – women's rights to self-definition and boundaries; children's well-being and safety; and gay people's ability to be out and proud about their same-sex attraction – it has grown beyond anything I could have predicted. Telling their story has been a privilege.

ACKNOWLEDGEMENTS

My deepest gratitude goes to my agent, Caroline Hardman, who picked up my proposal when others were too timid, and to my editor, Cecilia Stein, who not only has a spine of steel but provided invaluable guidance on matters of structure and tone.

I would like to thank the women of Vancouver and Toronto, who helped me understand Canada's erasure of sex-based rights, and the women of gender-critical Twitter, who responded with wit and insight to my many questions. I learned a great deal from other women who use their media platforms to write about the harms of gender-identity ideology, in particular Jo Bartosch, Julie Bindel, Sarah Ditum, Madeleine Kearns, Victoria Smith and Janice Turner. I was inspired by the staunchness of Stephanie Davies-Arai, Maya Forstater, Jane Clare Jones, Meghan Murphy, Kathleen Stock and Nicola Williams, and by the generosity of spirit of Nick Cohen, Simon Fanshawe, Jon Kay and James Kirkup.

And finally, I salute the women responsible for the resurgence of grassroots feminism in the UK: FiLiA, Fair Play for Women, Woman's Place UK, Legal Feminist, Sex Matters, For Women Scotland, MBM Policy Analysis and many others.

FURTHER READING

All online sources were last accessed on 3 March 2021.

Chapter 1

Ashley, A., Thompson, D., *The First Lady* (Blake Publishing, 2006).

Colapinto, J., *As Nature Made Him: The Boy Who Was Raised as a Girl* (Harper Perennial, 2006).

Hoyer, N. [Lili Elbe], *Man into Woman: The First Sex Change* (Canelo, New edition, 2015).

Jorgensen, C., *Christine Jorgensen: A Personal Autobiography* (Cleis Press, 2000).

Marinov, G.K., 'In humans, sex is binary and immutable', *Academic Questions*, 33 (2020), 279–288.

Meyerowitz, J., *How Sex Changed: A History of Transsexuality in the United States* (Harvard University Press, 2004).

Morris, J., *Conundrum* (Faber & Faber, 2018).

Wolff, C., *Magnus Hirschfeld: A Portrait of a Pioneer in Sexology* (Quartet Books, 1986).

Chapter 2

Bailey, M., *The Man Who Would Be Queen: The Science of Gender-Bending and Transsexualism* (Joseph Henry Press, 2003).

Bailey, M., Blanchard, R., 'Gender dysphoria is not one thing', *4thWave Now* (7 December 2017), https://4thwavenow.com/2017/12/07/gender-dysphoria-is-not-one-thing/.

Bartlett, N., Vasey, P., Bukowski, W., 'Is gender identity disorder in children a mental disorder?', *Sex Roles*, 43 (2000), 753–785.

Blanchard, R., 'Clinical observations and systematic studies of autogynephilia', *Journal of Sex & Marital Therapy*, 17 (1991), 235–251.

Blanchard, R., 'Early history of the concept of autogynephilia', *Archives of Sexual Behavior*, 34 (2005), 439–446.

Blanchard, R., 'The classification and labeling of nonhomosexual gender dysphorias', *Archives of Sexual Behavior*, 18 (1989), 315–334.

Bloom, A., 'Conservative men in conservative dresses', *Atlantic Monthly* (March 2002).

Dreger, A.D., *Galileo's Middle Finger: Heretics, Activists, and One Scholar's Search for Justice* (Penguin Books, 2017).

Gómez Jiménez, F.R, Court, L., Vasey, P.L., 'A retrospective study of childhood gendered behavior in Istmo Zapotec men, women and muxes', *Archives of Sexual Behavior*, 49 (2020), 467–477.

Green, R., *The 'Sissy Boy Syndrome' and the Development of Homosexuality* (Yale University Press, 1987).

Lawrence, A., *Men Trapped in Men's Bodies: Narratives of Autogynephilic Transsexualism* (Springer, 2012).

McCloskey, D.N., *Crossing: A Memoir* (University of Chicago Press, 2000).

Vasey, P.L., Bartlett, N.H., 'What can the Samoan fa'afafine teach us about the Western concept of "gender identity disorder in childhood"?', *Perspectives in Biology and Medicine*, 50 (2007), 481–490.

Chapter 3

Currin, J.M., Lee, F.M., Brown, C., Hammer, T.R., 'Taking the red pill: using *The Matrix* to explore transgender identity development', *Journal of Creativity in Mental Health*, 12:3 (2017), 402–409.

De Beauvoir, S., *The Second Sex* (Vintage, 2010).

Epstein, R., 'The empty brain', *Aeon* (18 May 2016), https://aeon.co/essays/your-brain-does-not-process-information-and-it-is-not-a-computer.

Sax, L., 'How common is intersex? A response to Anne Fausto-Sterling', *Journal of Sex Research*, 39:3 (2002), 174–178.

Chapter 4

Bailey, M., Blanchard, R., 'Suicide or transition: the only options for gender dysphoric kids?', *4thWaveNow* (8 September 2017), https://4thwavenow.com/2017/09/08/suicide-or-transition-the-only-options-for-gender-dysphoric-kids/.

Biggs, M., 'Puberty blockers and suicidality in adolescents suffering from gender dysphoria', *Archives of Sexual Behavior*, 49 (2020), 2227–2229.

Biggs, M., 'The Tavistock's Experimentation with Puberty Blockers', *Transgender Trend*, https://www.transgendertrend.com/product/the-tavistocks-experimentation-with-puberty-blockers/.

Cantor, J., 'Do trans- kids stay trans- when they grow up?', *Sexology Today* (11 January 2016), http://www.sexologytoday.org/2016/01/do-trans-kids-stay-trans-when-they-grow_99.html.

Cantor, J.M., 'Transgender and gender diverse children and adolescents: fact-checking of AAP policy', *Journal of Sex & Marital Therapy*, 46:4 (2020), 307–313.

D'Angelo, R., Syrulnik, E., Ayad, S., et al., 'One size does not fit all: in support of psychotherapy for gender dysphoria', *Archives of Sexual Behavior*, 50 (2021), 7–16.

De Vries, A.L.C., McGuire, J.K., et al., 'Young adult psychological outcome after puberty suppression and gender reassignment', *Pediatrics*, 134:4 (2014), 696–704.

De Vries, A.L.C., Steensma, T.D., et al., 'Puberty suppression in adolescents with gender identity disorder: a prospective follow-up study', *Journal of Sexual Medicine*, 8:8 (2011), 2276–2283.

Shappley, K., 'I had 4 boys – until one of them told me she was really a girl', *Good Housekeeping* (April 2017).

Singal, J., 'How the fight over transgender kids got a leading sex researcher fired', *The Cut* (7 February 2016), https://www.thecut.com/2016/02/fight-over-trans-kids-got-a-researcher-fired.html.

Chapter 5

Acocella, J., *Creating Hysteria: Women and Multiple Personality Disorder* (Jossey-Bass, 1999).

Bailey, J. M., Zucker, K. J., 'Childhood sex-typed behavior and sexual orientation: a conceptual analysis and quantitative review', *Developmental Psychology*, 31 (1995), 43–55.

Du Preez, M., Dronfeld, J., *Dr James Barry: A Woman Ahead of Her Time* (Oneworld, 2016).

Laws, R.D., O'Donohue, W.T. (eds), *Sexual Deviance: Theory, Assessment, and Treatment* (Guilford Press, 2nd edition, 2008).

Littman, L., 'Parent reports of adolescents and young adults perceived to show signs of a rapid onset of gender dysphoria', *PLOS ONE*, 13:8 (2018), e0202330.

Ofshe, R., Watters, E., *Making Monsters: False Memories, Psychotherapy, and Sexual Hysteria* (University of California Press, 1996).

Shorter, E., *From Paralysis to Fatigue: A History of Psychosomatic Illness in the Modern Era* (Free Press, 1992).

Watters, E., *Crazy Like Us: The Globalisation of the American Psyche* (Simon & Schuster, 2010).

Chapter 6

De Castella, T. and Heyden, T., 'How did the pro-paedophile group PIE exist openly for 10 years?', *BBC News* (27 February 2014), https://www.bbc.co.uk/news/magazine-26352378.

Doward, J., 'How paedophiles infiltrated the left and hijacked the fight for civil rights', *Guardian* (1 March 2014).

Fairweather, E., 'WITNESS: Stalinist reluctance to study the facts', *Independent* (29 May 1995).

Fleischhauer, J., Müller, A.K., Pfister, R., 'Pedophile links haunt Green Party', *Spiegel International* (13 May 2013), https://www.spiegel.de/international/germany/past-pedophile-links-haunt-german-green-party-a-899544.html.

Gebhardt, W., 'The dark legacy of sexual liberation in Germany', *DW.com* (17 June 2020), https://www.dw.com/en/germany-allowed-pedophiles-to-foster-children/a-53839291.

Hamann, G., 'Greens research pedophilic past', *DW.com* (17 August 2013), https://www.dw.com/en/greens-research-pedophilic-past/a-17026612.

Harris, P., Bright, M., 'The whistleblower's story', *Guardian* (6 July 2003).

Hunt, G. (ed.), *Whistleblowing in the Social Services: Public Accountability and Professional Practice* (Hodder Education, 1998).

Moore, M., Brunskell-Evans, H. (eds), *Inventing Transgender Children and Young People* (Cambridge Scholars Publishing, 2019).

Moore, M., Brunskell-Evans, H. (eds), *Transgender Children and Young People: Born in Your Own Body* (Cambridge Scholars Publishing, 2018).

Rogers, T., 'A major German political party used to support pedophilia – and it's coming back to haunt them', *New Republic* (24 November 2014).

Shrier, A., *Irreversible Damage: Teenage Girls and the Transgender Craze* (Swift Press, 2020).

Chapter 7

Allen, S., Jones, J.C., et al., 'Doing better in arguments about sex, gender, and trans rights', *Medium* (23 May 2019), https://medium.com/@kathleen-stock/doing-better-in-arguments-about-sex-and-gender-3bec3fc4bdb6.

Benvenuto, C., *Sex Changes: A Memoir of Marriage, Gender and Moving On* (St. Martin's Press, 2012).

Bogardus, T., 'Some internal problems with revisionary gender concepts', *Philosophia*, 48 (2020), 55–75.

Chappell, S.-G., Lawford-Smith, H., 'Transgender: a dialogue', *Aeon* (15 November 2018), https://aeon.co/essays/transgender-identities-a-conversation-between-two-philosophers.

Ladin, J., *Through the Door of Life: A Jewish Journey Between Genders* (University of Wisconsin Press, 2013).

Lawford-Smith, H., 'The adoption analogy revisited', https://hollylawford-smith.files.wordpress.com/2020/10/the_adoption_analogy_revisited.pdf.

Nussbaum, M., 'The professor of parody', *New Republic* (27 February 1999).

Rich, A., *Of Woman Born: Motherhood as Experience and Institution* (Norton Paperback, 1996).

Trans Widows Voices, https://www.transwidowsvoices.org/.

Tuvel, R., 'In defense of transracialism', *Hypatia*, 32:2 (2017), 263–278.

Chapter 8

Biggs, M., 'The transition from sex to gender in English prisons: human rights and queer theory', *SocArXiv* (16 May 2020).

Carter, W.B., 'Sexism in the "bathroom debates": how bathrooms really became separated by sex', *Yale Law & Policy Review*, 37 (2019).

Dillon, S., '#TERF/Bigot/Transphobe – "We found the witch, burn her!"' (Ph.D. diss., University of Portsmouth).

Gilligan, A., 'Unisex changing rooms put women in danger', *Sunday Times* (2 September 2018), https://www.thetimes.co.uk/article/unisex-changing-rooms-put-women-in-danger-8lwbp8kgk.

Halley, A., 'Male-bodied rapists are being imprisoned with women. Why do so few people care?', *Quillette* (12 October 2019), https://quillette.com/2019/10/12/male-bodied-rapists-are-being-imprisoned-with-women-why-do-so-few-people-care/.

Lifton, R.J., *Thought Reform and the Psychology of Totalism: A Study of 'Brainwashing' in Communist China* (University of North Carolina Press, 1989).

Chapter 9

Ballantyne, N.K., Kayser, M., Grootegoed, J.A., 'Sex and gender issues in competitive sports: investigation of a historical case leads to a new viewpoint', *British Journal of Sports Medicine*, 46 (2012), 614–617.

Bazelon, E., 'Cross-court winner', *Slate* (25 October 2012) https://slate.com/culture/2012/10/jewish-jocks-and-renee-richards-the-life-of-the-transsexual-tennis-legend.html.

Coleman-Phillips, C., 'Transgender rugby player playing with "smile on my face"', *BBC Sport* (22 August 2019), https://www.bbc.co.uk/sport/rugby-union/49298550.

Fenichel, P., Paris, F., et al., 'Molecular diagnosis of 5α-reductase deficiency in 4 elite young female athletes through hormonal screening for hyperandrogenism', *Journal of Clinical Endocrinology and Metabolism*, 98:6 (2013), E1055–E1059.

Ferguson-Smith, M.A., Ferris, E.A. 'Gender verification in sport: the need for change?', *British Journal of Sports Medicine*, 25:2 (1991), 104.

Harper, J., 'Race times for transgender athletes', *Journal of Sporting Cultures and Identities*, 6:1 (2015), 1–9.

Hilton, E., Lundberg, T., 'Transgender women in the female category of sport: perspectives on testosterone suppression and performance advantage', *Journal of Sports Medicine*, 51 (2021), 199–214.

'Male high school athletes vs. female Olympians', http://boysvswomen.com/#/.

Martínez-Patiño, M.J., 'Personal account: a woman tried and tested', *Lancet*, 366 (2005), 538.

Shabir, I., Khuruna, M.L., et al., 'Phenotype, genotype and gender identity in a large cohort of patients from India with 5α-reductase 2 deficiency', *Andrology*, 3:6 (2015), 1132–1139.

Switzer, K., *Marathon Woman: Running the Race to Revolutionize Women's Sports* (Da Capo Press, 2009).

Wertheim, J., 'She's a transgender pioneer, but Renée Richards prefers to stay out of the spotlight', *Sports Illustrated* (28 June 2019).

Chapter 10

Biggs, M., 'LGBT facts and figures', http://users.ox.ac.uk/~sfos0060/LGBT_figures.shtml.

Burt, C.H., 'Scrutinizing the U.S. Equality Act 2019: a feminist examination of definitional changes and sociolegal ramifications', *Feminist Criminology* (1 June 2020).

US 4th Circuit Court of Appeals, Grimm v. Gloucester County School Board (26 August 2020), https://www.ca4.uscourts.gov/opinions/191952.P.pdf.

US Departments of Justice and Education, 'Dear Colleague Letter on Transgender Students' (13 May 2016), https://www2.ed.gov/about/offices/list/ocr/letters/colleague-201605-title-ix-transgender.pdf.

US Supreme Court, Bostock v. Clayton County (15 June 2020), https://www.supremecourt.gov/opinions/19pdf/17-1618_hfci.pdf.

Chapter 11

Burt, C.H., 'Scrutinizing the Equality Act: online supplemental information', https://callieburt.org/research-projects/oscl/scrueqact-online-supplement/.

Campbell, S., 'Abolishing women', *Wings over Scotland* (8 May 2020), https://wingsoverscotland.com/abolishing-women/.

Fair Play For Women, 'The British public knows that males can't become female and wants public policies to reflect that' (16 September 2020), https://fairplayforwomen.com/polldata/.

Fair Play For Women, 'The results of the Populus on-line survey following the UK Gender Recognition Act consultation 2018' (15 November 2018), https://fairplayforwomen.com/poll/.

Fair Play For Women, 'Where does the British public stand on transgender rights?' (16 July 2020), https://yougov.co.uk/topics/politics/articles-reports/2020/07/16/where-does-british-public-stand-transgender-rights.

IGLYO, Thomson Reuters Foundation, and Dentons, *Only Adults? Good Practices in Legal Gender Recognition for Youth* (November 2019), https://www.iglyo.com/wp-content/uploads/2019/11/IGLYO_v3-1.pdf.

Jones, J.C., Mackenzie, L., *The Political Erasure of Sex: Sex and the Census. Appendix: A Brief History of Transgender Ideology* (2020), https://thepoliticalerasureofsex.org/appendix/.

Kaufmann, E., 'How the trans pledge damaged the Labour Party', *Quillette* (27 February 2020), https://quillette.com/2020/02/27/how-the-trans-pledge-damaged-the-labour-party/.

Schilling, T., 'Battleground state polling', *American Principles Project* (28 July 2020), https://americanprinciplesproject.org/wp-content/uploads/2020/07/APP-Swing-State-Polling-Memo-7-28-20.pdf.

The Yogyakarta Principles Plus 10 (Geneva, 10 November 2017), http://yogyakartaprinciples.org/wp-content/uploads/2017/11/A5_yogyakartaWEB-2.pdf.

Women's Liberation Front, 'WoLF releases groundbreaking poll results: gender identity policies flop with voters' (4 September 2020), https://www.womensliberationfront.org/news/wolf-releases-groundbreaking-poll-results-gender-identity-policies-flop-with-voters.

Chapter 12

Brassil, G.R., Longman, J., 'World Rugby bars transgender women, baffling players', *New York Times* (31 October 2020), https://www.nytimes.com/2020/10/26/sports/olympics/world-rugby-transgender-women.html.

Reddick, N., 'USA Rugby's Naima Reddick: let trans women play', *Advocate* (31 August 2020), https://www.advocate.com/commentary/2020/8/31/usa-rugbys-naima-reddick-let-trans-women-play.

Showalter, B., 'Is there a secret plan to legalize sex trafficking of minors? Feminist activist tells all', *Christian Post* (26 April 2018), https://www.christianpost.com/news/is-there-a-secret-plan-legalize-sex-trafficking-minors-feminist-activist-tells-all.html.

Stock, K., 'Are academics freely able to criticise the idea of "gender identity" in UK universities?', *Medium* (3 July 2019), https://medium.com/@kathleenstock/are-academics-freely-able-to-criticise-the-idea-of-gender-identity-in-uk-universities-67b97c6e04be.

Stock, K., 'Trans policies in UK universities: some highlights' (29 December 2020), https://kathleenstock.com/highlights-of-trans-policies-in-uk-universities/.

Chapter 13

Henness, A., 'Sex. Not gender. It's in black & white. In the Equality Act', sexnotgender.info.

Pedersen, S., *The Politicization of Mumsnet* (Emerald, 2020).

Supporting Gender Non-Conforming and Trans-Identified Students in Schools (Transgender Trend, 3rd edition, 2020).

Whittle, S., Simkiss, F., *A Perfect Storm: The UK Government's Failed Consultation on the Gender Recognition Act 2004* (Edward Elgar, 2020).

Whittle, S., Turner, L., ' "Sex changes"? Paradigm shifts in "sex" and "gender" following the Gender Recognition Act?', *Sociological Research Online*, 12:1 (2007), http://www.socresonline.org.uk/12/1/whittle.html.

Conclusion

Bull, R., Asteriti, A., 'Gender self-declaration and women's rights: how self-identification undermines women's rights and will lead to an increase in harms', *Modern Law Review*, 83:3 (2020).

Fisher, R., Ury, W., *Getting to Yes: Negotiating Agreement Without Giving In* (Random House Business, 2012).

Pike, J., 'Safety, fairness, and inclusion: transgender athletes and the essence of rugby', *Journal of the Philosophy of Sport* (20 December 2020).

Rowling, J.K., 'J.K. Rowling writes about her reasons for speaking out on sex and gender issues' (10 June 2020), https://www.jkrowling.com/opinions/j-k-rowling-writes-about-her-reasons-for-speaking-out-on-sex-and-gender-issues/.

Simler, K., 'Crony beliefs' (2 November 2016), https://meltingasphalt.com/crony-beliefs/.

HELEN JOYCE is Britain editor of *The Economist*, where she has held several senior positions, including Finance editor and International editor. Before joining *The Economist* in 2005 she edited *Plus*, an online magazine about mathematics published by the University of Cambridge. She has a PhD in mathematics from University College London. Since becoming interested in gender-identity ideology, she has written for several outlets on the subject. On Twitter, she is @HJoyceGender.